Managerial Accounting and Analysis in Multinational Enterprises

Editors: H. P. Holzer · H.-M. W. Schoenfeld

Managerial Accounting and Analysis in Multinational Enterprises

Editors
H. Peter Holzer
Hanns-Martin W. Schoenfeld

Walter de Gruyter · Berlin · New York 1986

Dr. H. Peter Holzer
Deloitte Haskins and Sells Professor of Accountancy at the University of Illinois at Urbana-Champaign

Dr. Hanns-Martin W. Schoenfeld
Professor of Accountancy and Business Administration at the University of Illinois at Urbana-Champaign

Library of Congress Cataloging in Publication Data

Managerial accounting and analysis in multinational enterprises.
Bibliography: p.
Includes index.
1. International business enterprises--Accounting.
2. Managerial accounting. I. Holzer, H. Peter.
II. Schönfeld, Hanns-Martin.
HF5686.I56M36 1986 658.1'511 86-16533
ISBN 0-89925-087-4 (U.S.)

CIP-Kurztitelaufnahme der Deutschen Bibliothek

Managerial accounting and analysis in multinational enterprises / ed.: H. Peter Holzer ; Hanns-Martin W. Schoenfeld. – Berlin ; New York : de Gruyter, 1986
ISBN 3-11-010081-9

NE: Holzer, H. Peter [Hrsg.]

 – Typesetting and Printing: Tutte GmbH – Binding: D. Mikolai, Berlin – Cover Design: K. Lothar Hildebrand, Berlin – Printed in Germany

Preface

The increasing internationalization of business during the last three decades has focused attention on the specific accounting problems of multinational companies, in addition to other issues. Particularly, financial accounting and reporting have received wide attention by practitioners of public and industrial accounting. Accounting scholars have also widely discussed international issues of financial accounting. This is clearly indicated by the growing body of literature dealing with these issues. In addition, standard-setting bodies such as the *International Accounting Standards Committee (IASC)* in the area of financial accounting standards and the *International Federation of Accountants (IFAC)* in the field of auditing standards have made progress toward an eventual harmonization of financial reporting and auditing standards. These efforts toward the harmonization of international financial reporting continue and will undoubtedly receive considerable attention from both practitioners and scholars. The goal of full harmonization or even standardization will probably remain elusive, because important differences in national environmental factors will remain. Multinational companies will continue to be faced with different accounting regulations for their individual subsidiaries. These conditions will, of course, cause problems in consolidating financial statements and – even more important – in evaluating the operational results of subsidiaries in different countries.

The entire area of managerial accounting for multinational companies has received considerably less public attention in the literature than have international financial accounting problems. The lack of research in this area can, however, be easily explained. Management accounting is not in the public domain. Information on management accounting systems and procedures are not readily available to researchers. There are no standard-setting bodies, and the development of adequate systems is left entirely to the individual companies.

One of the important functions of international management accounting is the evaluation of international subsidiary performance. Because measures of performance are developed in accordance with perceived needs, it can be expected that companies will change their systems whenever such needs arise. Consequently, one would expect to find little uniformity in the early stages of multinational operations. Only after companies have gathered international experience for a number of years and have encountered similar problems in various locations can one expect the evolution of distinctive patterns in their systems. The issues involved in performance evaluation in a multinational environment are considerably more complex than those in a strictly domestic environment due to such factors as different national environments, different inflation rates, different conditions of financing, varying constraints imposed on subsidiary managements, and so on. These and many other influences individually and jointly distort traditional performance measures.

The international management accounting literature, as previously mentioned, is still limited. The results of several surveys on performance evaluation for international operations will be discussed in a subsequent section of these proceedings. These surveys, although very informative, have some unavoidable limitations. Their results are rather general and do not always allow an assessment of the systems and procedures developed by respondents. So far, only a few case studies have been published. By asking some leading U.S. – based multinationals to present and explain their systems, the organizers of this colloquium hope to contribute to the existing literature on the subject. Such case presentations have the advantage of giving a detailed analysis. They should permit insights into the rationale used when systems were developed and, hopefully, will clearly indicate the differences between domestic and international evaluation systems. A disadvantage of case presentations is, of course, that they do not permit general conclusions. We hope to add to the knowledge of prevailing practices by including case presentations on the systems of two multinationals from Europe and one from Korea. Presentations by three large international accounting firms which can draw on their experiences with a large number of multinational clients will further enhance the contribution of these proceedings. We are confident that the proceedings will give the reader some useful insights into the present state of the art.

We would like to thank all participants for their cooperation in making the colloquium possible, and especially Professor Kenneth Most of Florida International University who, in his own inimitable fashion, acted as moderator for the two discussion sessions. Particular thanks are due to the Center for International Education and Research in Accounting of the University of Illinois at Urbana-Champaign for sponsoring the colloquium, and to Deloitte Haskins and Sells for providing financial support through the Deloitte Haskins and Sells Professorship. Progress in management accounting is facilitated when practitioners are willing to share experience and insights with the academic community. We hope that the proceedings of this colloquium will, in a small way, advance the discipline of management accounting.

H. Peter Holzer
Hanns-Martin W. Schoenfeld

Contents

Company Approaches

View of Independent Accountants

Past Research on Performance Evaluation of International Subsidiaries

H. Peter Holzer

1. Introduction

The review of the literature that follows is intended to present a historical introduction to the topic of this colloquium. As international operations become more important and multinational enterprises (MNEs) begin to recognize the importance of performance evaluation systems, we find that scholars and researchers begin to be interested in this problem area. The results of the most important research projects published during the past twenty-five years in leading business and accounting periodicals are discussed and analyzed in the sections that follow.

2. Evolution of the Topic

Prior to the sixties, the topic of international aspects of managerial accounting received little attention. In a paper published in 1965, Hawkins reported that most U.S. companies with overseas subsidiaries use the same system for the control of foreign operations that is used for the control of domestic operations. The primary reason given was that the system is less expensive, that the information can be more readily consolidated, and that domestic executives are more comfortable with a system with which they are already familiar. But Hawkins also reported that these exported systems are seldom as effective internationally as they are at home, because (1) objectives for foreign subsidiaries are often not identical to the goals of domestic operations; (2) organizational and environmental differences and different economic factors exist; and

(3) foreign operations are usually not as independent as domestic profit centers.[1]

In 1967, David Zenoff reported the results of interviews with financial executives of thirty prominent U. S. – based multinational enterprises. He claimed that at that time, many foreign operations were considered as "step children," as tools for tax minimizing and as "cash cows." Only a few companies viewed their overseas subsidiaries as bona fide business operations and had developed a long-term international outlook. At the time, U.S. MNEs were primarily concerned with the safety of their overseas investment and related cash flows. Long-term profitability apparently was a secondary problem, and little attention was paid to problems of its measurement.[2]

The Mauriel Survey (1969) was one of the earliest surveys dealing with performance measurement and control systems of international operations. It reported the results of interviews with fifteen large MNEs. Some of the important findings were that a MNE's domestic financial control systems were used without modification in foreign operations. Profit and investment center concepts were applied, and return on investment (ROI), as well as residual income (RI), was growing in popularity as a measure of performance — but frequently profit on sales was considered a more important measure. Companies felt that it was too early to be periodically examining ROI because their foreign operations were fighting to establish a foothold in new markets.[3]

3. Research in the 1970s

The McInnes Survey (1971) analyzed the financial reporting and evaluations systems of thirty U.S. MNEs. It was again found that only minor differences existed among the reporting systems used by domestic and foreign units. It can be considered significant, however, that approximately 50 percent of the firms required reports in both dollars and local currencies. The most frequent evaluation measures used were ROI, followed by budget comparisons and historical comparisons.[4]

The Financial Executives Research Foundation Study (1974) covered thirty-four MNEs. An interesting finding was that the primary emphasis had shifted to a comparison of actual versus budgeted profits. ROI followed by a comparison of actual and budgeted sales ranked next in popularity. The study strongly recommended that methods should be developed to permit *separate evaluation* of the performances of managers from those of their activities.[5]

The Report of the American Accounting Association Committee on International Accounting represents the most comprehensive theoretical analysis of financial control and reporting problems of a MNE. The committee attempted to identify the differences in modes of operations between domestic and multinational companies and describe in detail financial control, reporting, and other accounting problems peculiar to international operations. In this context, they also analyzed performance problems. Some results of the committee's comprehensive analysis are the following:

1. A profit center approach usually is not appropriate because overseas units lack independence, that is, they do not have sufficient control over profit influencing factors, and
2. Profits are too much influenced by transfer prices which are also presumed outside the control of the subsidiary manager.

The committee suggests the use of a budget-based approach which should include a careful distinction between controllable and non-controllable variances and thus make possible a distinctive evaluation of managers and units. They also suggest the use of additional non-financial quantitative measures (for example, employee hours of executive training) and management and performance audits. For transfer pricing, they suggested a system of two or more transfer prices, each serving a different purpose.[6]

In a 1973 survey, Robbins and Stobaugh interviewed representatives of thirty-nine enterprises to identify their evaluation practices of international operations. They found that 95 percent of firms evaluate foreign units in exactly the same way as they do domestic units and that no distinction is made between the evaluation of the managers and the unit. The principal measure used was ROI. Budgets were utilized for supplementary information purposes only. The survey indicated that 44 percent of multinational companies measured in foreign currencies, 44 percent in U.S. dollars, and 12 percent used both. Robbins and Stobaugh recommended that ROI be replaced by a budget-actual-comparison with objectives developed individually for each subsidiary. They also pleaded for the use of so-called secondary criteria, that is, individual elements of budgets, related to the strategic objectives.[7]

Persen and Lessig's Financial Executives Research Foundation study of 1979 covered four hundred U.S. MNEs. Of the 400 questioned, 125 responded. The questionnaires were followed by interviews of executives with twenty companies. The study's objective was the evaluation of systems used for wholly owned, on-going overseas subsidiaries over time. In other words, the executives were queried about the evaluation techniques they employed at that time, five years before and five years after. A major finding was the lack of uniformity in approaches. Systems varied because environmental differences were considered, changes in these factors were noted, and judgment was used to supplement objective quantitative measures. Although "operating budget comparisons" seemed to be the most prevalent at the beginning of the period covered by the research, ROI becomes an important measure five years later. Other interesting results are that for international operations, return on sales was rated higher than for domestic operations. Inflation-adjusted ROI had gained increasing acceptance by the end of the period.

For companies with high percentage of international sales, the most common transfer pricing base was cost plus markup. The other financial measures used were contributions to earnings per share, corporate cash flow, and discounted cash flows or internal rate of return (IRR). Fifty-eight percent used both local currency and parent currency in measuring performance criteria. Some non-accounting measures were market share, quality control (especially important in cost centers), and labor turnover. These measures were primarily used for the evaluation of individual managers.[8]

4. Recent Developments

Morsicato (1980) studied seventy MN corporations in the chemical industry to determine how these companies evaluate the internal performance of their foreign managers. The most commonly used measures were in U.S. dollars; measures used included profit, ROI, budgeted versus actual profits, budgeted versus actual sales, cash flow potential, budgeted versus actual ROI, with RI last. Whenever foreign currency was used to measure performance, the list was headed by budgeted versus actual profits.

MNEs still used more U.S. – dollar information for internal evaluation purposes, although most executives believed that foreign currency statements provide better information for the evaluation of subsidiaries and managers. In the majority of cases, the same basic techniques were used for the evaluation of foreign units and the evaluation of their manager.[9]

The Czechowicz study (1982) covered eighty-eight MNEs, of which twenty-four were European based. They were first surveyed by questionnaires, responses to questionnaires were then supplemented by personal and telephone interviews, and three roundtable discussions (which included participants of fifty U.S. – based corporations).

One of the more important findings was that both European and U.S. corporations established foreign operations for strategic reasons. Both viewed foreign operations as part of an integrated system, although European-based MNEs seemed to allow their foreign operations a greater degree of autonomy in terms of organization than do U.S. companies. This difference in style seemed to be reflected in the way performance is measured.

Performance criteria employed were both financial and non-financial. Financial criteria tended to dominate; most popular were *budget comparisons*, followed by ROI. Of the non-financial criteria, *market share* and *relations with host governments* were the most important. Both U.S. and European MNEs considered budgets and historical performance useful standards for comparing the performance of foreign units and managers. European MNEs tended to attach more importance to the performance of local competitors as a benchmark than do U.S. MNEs. Few companies made a clear distinction between the evaluation of the manager and the unit. Approximately the same measurements were used, although additional judgmental factors seem to enter into the picture when evaluating managers.

Although criteria seemed similar, (budget and ROI) measures employed varied. U.S. – based companies used both pretax and after-tax data in evaluating ROI and return on total assets (ROA). European companies tended to emphasize pretax numbers.

U.S. companies were divided when deciding whether to include headquarters' expenses and foreign exchange adjustments in the reports of foreign subsidiaries. European companies tended to exclude them. Opinions were divided as to whether intercompany services should be allocated to foreign operations, and what methods to use. Europeans tended to allocate less frequently than did U.S. MNEs.

U.S. companies tended to employ a parent currency perspective. Non – U.S. MNEs generally preferred a local currency perspective when evaluating both the foreign unit and its manager. *Transaction gains and losses* were generally included in the evaluation of both the units and the managers. Unit managers were held accountable for those gains and losses since they had the authority to hedge this form of risk. U.S. – based MNEs sometimes assigned *translation gains or losses* to units and managers while European-based MNEs did not.

In the case of U.S. – based MNEs, the formal incorporation of inflation adjustments was limited to the budgetary process. Assets were not restated. Non – U.S. MNEs used a far more comprehensive approach. There seemed to be a European consensus that inflation-adjusted numbers (no matter how crude) provide more useful measures of performance than do unadjusted cost figures.

U.S. MNEs tended to use cost-based transfer prices, and these were usually set by headquarters. Non – U.S. enterprises generally employed market value to set transfer prices — and this was subject to negotiations by subsidiary managers. In general, the same transfer price was used for internal performance evaluation and tax purposes.

Most MNEs, both U.S. and European, did not incorporate risk into their performance evaluation system. The significant minority that did usually added a subjective risk premium to the performance standards for foreign operations.

Most MNEs expressed satisfaction with their systems of evaluating both domestic and foreign operations. Only a small minority thought that their system led overseas managers to suboptimal behavior, with 14 percent of U.S. MNEs and 21 percent of non – U.S. MNEs believing there was room for improvement in their systems. One-fourth of U.S. MNEs and one-third of European MNEs expected that their existing performance evaluation systems would be modified in the future. The most cited reason for this was *foreign inflation.*

At the conclusion, the study recommends that systems should be evaluated and, if necessary, modified to ensure that short-term goals and related incentives conform with strategic goals.[10]

Elwood Miller's book contains an extensive treatment of MN performance evaluation problems and an excellent discussion of the literature, in addition to studies of two companies: 3 M Company and Monsanto (an updated version of the latter is included in these proceedings). They reveal how U.S. companies formally state their strategic objectives and the financial goals and show how financial and non-financial criteria are used in evaluating the performance of overseas units.

Through these studies, we discussed how MNEs deal with the problem of foreign exchange and foreign inflation, what transfer pricing practices are employed, and how performance standards are set.[11] Table 1 summarizes the performance measures and their ranking as reported in the research discussed.

Donaldson and Pai describe the Burroughs system. It is the most recently published article on the subject and gives some insight into the operational and procedural approach presently employed.

Burroughs has subsidiaries in countries with chronic inflation (Brazil, Mexico, and Argentina), in countries with currencies that have been strongly devalued with respect to the dollar, and in countries such as Germany and Japan with stable currencies. This is in addition to other differences in the cultural, political, and economic environment. They list nine important characteristics of a performance evaluation system — some of the more important are as follows:

1. It should define "performance"; for example, orders and sales, timely delivery, quality, and so on;
2. Criteria used should be measurable and not abstract factors; for example, if customer satisfaction is an important criteria — order and lease cancellation may be used as surrogate measures;
3. It should clearly define accountability; for example, responsibility for cancellation cannot be assigned unless cause is determined (sales person of manufacturer?);
4. It should communicate positive as well as negative performance — emphasis should be on motivational rather than punitive aspects;
5. It should be aggressive yet fair and flexible (we can readily understand this given the rapidly changing conditions in the international environment); and
6. It should help management anticipate problems in time to take corrective action. That is, the system should monitor performance against corporate targets.

Burroughs uses both financial and nonfinancial criteria; examples of the

Table 1. Rankings of Financial Performance Measures Reported 1969–1982 and Projected to 1984 Regarding MNCs (adopted from Miller, p. 127)

Performance measures	Studies: Mauriel 1969	Financial Executive 1971	McInnes 1971	Robbins and Stobaugh 1973	Financial Executive: Actual	Financial Executive: Projected to 1984	Morsicato (1)	Morsicato (2)	Czechowicz 1982: U.S. MN	Czechowicz 1982: Non U.S.
Sales budgets		3								
Profit (ROS)	1	1			5	7	2	1	4	2
Operating budgets			2	2	1	1				
ROI	2		1	1	3	3	3	2	2	3
ROI and RI		2								
Historical comparison										
Contribution to EPS	3		3		2	5			8	11
Contribution corporate cash flow							6	5	5	6
ROA					4	2			5	4
Asset/Liability management					5	6				
RI							7	7	11	10
Operating cash flow to subsidiaries									6	7
Budget compared to actual profit							1	3	1	1
Budget compared to actual sales							4	4	3	2
Budget compared to actual ROI							5	6	5	5
Budget compared to actual ROE									10	9
ROE									9	8
Other					6	4				

(1) Before translation. (2) After translation.

latter are orders, productivity, employee turnover, profit, cash flow, contribution margins, ROA, receivable days, inventory levels, and manpower.

Burroughs uses a U.S. – dollar perspective for all financial criteria — it wants to motivate subsidiaries to maximize U.S. – dollar results. Transaction gains and losses are excluded from subsidiary evaluation. Corporate services such as research and development (R & D) management and royalties are allocated, but only on the basic of budgeted numbers. Depending on conditions, before- and after-tax profits are used (for ROI).[12]

5. Unresolved Issues

Let us briefly summarize the key issues and concepts that emerged from the preceding review of the literature on the performance evaluation of international subsidiaries. We began by restating the purpose of performance evaluation systems in general. Such systems should permit the parent's management: (1) to evaluate the economic performance of its international operations: this is frequently referred to as an evaluation of the unit's economic performance; (2) to evaluate the unit's management performance; (3) to monitor progress toward corporate objectives including strategic goals; and (4) to assist in the efficient allocation of resources.

The problems involved in achieving these objectives for domestic units are widely discussed in the literature and in textbooks. The issues involved for attaining the objectives for international subsidiaries that operate in a much more complex environment are not only more numerous but also more complex. Our review shows that the performance evaluation systems for international units described in the literature during two decades became increasingly more sophisticated. Domestic systems are frequently modified to consider the different environment and operating conditions of overseas units. Performance criteria show a tendency to include several financial criteria and are frequently supplemented by nonfinancial ones. Performance is often measured in foreign currencies. In some cases, companies have begun to separate the evaluation of the managers from the evaluation of the economic performance of the unit. Increasingly, due recognition seems to be given to the motivational impact of the measures employed. To conclude our review of the literature, we will list the key issues involved in the design and operation of performance evaluation systems for international subsidiaries.

1. The concept of performance must be clearly defined. This may be expressed as realizing budgeted operating profits, achieving a certain degree of market penetration, or a target rate of return on invested capital. Unless clearly defined, it may mean different things to different people. A clear understanding of what performance is is even more important for the evaluation of managers because of motivational implications.
2. The financial and nonfinancial criteria used in evaluating performance must be stated. Nonfinancial criteria may include such items as timely delivery, and timely billing and collecting of accounts receivable or increased market shares.
3. How are the criteria to be measured? For example, if timely delivery is viewed as an important performance criterion, the system must provide information that permits us to measure the criterion. In this case, for example, a comparison between promised and actual delivery dates may give a satisfactory measure. The use of profitability measures such as rate of return on investment, residual income, and comparisons between planned and actual profits have been frequently discussed in the literature and are often referred to in these proceedings.
4. Should a distinction be made between the performance of the unit and the performance of its management? Here the degree of autonomy and independence afforded to the foreign unit's management may be of critical importance. Fully autonomous subsidiaries of a conglomerate may make it possible to evaluate the economic performance of the unit and the effectiveness of its management with a single measure of profitability because practically all important factors affecting the unit's profit are under the control of the unit's management. With decreasing autonomy of the unit's management, this will probably no longer be possible because key factors affecting the overall profitability of the unit will no longer be under the control of its management.
5. Should performance criteria be measured in foreign currencies or in U.S. dollars? The Burroughs case mentioned in the review of the literature is an example of dollar measures being appropriate because the parent's management considers short-run dollar profitability an

important objective. The rate of inflation affecting a subsidiary's currency and the existence of price controls and other constraints may be important factors in deciding which currency to use.

6. Should exchange gains and losses be reflected in the performance evaluation? Transaction gains or losses should be included in the evaluation of the unit's performance. Whether they should be factored into management's performance evaluation depends, at least to some extent, on whether managers can influence transaction gains and losses related to the unit's operation. If they can influence them, they should probably be reflected in the evaluation. Many accountants consider translation gains and losses as having no economic substance and should therefore be disregarded.

7. What should be done about foreign inflation? Doubtless, high inflation rates render accounting numbers fairly useless for performance evaluation. Without adjustments, realistic evaluations of units and management would be very difficult. The guidelines of Financial Accounting Standard 52 may even prove useful for management accounting purposes.

8. How should transfer prices be set? This issue is complicated by the fact that tax and custom authorities of different countries take an active interest in the methods employed. The transfer prices used should not distort the subsidiaries' performance measures. This ideal can be accomplished only when true arms'-length prices are available. Because this is frequently not the case, other pricing methods based on cost must be used.

9. Should corporate costs be allocated to subsidaries for performance evaluation purposes? This issue includes not only charges for corporate services but also charges for corporate capital, especially when residual income is used as a performance measure. Factoring the cost of capital into the performance evaluation systems raises the question of whether there is such a thing as a worldwide cost of capital for a MNE. Is this cost of capital uniform, or should rates be adjusted for differences in risk? Opinions are also divided concerning charges for other headquarters' services such as research and development fees, management fees, franchises, and others.

10. A final issue deals with income taxes. Should foreign income taxes be included when units and managers are evaluated? A good argument can be made for including taxes in the evaluation of the units' profit-

ability. Including taxes in the evaluation of management, on the other hand, would imply at least a degree of controllability which may be appropriate in some circumstances.

These and other issues are discussed in the following sections of the proceedings in the context of the conditions faced by different multinational companies.

The organizers of this colloquium appreciate the willingness of the participating firms and companies to share their experiences and to contribute reports on their international performance evaluation systems. We are confident that these proceedings will make a contribution to the literature on an important management accounting issue.

Notes

[1] David E. Hawkins: "Controlling Foreign Operations", *Financial Executive*, 33 (February 1965): 25–32.

[2] David Zenoff: "Profitable, Fast Growing, But Still the Stepchild", *Columbia Journal of World Business* (July – August 1967): 51–56.

[3] John J. Mauriel: "Evaluation and Control of Overseas Operations", *Management Accounting* (May 1969): 35–39, 52.

[4] J. M. McInnes: "Financial Control Systems for Multinational Operations: An Empirical Investigation", *Journal of International Business Studies* (Fall 1971): 11, 21.

[5] Edward C. Bursk, John Dearden, David F. Hawkins, and Victor M. Longstreet: *Financial Control of Multinational Operations* (New York: Financial Executives Research Foundation, 1971).

[6] American Accounting Association, Committee on International Accounting: "Report of the Committee on International Accounting", *Accounting Review*, supplement to vol. A 7 (1973): 120–167.

[7] Sidney M. Robbins and Robert B. Stobaugh: "The Bent Measuring Stick for Foreign Subsidiaries", *Harvard Business Review* (September – October 1973): 80–88.

[8] William Persen and Van Lessig: *Evaluating the Financial Performance of Overseas Operations* (New York: Financial Executives Research Foundation, 1979).

[9] Helen Gernon Morsicato: *Currency Translation and Performance Evaluation in Multinationals* (Ann Arbor, Mich.: U. M. I. Research Press, 1980).

[10] I. James Czechowicz, Frederick D. S. Choi, and Vinod Bavishi: *Assessing Foreign Subsidiary Performance Systems' Practices of Loading Multinational Companies* (New York: Business International Corporation, 1982).

[11] Elwood L. Miller: *Responsibility Accounting and Performance Evaluations* (New York: Van Nostrand Reinhold Company, 1982).

[12] Howard M. Donaldson and Amar K. Pai: "Management Performance Evaluation", in *Managerial Accounting: An Analysis of Current International Applications*, ed. V. K: Zimmerman (University of Illinois: Center for International Education and Research in Accounting, 1984): 1–22.

COMPANY APPROACHES

Accounting Techniques Utilized for the Evaluation of International Subsidiaries: The IBM Case

R. J. Rubino

1. Introduction

The effective evaluation of an enterprise requires knowledge and imagination. "Knowledge" is defined here as the ability to perceive historical events accurately, and "imagination" is viewed as a creative characteristic used to transform historical knowledge into a form which provides maximum utility for management decision processes. This paper focuses on the use of these key elements as they apply to the accounting evaluation of the international operations of International Business Machines Corporation (IBM).

The theory that accounting is an art implies that a fixed and finite set of accounting techniques does not exist. Techniques represent the imagination element of the aforementioned elemental relationship, and to the extent that techniques result in additional knowledge, a cyclical and constantly improving evaluation process results. The cycle cannot begin, however, without a base of knowledge. Techniques must be designed to accommodate the business and to satisfy the needs of management. Such can be achieved only if the architect of the technique, the accountant, understands the business and the organizational structure.

2. Business and Organization

IBM is the largest manufacturer of data processing equipment and systems in the information handling field. It had approximately 370,000 employees worldwide as of December 31, 1983. Its gross income for 1983 totaled over $40 billion. Operations in the United States are organized into three principal groups. The *Information Systems Group* (ISG) provides direction to its six constituent divisions, whose responsibilities include the marketing and maintenance of IBM products, the assurance that development and manufacturing groups develop products and services to satisfy the needs of U.S. customers, and the identification of present and future marketplace requirements. The four divisions of the *Information Systems and Technology Group* (IS & TG) are responsible for the worldwide product development and the U.S. manufacturing of large systems, storage systems, program products, semiconductors and ceramics, circuit packaging, and intermediate processors and printers. An *Information Systems and Communication Group* (IS & CG) consists of four divisions and is responsible for worldwide development and the U.S. manufacturing of telecommunications and office systems, displays, personal computers, typewriters, copiers, and small and intermediate-sized general purpose systems. The overall organization of IBM is captured in Figure 1.

The group concept has maximized the manageability of this very large company by placing similar/related products under common management. It has simplified the marketing interface, improved marketing sensitivity, and promoted strong strategic focus by business areas.

In addition to the three U.S. groups, independent business units have been established as vehicles for entering new business areas with promising growth opportunity. An independent business unit owns or adequately controls all essential business functions, including development, manufacturing, marketing, service, and finance. Such an arrangement provides minimum dependency on IBM's mainstream business, and there is assurance that an embryonic endeavor is afforded specialized management attention.

IBM has two subsidiaries responsible for the execution of business operations outside the United States. IBM World Trade Europe/Middle East/Africa Corporation (E/ME/A) is responsible for operations in eighty-five countries. Generally, each country represents a subsidiary re-

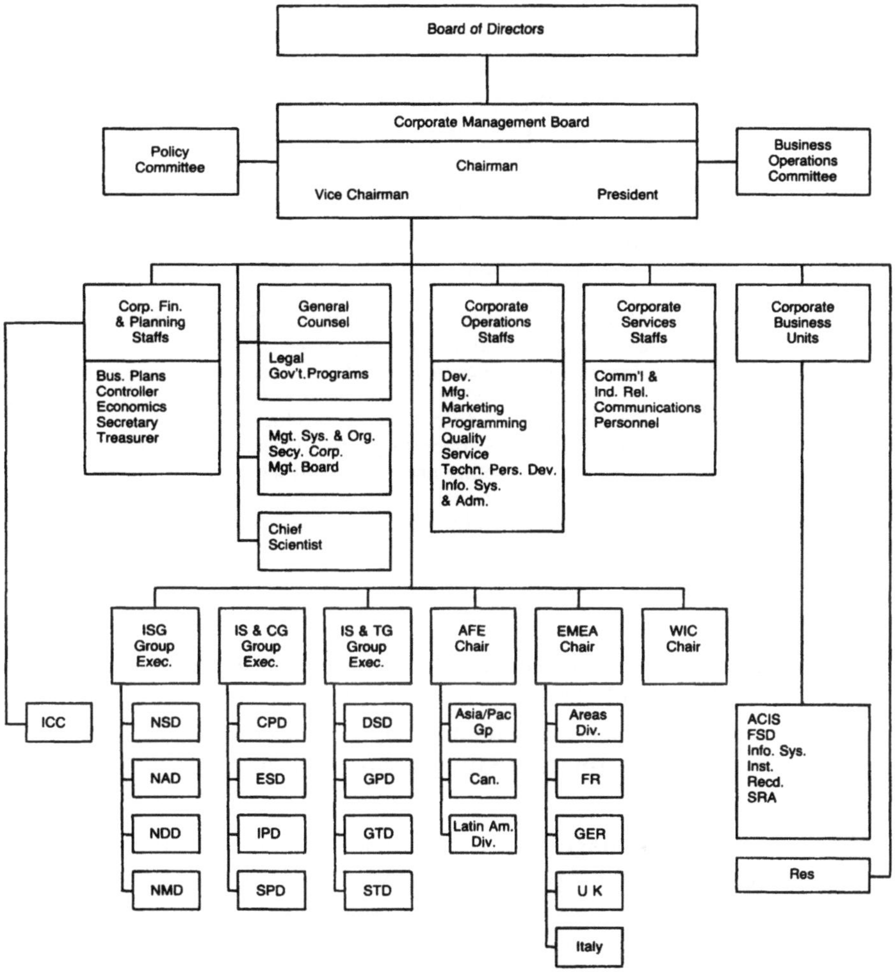

Figure 1.

sponsible for marketing all products and sometimes for manufacturing. Most products marketed in E/ME/A are also manufactured by E/ME/A. An overview of E/ME/A can be found in Table 1.

The remaining part of the globe falls within the territory of IBM World Trade Americas/Far East Corporation (A/FE), which spans four continents and is responsible for operations in forty-six countries. E/ME/A and A/FE objectives include the application of IBM policies and principles consistent with the customs and laws of the various countries. They

Table 1. E/ME/A Overview

Mission	Conduct IBM's business in areas outside the United States in a manner that will result in Continued growth Maximized profits Optimum stockholder, customer, and employee satisfaction
Responsibilities	Apply IBM policies, principles, practices, and standards of performance in a manner consistent with customs and laws of various countries Marketing, installing, and maintaining IBM products and services Satisfy revenue and profit objectives Protect the sources of revenue Manufacture IBM products and devices for marketing needs Develop and produce program products Ensure that U.S. operating units develop products and services satisfying marketing needs of countries Identify marketplace requirements, investigate new business opportunities, and propose new business ventures to achieve future growth

are responsible for manufacturing, marketing, installing, and maintaining IBM products and services, for ensuring that U.S. operating units develop products and services which satisfy country marketing needs, and for identifying marketplace requirements and new business opportunities.

IBM Corporation management is responsible for integrating the entire global process of IBM operations. IBM Corporation establishes the overall objectives, principles, policies, missions, standards, and measurements. The corporate function is responsible for the approval of plans, budgets, senior management appointments, salary structure and benefits, contributions, and real estate activity. A corporate management board provides overall direction to the company, while the Business Operations Committee focuses on the daily operations of the business, and the Policy Committee develops long-term plans regarding the policies, resources, and finances.

The complexity and sheer size of the IBM organization worldwide make effective accounting evaluation quite a challenge which is magnified when the entire structure is immersed in an environment of dynamics so volatile that the needs for accounting data seem to increase on a daily basis. With such demands, the IBM accounting community does not react to the ever-broadening stream of business requirements but is part of that stream.

3. European/Middle East and African (E/ME/A) Accounting System

E/ME/A generated aproximately 11.6 billion in revenue in 1983, prior to eliminations. The comparison of E/ME/A with IBM totals is given in Table 2.

As is evident, E/ME/A is sizeable from both geographical and operational perspectives. The E / ME / A Headquarters Accounting function is responsible for reporting consolidated E / ME / A – wide accounting information

Table 2. IBM World Trade E/ME/A Comparative

	IBM	E/ME/A
Revenue	$40.2	$11.6*
Net earnings	$ 5.5	$ 1.6*
Employees	370,000	105,000
Countries with marketing service	132	85

* Prior to eliminations

Table 3. E/ME/A Headquarters Accounting Business Controls Country Accounting Review Program

Purpose	Develop in-depth understanding of individual country accounting organizations and determine their integrity and effectiveness
Areas reviewed	All aspects that affect the reliability of accounting information (data and communication) Organization Personnel Accounting systems Business controls Other ... on a Rotational Basis
Results	Confirmation and/or recommendations – 1. To director of headquarters accounting 2. Then to country accounting management • Current workload and control posture • Ability to cope with business changes • Accounting vitality
Benefits	Enables financial management to take time from operational involvement to analyze the overall effectiveness of the accounting function Focuses on key concerns and affects resolutions

to the corporate accounting function. E/ME/A Headquarters Accounting performs a dual role regarding the evaluation process. One role is to ensure that the accounting organization in each country is providing quality information. The other involves the overall evaluation of the business performance reflected by the data. The organizational chart of E/ME/A is shown in Figure 2.

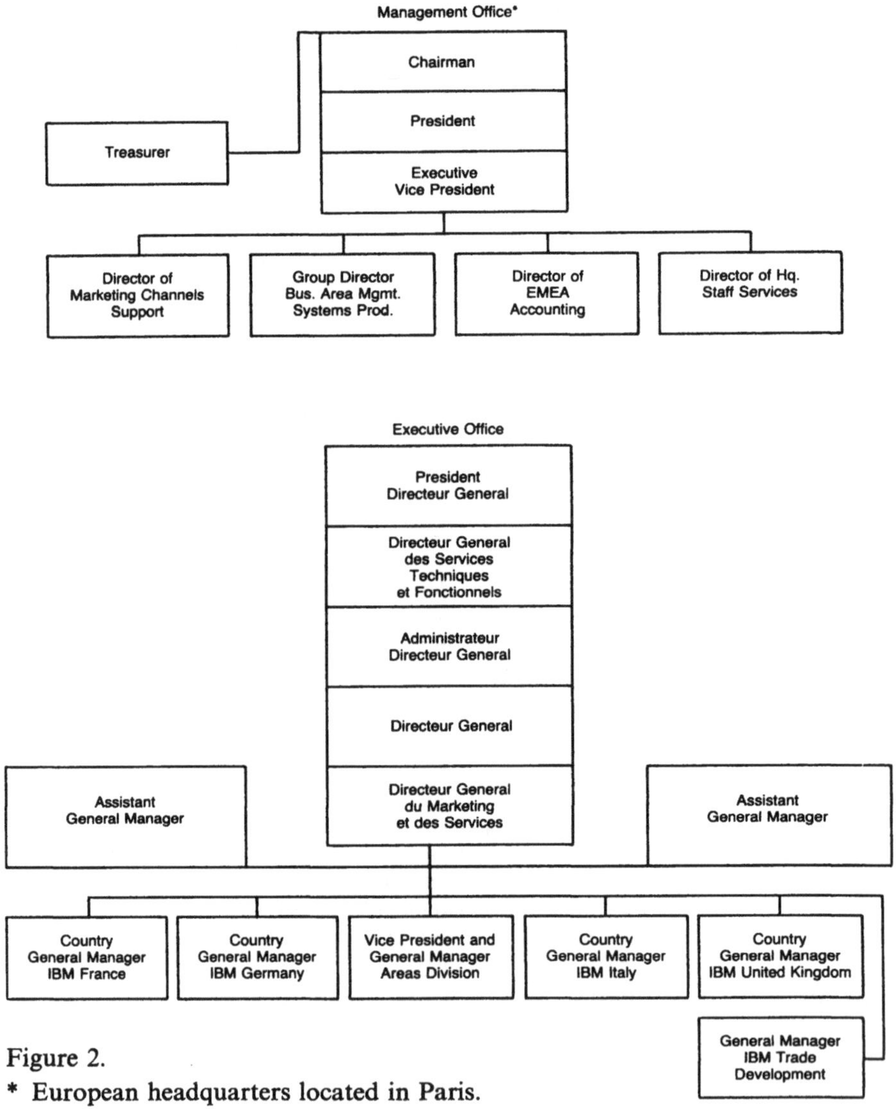

Figure 2.
* European headquarters located in Paris.

The dual role can be further segmented into three subsets. To evaluate a subsidiary's (country's) operation effectively, E/ME/A Headquarters Accounting will (1) have knowledge of existing controls in place which assure reliable data, and have techniques available for ongoing evaluation of the controls; (2) have techniques to ensure that information is received in the form and time frame needed; and (3) apply appropriate measurement techniques based on information received. The E/ME/A Headquarters Accounting organizational chart is shown in Figure 3.

4. Business Controls

A Business Controls function is integrated into E/ME/A Headquarters Accounting with a primary mission of evaluating the overall control posture in E/ME/A from a local country, as well as consolidated, perspective. In a company the size of E/ME/A, a business controls department at headquarters would appear to have nominal likelihood of effectiveness. The mission of the function is not to control, but rather understand, monitor, and evaluate, as well as promote, locally supported control activities within each country.

The most formidable input into the overall understanding process results from business controls' Country Review Program, as summarized in Table 3.

In short, this program entails a thorough review of a particular country's accounting organization, personnel, systems, controls, and overall quality. A sample country review program checklist and a description of key components follows:

Organization
- The Accounting Organization
  - Organization Structure
  - Checks and Balances between Departments
  - Separation of Duties within a Department
- Headcount
  - Adequacy
  - Managerial Span of Control
  - Overtime and Trends

Interfunctional Relationship
Chain of Command
Involvement in Review Processes (Monthly Meetings to Discuss Financial Statements)
Interfunctional
Accounting with Management

Personnel
Hiring Practices (External and Internal)
Adequacy of Academic Background and Prior Experience
Internal Transfers
Future Potential
Turnover
Vitality
Managerial Replacement
Tracking
Special Training
Education/Training
Plans and Achievements
Internal and External Programs
Career Path
Opinion Survey
Prior Results
Exposures
Action Programs and Results
Job Descriptions
Existing and Up-to-Date
Communication to Staff
Levels
Matching Responsibility
Functional Comparison
Country-to-Country Comparison (E/ME/A Accounting Responsibility)
Staff Performance
Excessive or Unfavorable Situations and Action Plans
General
Ratio Part-Time, Full-Time
Use of Outside Contractors

Accounting Systems
Existing Systems

- Adequacy of Each
- Problems and Actions
- Identification of Ownership
- Manual Workload
  - Significant Areas
  - Actions to Eliminate
- Common Accounting Systems
  - Participation
  - Concerns/Problems and Actions
  - Planned Installations
- Accounting/EDP Interface
  - How/What/Why
  - Communication Channels
  - EDP Effectiveness
  - User Support
  - Accounting Strategy
  - History of Enhancements

Business Controls
- Organization
  - Accounting Coordinator
  - Country Business Controls Manager
  - Internal Auditor
- Performance
  - Understanding of Definitions
  - Involvement in Locally Written Procedures
  - Test Calculations
  - Review Performance
    - Problems
    - Actions
  - Local Indicators — Actions
  - Communication
- Self-Analysis Checklist/Audit Digest
  - Review
  - Problems and Actions
  - Management Involvement
- Audits
  - Follow-up
    - Status Report

Country Auditor
Fulfilling Responsibilities
Critique Internal and External Audits

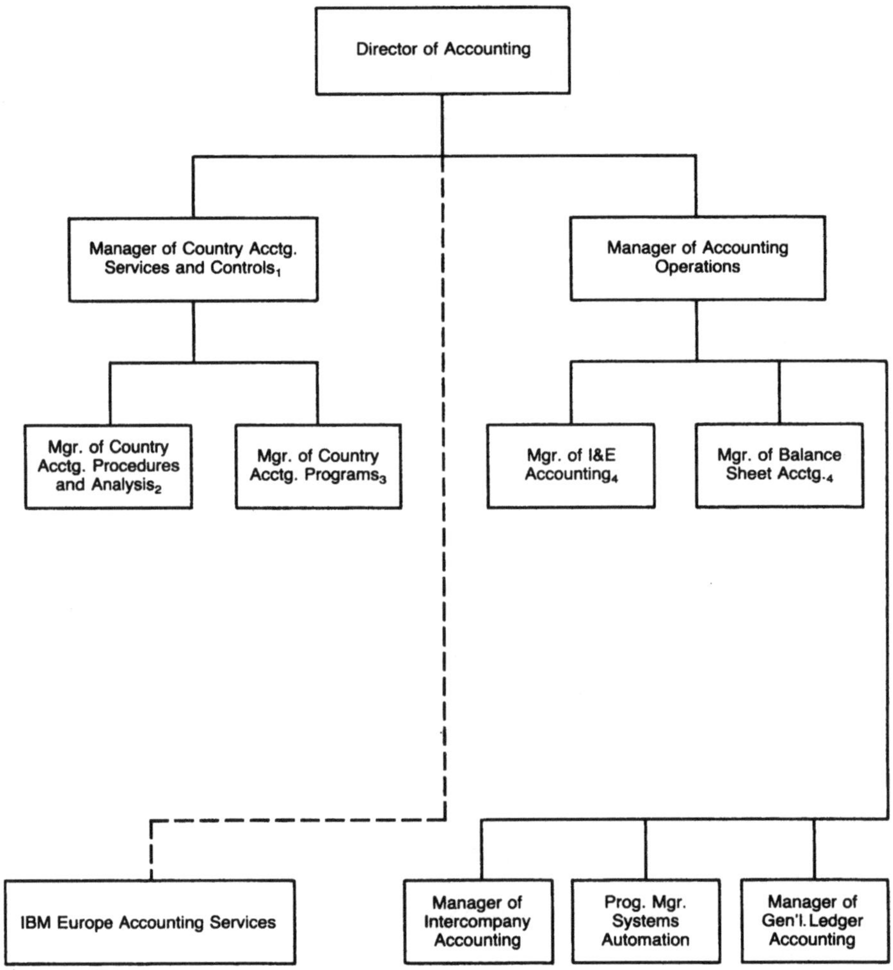

Figure 3. Headquarters Accounting (White Plains, N.Y.)

[1] Country focus.
[2] Review of individual country results and development of country accounting procedures
[3] Business controls.
[4] Integrity of consolidated financial statements.

The first step when performing a country review is usually to review the organizational structure of accounting. The structure is analyzed from an objective-achievement perspective. Management control, chain of command, interfunctional relationships, and the overall communication process are reviewed to determine the levels of integration, efficiency, international control, and quality which can be generated.

Once the inner workings of the organizational structure are understood, the next step in the review process addresses the individuals comprising the organization. The program is designed in full cognizance of the fact that the individual is the most valuable component of any business operation. People who are conscientious, qualified, satisfied, challenged, and achieve their objectives are key contributors to the overall internal control plan. A detailed review of employee hiring practices, turnover, education/training, staff performance, and growth opportunities is executed to develop an understanding of the quality of output which can be expected from the particular accounting function.

Accounting management is reviewed in great detail. Vitality is a key consideration in the management arena, and the management preparation/replacement procedure is closely analyzed to determine the expected effectiveness of present and future members in the chain of command. Employee-prepared opinion surveys of management are reviewed to evaluate the appropriateness of management performance from an employee perspective. The formal review process is augmented by discussions with control operational management and E/ME/A Headquaters Accounting Management who can often provide information regarding country accounting management's technical ability, general business knowledge, and communication effectiveness. Vitality analysis ranges from staff turnover to management turnover and is regarded as a key to keeping new ideas, approaches, and techniques flowing within the system.

Since professional growth of the individual is viewed throughout IBM as very important, countless educational programs have been established throughout the organization. Such a program directed by E/ME/A Headquarters Business Controls offers several courses each year to staff levels, as well as higher-level accounting management. Courses often cover a broad range of topics from financial statement theory to current business developments. Participants are typically from various E/ME/A countries, and the entire process is a principal factor in promoting accounting enrichment.

Accounting systems are a crucial consideration when attempting to evaluate the quality or reliability of accounting data generated at the country level. The first objective of the systems review is to identify systems in place. Once identified, the adequacy of each is analyzed from a logistical and accounting control perspective. A workload review determines the degree of manual effort compared to mechanized tasks, and an electronic data processing (EDP) review determines the appropriateness of system integration, input/output controls, and overall efficiency and reliability. The review also addresses the effectiveness of communication channels between accounting and the EDP support function, as well as the ability of accounting management to establish and develop a mechanization process. That a strategy is in place, or in other words, that an objective is established by local accounting to ensure that maximum unity is derived from EDP, should be ascertained in every case.

That the country review process is necessary is evident since it provides Headquarters Accounting Management with valuable information on the control status of a particular country's accounting function. IBM is very concerned to keep up-to-date with business, and the company stresses the communication between the local accounting function and local business management to facilitate decision making. Local business controls functions are established at the country level to afford a more local quality assurance and maintenance approach rather than relying on an externally mounted quality control approach. The Headquarters Business Controls function assists in the establishment and review of the adequacy of local business controls functions.

A principal purpose of a local business controls organization is to perform the task of E/ME/A Headquarters Business Controls on a daily basis, thus expanding the exercise from one of developing a base of knowledge to one of using techniques based on the knowledge to improve the business. The most important technique to arise from this concept is that of self-assessment.

Self-assessment is designed for accounting management to test itself periodically on compliance with control requirements. It permits local accounting to evaluate its operation in a structured and systematic manner, and it can be considered a "check-up" on the level of execution of procedures. The entire process is based on the sound theory that no one knows firsthand the strengths, weaknesses, people, and concerns better than management directly responsible for the operations.

The local business controls function affects the development of custom audit checklists and self-analysis programs for each accounting function in the country. From a practical perspective, an effective self-assessment program is a self-initiated one which creates an awareness of identified concerns, puts in action plans to correct any problems, and allows the function to be in control and retain a positive posture. The business controls objectives regarding self-assessment are to ensure integrity in the process, review the results, and assist in any decision-making process.

When the country review process has been completed by E/ME/A Headquarters Business Controls, and when local business control functions are operating effectively, the monitoring process continues via the utilization of a measurement plan of key indicators. These represent a set of standard detailed accounting measurements utilized to measure the health of the overall accounting data base and particular financial statement line items.

There are two types of key indicators, one measuring the potential problems that might affect the reliability of the data base and the other addressing the direction or the trend of the business. The first set of key indicators could be numbers of unreconciled items, number of disagreements between detailed accounts and general ledger accounts, and number of unprocessed invoices. Examples of a second set of key indicators include accounts receivable, and field and manufacturing inventory turnovers.

The key indicator results serve as a quantifiable barometer of discretely identifiable trends within a country and, because of the commonality of the measurements, offer headquarters management an excellent data set on which to base country comparisons. Consequently, they provide a frame of reference which could be used for transferring ideas from one country to another depending on the similarities in the operations.

The business controls effort results in the accumulation of an expansive data base of both qualitative and quantitative information. A cycle has developed in which knowledge feeds techniques, and technique advancement leads to increased knowledge. Through the advancement of techniques, the quality of information provided management has improved dramatically, and management can much more easily determine the course of action in the controls arena.

5. Evaluation Techniques

An open communication process between headquarters and country accounting functions provides for an extensive exchange of ideas regarding technical accounting issues, reporting requirements, business needs for information, and countless other topics. Two key publications, however, truly provide the foundation for the entire E/ME/A reporting plan. The *E/ME/A Accounting Manual* and the *E/ME/A Manufacturing Accounting Manual* provide to countries detailed guidance on specific accounting procedures, specific accounting classifications, theoretical support, explanation of terms, and all reporting requirements from a format and timing perspective. Both manuals are constantly updated and improved to reflect new business requirements, new techniques and modes of analysis, and new accounting pronouncements. The fact that the manuals are so well maintained adds a strong amount of credibility and reliability which ultimately results in a higher-grade end product. The accounting manuals provide for standard data reporting to headquaters for consolidation purposes. Headquarters Accounting reviews the monthly financial statements of each country, in conjunction with related analyses and comments submitted as part of the normal closing process. Various financial analyses, based on data received at the headquarters level, are performed to measure individual country performance and E/ME/A – wide performance. For management, local currency statements are more important. For reporting to shareholders, however, U.S. dollar figures are used.

Until recently, a cost-plus – mark-up transfer pricing policy was used. At present, transfer pricing based on market value is in the testing process. Such policy will lead local management to accept more risk, and it is also hoped that tax issues can be handled more appropriately.

The organization of E/ME/A Accounting is the key to the effectiveness of the analysis process. In general terms, E/ME/A Accounting is structured into a country-level analytical function, and a consolidated analytical function. Both functions perform the financial statement analyses, though from different perspectives. Country analysts address results in terms of particular country management, performance, and environment, and are the primary contact with local accounting management. Monthly joint financial statement reviews involving all country analysts and E/ME/A Accounting Management provide an outstanding vehicle for the exchange for knowledge about particular country results, problems, and trends. This vehicle results in the recognition of common, as well as particular, elements of each country's operation, and affords effective action plan development when necessary. In each country, U.S. books are formatted according to headquarters' needs (in U.S. dollars) using IBM general ledger accounts. Also, in each country, statuary accounts exist for statuary reporting. Usually both systems require different data bases. When the accounting requirements are similar (such as the U.S. and U.K. generally accepted accounting principles), the same data base might be used with minor adjustments.

The consolidated analytical function is principally concerned with the aggregate E/ME/A results. Income statement and balance sheet departments are responsible for logistically preparing and comprehensively analyzing the consolidated financial statements from an individual line item, line-item interrelationship, and integrated perspective. A constant communication channel between the consolidation and country-level departments, as well as an integrated management review, assures that overall E/ME/A results accurately reflect the sum of the parts. Also, all intercompany profits which could result from transfer pricing are eliminated in the process of consolidation. To reach these objectives, everyone must understand the accounting principles of both the host country and the United States.

The financial statements are analyzed from a business perspective. Given the fact that the data received reflect the business, we can view the income statement as a motion picture of the operational activities of the business, and view the balance sheet as a still life of the business. Conclusions are drawn from the data when the following key questions are answered from both local country and consolidated results:

1. What is the present health of the business?
2. What was the health of the business for other periods being compared?
3. Why has the business changed? Why has the business not changed?
4. Why is one country performing differently than another?
5. Does the present business reflect the direction desired or expected by management? In other words, are we meeting management's objectives?
6. What is under management's control and what is not? What is the impact of changes in currency exchange rates?
7. What information does management need now? In the future?

Evaluation techniques and reporting procedures are shown in Tables 4 and 5.

The income statement is analyzed in detail on a month versus prior month basis and a year-to-date versus prior year-to-date basis. Both monthly and year-to-date amounts are also compared to plan data. A prime

Table 4. E/ME/A Headquarters Accounting Evaluation Techniques Reporting and Form of Data

Key concerns
- Adequacy
- Accuracy
- Timeliness
- Commonality (comparability/consistency)

Controlled by
- Communication – most important for E/ME/A accounting community to understand
  - Why it is needed
  - How it is needed
  - Relative importance
  - How it is used

E/ME/A accounting manual
- Accounting procedures
- Reporting procedures/dates
- Accounting codes
- Company accounting standards
- Definitions of terms/acronyms

E/ME/A Manufacturing Accounting Manual

benefit to this approach is that the current activity is being compared to a known and previously understood data set. The task is somewhat complicated by the fact that movements in exchange rates will impact results in U.S. dollars. In times when foreign currency exchange rates become significantly different than those assumed in the plan, a comparison of actual at plan rates versus plan is performed. The restatement of actual to plan rates often provides optimal insight into true business activity.

Detailed income statement enhancement and erosion data are compiled to provide additional information regarding changes from period to period in the interrelationships between particular line items. This provides an excellent source for trend analyses for country-to-country and period-to-period comparisons.

The statement of financial position is analyzed on a month versus prior month, month versus prior year end, month versus same month prior year, and actual versus plan basis. All changes in account balance from period to period are segregated into the portion attributable to currency movements and that attributable to business activity. The balance sheet is transformed from a static to dynamic statement via transformation to the funds flow statement. The statement indicates activity between two bal-

Table 5. E/ME/A Headquarters Accounting Evaluation Techniques Technical Tools

Financial statement analyses

Period-to-period comparisons
- Year to year
- Month to month
- Year to date v. prior year to date
- Month this year vs. same month last year

Actual-to-plan comparisons
- One plan and three plan updated per year (Updates usually driven by new currency rate plans)
- Plans always useful and never outdated
- Constant communication with Planning Functions

Business vs. currency analyses
- Impact of currency
- Impact of business decisions

Enhancements and erosions
- Impact of product mix on margins
- Impact of volumes on profits
- Interaction of different financial statement lines

Ratio analyses – Used for comparison and to indicate direction
- Ratios utilized
    - Gross profit margin
    - Expense/revenue
    - A/R collection
    - Inventory turnover
    - Return on controllable assets

ance sheet dates from the perspective of cash flow. In essence, the funds flow statement is a documentary of the direction applied to resources for the generation of positive business results.

Given the complexity and dynamic nature of the business, and the environment in which it operates, it is not possible to create an equation or list of analytical tools which will by themselves lead to success. Integration of the income statement and balance sheet review process, as well as the study of the relative significance of financial statement interrelationships and intrarelationships, is achieved via the use of ratio analyses. Ratios provide useful gauges of each country's and E/ME/A's performance. The ratios most commonly used include the profitability ratios of gross profit margin, expense to revenue, operating margin, and net profit margin; the activity ratios of collection period, inventory turnover, and asset turnover; the return on assets efficiency ratio; and quick ratio. The headquarters analysis process succeeds only partially as the result of the availability of quantitative data. None of the key questions can be answered without communication. E/ME/A's analysis is understood, because the business of each country comprising E/ME/A is fully understood. Communication techniques ranging from telexes to personal visits all ensure that financial data appropriately reflect the business.

6. Conclusion

In conclusion, it is evident that an effective evaluation process for a company of E/ME/A's magnitude requires a series of concurrent quality efforts. A highly integrated business controls function ensures adequate controls at the country level. Financial analysis techniques utilized in each country provide for a comprehensive evaluation of all facets of the local business. With the help of country reporting and communication channels, E/ME/A Headquarters Accounting is able to evaluate the consolidated financial statements from a total business perspective. By using supporting graphs and pie charts for all countries, major influences are made visible, and it becomes easier to separate areas of direct management responsibility from outside influences.

Monsanto Company — Managing Change

Elwood L. Miller

The Monsanto Company has been in a state of flux since the late 1970s. It will continue to evolve for some time, according to the best estimates. Restructuring ways of thinking and ways of doing things have been both in response to and in anticipation of change. A major corporate reorganization was initiated in 1983. Although the reorganization was implemented quite rapidly and is generating the desired benefits, some reverberations in certain parts of the organization have continued into 1984. Chief executives note that "the company's product lines in 1990 will look quite different" than they do today.

1. Monsanto Company in Perspective[1]

Monsanto originated in 1901 as the Monsanto Chemical Works in Saint Louis, Missouri. In 1933, the successor Monsanto Company was incorporated under Delaware law. Monsanto's world headquarters are located on a 285-acre campus in Saint Louis County. A "world class" research center is also being completed on a separate 210-acre tract of prime Saint Louis County land.

From its beginnings with saccharin, Monsanto has become the fourth largest firm (of seven) in the U.S. chemical industry. In 1983, worldwide sales were $ 6.3 billion.

Today, Monsanto produces a variety of chemicals, petrochemicals, and related products along with engineered products and process controls in a worldwide network of more than 160 plants and research centers located in twenty nations. The more than two thousand products are marketed, directly or through affiliates, in more than one hundred countries. As of December 1983, Monsanto represented, in terms of people, 69,787 common shareholders and some 50,889 employees. (These latter data are the lowest in the past eleven years. The number of common shareholders declined steadily each year from the 98,964 reported in 1973 — a decrease of 30 percent. Employees have been reduced by 20 percent or some 13,000 from the high of 63,926 reported in 1979.)

1.1 A Decade of Transition

Since 1973, Monsanto has evolved from a loosely knit group of chemical businesses with $2 billion in sales to a coordinated group of interdependent units with sales of $7 billion in 1981. The synergism created was welcomed, on the one hand, since the achievements of the corporation were greater than the sum of the results of the related activities standing alone. On the other hand, this synergism created problems regarding performance evaluations — as well as operational and strategic dilemmas. With which component activities should the synergistic surplus be related? How could raw materials be linked more closely with the several intermediate and end products produced by the various units? Given the interdependencies, how could the activities be managed as strategic units? How could plant and people resources be focused more efficiently?

Some of the problems have been solved. Others have been ameliorated. Still others remain.

1.2 Monsanto — Circa 1981

By January 1981, some restructurings had been accomplished although primarily in the form of divestitures rather than organizational changes. Figure 1 reflects the corporate structure existing as of January 1981, as well as the international restructuring being considered at that time.

Monsanto consisted of five operating companies, one majority-owned subsidiary, and an international operation. Each operating company was composed of from three to eight divisions (with twenty-four in total, counting the International and Fisher Control divisions) handling compatible product groups.

Interdependencies. A *modified matrix* system was employed to accommodate the interdependencies (inherent and created) as well as to achieve efficiency and effectiveness. The interdependencies existing within and

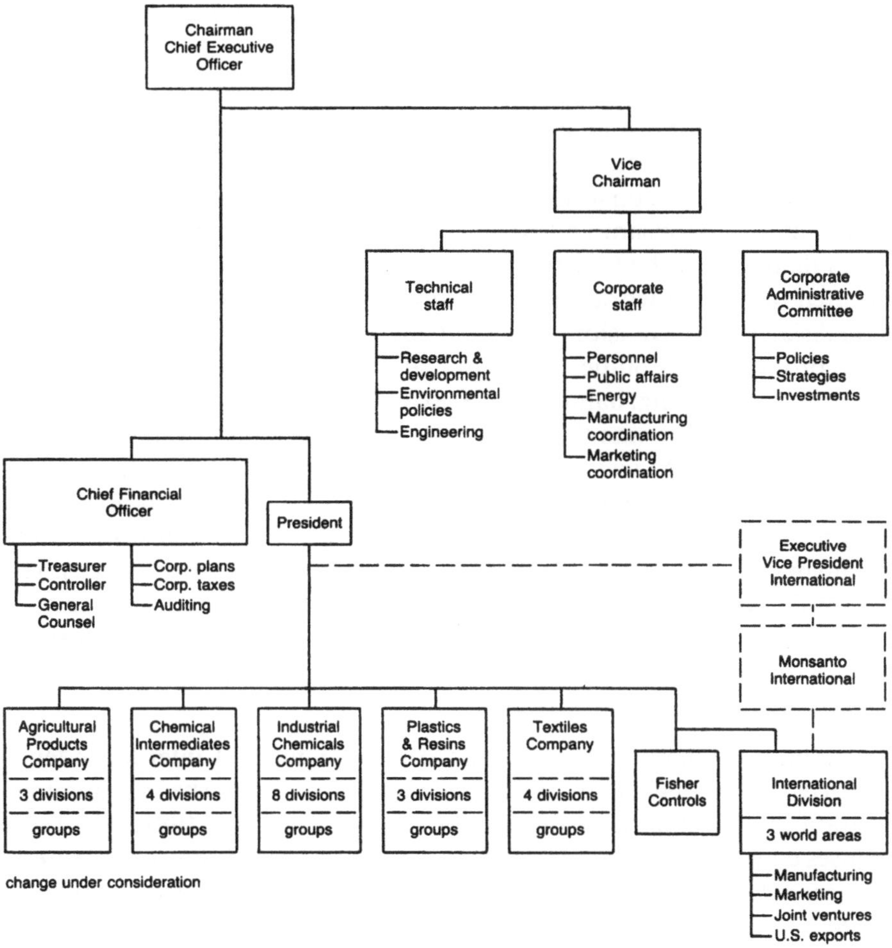

Figure 1. Monsanto Company, Corporate Organization, January 1981

among the operating companies were significant. The heads (vice presidents) of the five operating companies and the managers of their component divisions were charged with worldwide profit responsibility. One of the operating companies, Chemical Intermediates, functioned primarily as the supplier of its sister companies, however. Furthermore, many manufacturing plants within each operating-company responsibility center produced goods for several of the divisional responsibility centers within the company and also for other operating companies. As a result, with some effort, plant assets could be related with operating companies but only after much difficulty with divisional and product group components.

Also, international operations had developed significant proportions by 1980. U.S. exports and products manufactured and sold outside the United States represented $2 billion in 1979 (38 percent of consolidated sales) and $2.24 billion in 1980 (34 percent of sales). Also, at that time, the economies of Monsanto's former U.S. markets were growing at faster rates than that of the United States. The International Division was segmented into three world areas: Europe/Africa, Canada/Latin America, and Asia/Pacific. Division, area, and country managers were also tasked with profit responsibilities for all operations in their areas: on-site manufacturing, marketing, handling U.S. exports, and managing some sizeable joint ventures (one was the seventh largest of its kind in Japan; another was the largest in Mexico). Inter-area transfers were significant, yet Monsanto attempted to determine the total profits of international operations and relate the earnings with overseas areas and units, as well as operating companies and divisions (for their respective products — worldwide). The increasing importance of international operations led Monsanto to consider the establishment in 1981 of a sixth operating company (Monsanto International) to be headed by an executive vice president (represented by the dotted lines in Figure 1).

In addition to manufacturing costs, a final, significant interdependency involved the management of and accountability for marketing, administration, and technical resources (MAT expenses). By 1981, MAT expenses consumed more than $900 million per year and the annual rate of increase (15 percent) was greater than that of sales (9 percent). Plannings of MAT expenses were performed by some forty-four strategic planning units (SPUs) that crossed divisional but not operating company lines. Accountability was less than desired. Results of operating companies could be tracked, but many of the SPUs and divisions could not be monitored practicably.

Innovative solutions. To accommodate the desirable interdependencies, yet minimize their interferences with controls and performance evaluations, several innovative — although temporal — solutions were designed.

Concepts of income. Since operating assets could not be related readily with divisions (or their component business groups), traditional net income and return-on-capital concepts could not be employed. (Several experimental applications were attempted over time, particularly with respect to divisions, but these proved to be impracticable and/or too subjective to form the bases for official evaluations.)

From 1975 until 1983, profitabilities of divisions and groups were evaluated by means of their "*performance incomes*":

Sales	$
Cost of goods sold	
Gross profit	$
Less MAT expenses	
Marketing	$
Administration	
Technology	
Operating profit	$
plus: Other income and credits	
less: Working/Capital charge	
Performance income	$

Profitabilities of operating companies were carried to net income (the above performance income less corporate overhead allocations and provisions for taxes). Return on capital (ROC) was also computed (net income plus the adding back of the working capital charge, divided by the capital employed by each company).

Two additional innovative methods were employed — priority resource budgeting (PRB) and management by results (MBR). Each will be described later since they continue in use today.

1.3 Winds of Change

Over the past decade, the chemical industry was buffeted by two pervasive oil shocks and an inflation-plagued world environment. Concurrently, competition mandated ever-increasing levels of investment in research and development. Earnings suffered.

Moreover, the glamour segments of the industry since the 1930s — petro- and commodity chemicals — underwent significant structural changes. Oil-producing countries and the major oil companies upgraded their crude petroleum into higher value intermediates and represented serious market threats.

After a lengthy period of internal analysis, Monsanto determined that drastic changes were necessary. Some raw materials (notably oil) formed the nucleus of too many of their products. Assets were tied up in industries which, because of competitive structure or overcapacity, held little future promise. Existing interdependencies precluded strategic management (from raw materials to finished products) of desirable core and growth businesses.

On the positive side, Monsanto held world leadership positions in several industry segments, owned state-of-the-art technologies in other areas, and was on the cutting edge of emerging technologies in still others.

Beginning in 1979, Monsanto embarked on a series of major divestitures to rid itself of low or non-productive assets. These actions caused net income to fall below 2 percent of sales in 1980, from the normal 6 to 9 percent range of the prior decade. Results for the 1979–1983 period would have suffered even more were it not for some offsetting gains and tax benefits (Table 1).

Table 1. The Monsanto Company — Extraordinary Effects on Income, 1979–1983

Year	Event	After-tax gain (Loss)	
		Millions of $	Per share $
1979	Withdrew from nylon operations in Europe	(49)	(.53)
1980	Sold polyester business in United States	(69)	(1.90)
1981	Sold Conoco joint venture	68	1.75
	Sold Spanish polymer interests	(39)	(1.07)
1982	Sold European acrylic fibers business	(18)	(.46)
	Debt exchanged for common shares	23	.58
	Early retirement program cost	(11)	(.26)
1983	Use of ex – U.S. loss carry forwards	33	.81

Source: Compiled from annual reports.
Note: In addition, there were many smaller product line divestments. In total, Monsanto divested businesses with annual sales of about $ 2 Billion.

The divestitures cited primarily represented external restructurings. On January 1, 1983, Monsanto also completed its second phase of strategic redirection — a major corporate reorganization.

2. Monsanto Today

Monsanto is a somewhat leaner company today. Many of the interdependencies that were inherent or created have been eliminated or reduced. Also, administrative personnel have been reduced (by the elimination of one operating company) and/or reassigned (some staff-related functions were decentralized from corporate to operating companies).

Examination of the organizational structure that had evolved as of April 1984 (Figure 2) indicates an arrangement of three somewhat independent sectors: maturing chemicals and fibers businesses, emerging non-chemical businesses, and agricultural/nutritional products.

Operating companies — the largest units with a commonality of purpose and product — were reduced from five to four. The former Chemical Intermediates Company was eliminated, and its component parts were absorbed by the surviving companies for which the parts represented links in normal production chains.

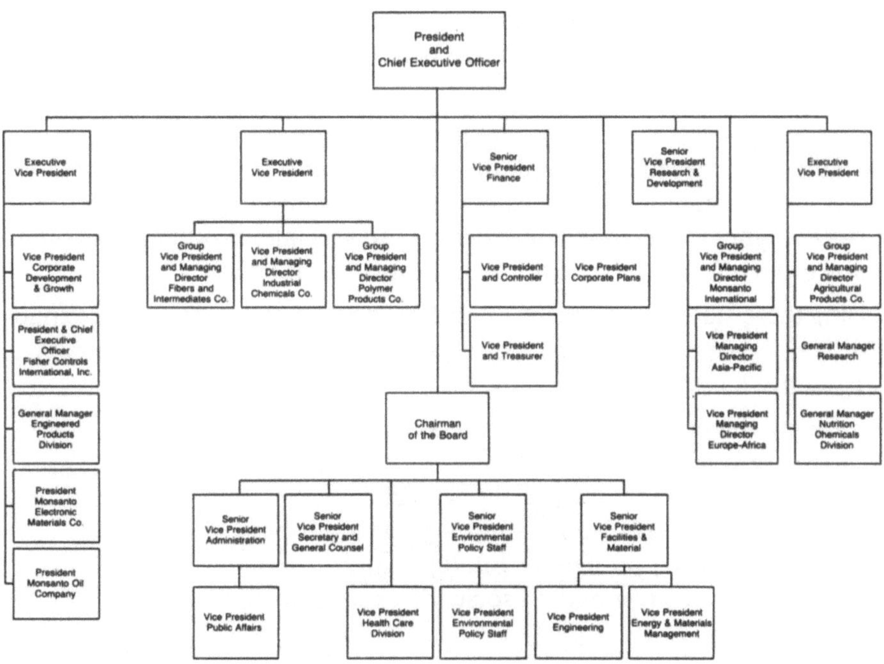

Figure 2. Monsanto Company, Corporate Organization, April 1984
Source: Courtesy of Monsanto Company

Four stand-alone divisions — units smaller and less complex than operating companies — were established for emerging businesses. When these divisions grow larger in scope, they will become operating companies. Commonalities of processes, product groups, and market areas were the criteria employed in the restructuring.

Two relatively free-standing, wholly owned subsidiaries (Fisher Controls and Monsanto Oil) are operated as subsidiaries with a certain degree of additional autonomy. Other product divisions and groups still exist within operating companies, but their exact numbers are not known.

The Monsanto organization is still undergoing response to change and should continue to evolve. The possibility of establishing a Latin American administrative headquarters nearer the region is now under consideration.

2.1 Strategic Planning Systems

Within Monsanto, strategic planning forms the critical direction for all management, control, and operating activities. All are interwoven into a cybernetic style of management and performance evaluations (Figure 3).

Strategies flow primarily from the top down. Top management sets corporate objectives and policy guidelines which currently are (1) to double earnings each decade *after* inflation; (2) to continue strategic redirection away from commodity petrochemicals; (3) to move product portfolios toward higher value-added proprietary and specialty products; and (4) to reduce the effects of cyclical fluctuations in economies.

Using these statements, senior operating executives develop more explicit "direction papers"outlining the strategies to be pursued. Elements of Monsanto's overall strategy are to

1. Renew the core chemical business;
2. Increase options for growth;
3. Emphasize growth around the world;
4. Extend the market leadership of growth businesses;
5. Create windows on new technology; and
6. Anticipate and respond to society's expectations.

Operating companies translate these materials into long-range and operating plans. Individual managers and other decision units then identify the specific results to be achieved in support of the operating plans.

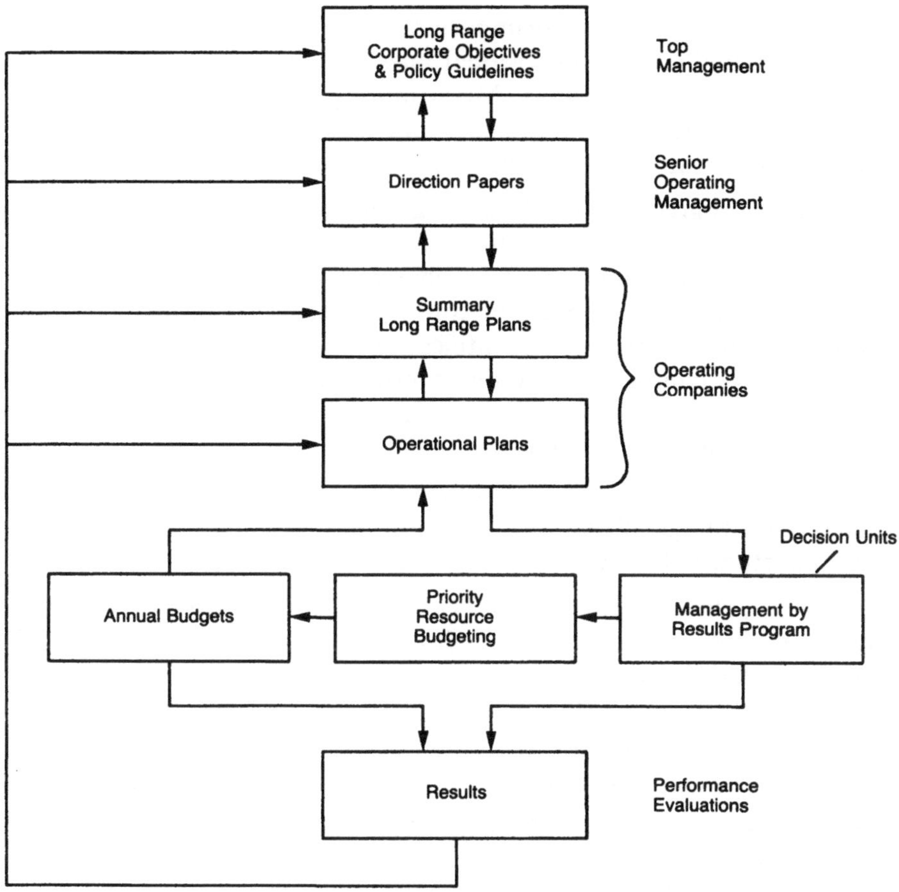

Figure 3. Monsanto Company: Cybernetic Style of Management and Performance Evaluation

Source: Courtesy of Monsanto Company

The end results are comprehensive annual budgets specifying the outputs sought and the inputs necessary to achieve them.

Recent divestitures and corporate reorganizations have been restructurings to enhance these goals, meet customers' needs better, and enhance the contributions of technology in more research-intensive (and less capital-intensive) undertakings.

Corporate realignments have reduced the number of SPUs slightly (from forty-four to forty-two). More importantly, the new operational structure has nearly eliminated the divisional lines that had to be crossed (and accommodated) by the SPUs. Much more planning can now be performed in-line (tied to management reportings), thereby enhancing both controls by and evaluations of the several divisions and their components.

To enhance progress toward the strategic goals further, a Corporate Development and Growth Committee was formed in January 1983, headed by a vice president. The committee is charged with assisting line managers with near-term strengthenings of core businesses and developments of growth businesses through identifications of attractive acquisitions. These are to be compatible, developed businesses with established market niches, high technologies, and potentials for attractive near-term (and increasing) returns on capital investments.

Monsanto employs an *evergreen* system to review/evaluate assumptions underlying strategic plans. Reviews are continuous and made as change and opportunity dictate.

Interface — strategic planning and capital budgeting. Monsanto's "total investment" level — capital expenditures, acquisitions/venture capital, and research and development (R & D) commitments — continues high, but with a pronounced shift in the underlying components.

During the 1979–1983 period, Monsanto's capital expenditures amounted to roughly $1 billion in average 1983 dollars. Decreases were made in the basic, core businesses where adequate productive capacity for growth was considered to exist. Increased investments were made in less capital-intensive, high-technology product areas.

Briefly, capital expenditure requests must support long-range plans. Projects in excess of $3 million must be submitted to the appropriate executive vice president for approval. Such appropriation requests usually comprise from ten to seventy-five pages. Lesser requests are approved at the group vice president or general manager levels as appropriate.

Interface — strategic planning and R & D. Monsanto has historically been dependent on R & D. Expenditures in nominal dollars have tripled over the last five years and amounted to 5 percent of sales in 1983. Emphasis on the development of new proprietary products and processes mandates that ever-increasing amounts of resources be allocated to R & D in three broad areas: (1) regeneration — increase values of existing technologies; (2) expansion — identify new and increase present markets for growth products; and (3) venture — explore new fields.

2.2 Operational Planning

The interrelationships of strategic and operational planning, shown in Figure 3, shroud some innovative programs that tend to involve everyone.

Management by results (MBR). In 1975, Monsanto initiated a key program called "management by results." The MBR program is employed actively today and is actually a variant form of management by objectives.

Briefly, managers and other decision units establish specific results to be accomplished in support of operating plans. These results (or goals) can be almost anything from specified earnings per share, increases in productivity, new products/technologies, and social responsibility commitments, to cost reductions in management reportings, correspondence, or housekeeping. The MBR program works because almost everyone is involved, and the MBR goals agreed on become important benchmarks for subsequent performance evaluations.

Priority resource budgeting (PRB). For decades, Monsanto has used sophisticated standard cost systems to monitor costs attached to products, including the costs of plant assets consumed — even though the latter were not always traceable to particular divisions. Allotments of resources were determined, however, on an operating unit basis.

In 1978, a system termed "priority resource budgeting" was introduced to assure that (1) available resources were allocated in support of strategic plans; (2) approved projects/products would be supported by adequate marketing, administration, and technology expenses; and (3) expenses would be consistent with the operating results budgeted. In effect, PRB (a modified form of zero-based budgeting) serves as the "missing link" needed by decision units to direct and control MAT and indirect manufacturing expenses. It also assures that the most important products/activities are being funded.

Decision units, according to Monsanto's PRB manual, are "the smallest meaningful group of people and/or other resources devoted to achieving a common significant business purpose." The person in charge of each decision unit (generally five to fifteen people with an annual budget of $150,000 to $400,000) defines its basic mission and the threshold level (minimum) of resources (people and money) necessary to remain viable. Incremental resources needed to achieve additional results (set forth in the MBR program) are then specified, justified, and ranked in their perceived order of importance or desirability.

Naturally, changes occur in rankings during the reviews and defenses required at the director, division, and operating-company levels. In the review process, the manager and all immediate subordinates meet and mutually agree on priority rankings. This improves the subordinates' understandings of and commitments to the activity's goals. On final approvals, the PRB process (1) identifies what is to be accomplished in support of strategic plans; (2) allocates the resources considered to be necessary to achieve the results; and (3) ranks activities above and below the "funding line" so that responses by decision units to future change might be facilitated.[2]

Comprehensive budget reviews. Operating companies submit operating budgets, incorporating the PRB levels of funding to the corporate review committee. Budget submissions include narrative summaries, financial exhibits, and supplemental information. Narrative summaries address basic assumptions and premises, assessments of future business and economic environments, and the results budgeted.

Financial exhibits consist of executive summaries supported by analyses of sales, net income, MAT expenses, manning tables, capital employed, and asset management. Changes in sales projected from the prior year are analyzed by cause: volumes, prices, product additions/deletions, and so forth. Changes in levels of significant MAT expenses are also explained, including the effects of inflation and cost reduction. Reviews of asset management focus primarily on return on capital and cash flows. Supporting data address projected levels of inventories, receivables, and capital expenditures.

Supplemental information usually highlights changes in key products, start-up expenses of major projects, changes in plant utilizations, and significant R & D commitments.

On approvals, budgets are considered to be "contracts" between the company and the managers and become parts of the "goals" for the year. Actual and budgeted results are reviewed monthly. Quarterly forecasts are prepared to minimize "surprises" should actual results differ from budgeted levels. The original annual budgets, as approved, however, are the official benchmarks with which actual results are compared and assessed.

As can be imagined, the paperwork involved in Monsanto's cybernetic management system can become burdensome. Consequently, efforts have been introduced recently to reduce the paperwork involved with monthly analyses of historical results, thereby freeing managers to spend more time assessing and managing the future.

2.3 Performance Evaluations

The corporate reorganization in 1983 enabled Monsanto to combine basic building-block facilities with the downstream users, thereby enhancing strategic planning. Some aspects of the reorganization, however, increased the use of the matrix system of management. In addition, interdependencies continue to exist between the operating companies and the international operations.

What follows are general synopses of the evalutions of activities and their managers. Adaptations made relative to international operations will be mentioned later.

Official performance evaluations of activities and individuals are reviewed shortly after the end of the calendar year. During the following March, incentive compensation is distributed.

Activity evaluations. Annual activity reviews, made at the corporate level, consist of comprehensive reviews of planned and actual results: that is, variances from original, approved budgets.

For the free-standing companies and divisions, the major financial criteria assessed are sales, net income, return on capital, asset management, and cash flow. Activity evaluations of groups and other units lesser than divisions may be able to focus only on sales, operating incomes, or gross margins.

Monsanto considers capital to include the investment necessary (1) to maintain the existing earnings base; and (2) to support future income growth. Proxies used to estimate the investment needed to maintain existing earnings are a LIFO-cost adjustment, current cost depreciation, and an estimate of "maintenance" R & D costs to sustain existing businesses.

A variety of financial and nonfinancial criteria is used to compare the company and its segments with competitors. The Competitive Report, prepared annually, compares Monsanto with the other "Big Six" chemical companies and nine smaller specialized chemical competitors.

Manager evaluations. The incentive compensations for managers are determined in a variety of ways, depending on the positions concerned.

Executives of operating companies and divisions are evaluated, in part, by the net income attributed to their operations. A second part of the evaluation is based on the level of achievement reflected by his or her MBR program. As mentioned earlier, the goals cited in approved MBR programs can be anything in support of strategic and operating plans. Consequently, MBR benchmarks can be financial and/or nonfinancial and encompass short-term and progress toward long-term goals. Moreover, both efficiency (doing something right) and effectiveness (doing the right something) can be assessed.

Performance evaluations of managers of decision units are determined by their immediate superiors. Where appropriate, net income of the division to which the manager is assigned is used as one segment. This encourages decision makers to keep the best interests of their activities in mind. MBR goals serve as the second segment. For most lower-level decision makers, the MBR inputs would represent the only items considered.

While weights assigned net incomes and MBR inputs are not known, presumably the relative emphasis placed on profitability would be a function of the decision maker's perceived impact on profits and the unit's strategic goals.

2.4 International Operations

Activities outside the United States have long since outgrown any stepchild status. At last report, one-third of Monsanto's consolidated sales and 30 percent of consolidated net income were attributed to former U.S. operations. (These results are significantly lower than in prior years because of a stronger U.S. dollar, increased competition, and depressed economic conditions overseas.) Nearly a full line of products is manufactured abroad; one-half of former U.S. sales were supplied by ex – U.S. plants. Monsanto is convinced that important segments of future growth will occur outside the United States. For example, within the next decade, three-fourths of the growth in chemicals is forecast to occur in ex – U.S. markets. Consequently, active investment programs are projected for international market developments, including strategic acquisitions. Major research centers (agricultural, pharmaceutical, and electronic) have been established during the last three years in Brazil, Belgium, and Japan. Also, venture-capital investments in high-technology businesses have been made in Europe and Asia-Pacific. Also, an Advent Eurofund consists of cooperative research ventures with major European and U.S. universities.

Interdependencies. International operations and the U.S. operating companies/divisions share joint responsibility for ex – U.S. profitabilities of product lines. Basically, worldwide strategies are established by the operating companies/divisions for their product lines. These strategies are then issued to the international operations for implementation and inclusion in their strategic and operating plans.

Monsanto International, headed by a group vice president, has been restructured from three to four world areas: Canada, Latin America, Asia-Pacific, and Europe-Africa. (Prior to 1984, Canada and Latin America comprised one area.) At present, Canada and Latin America are directed by the group vice president, with each of the remaining two areas headed by a vice president. (Monsanto is considering the appointment of a separate manager to head the Latin America area in the near future.)

Some decentralization of the headquarters' international staff occurred as a result of the 1983 corporate reorganization. A significant number of staff were reassigned to (1) operating companies, to improve coordination; and (2) the field, to assist operations in the world area locations.

Each ex – U.S. operation has a charter and a mission statement. These missions vary from generating net income, to local manufacturing required to protect patent rights, to obtaining freer access to markets, to providing economies of scale for U.S. companies, to introducting newly developed products, to merely furnishing technical support.

Risk evaluation procedures. With operations in more than one hundred countries, a full range of risks are encountered: currency fluctuations and regulations, wage and price controls, employment regulations, expropriations, and patent risks, among others.

Management admits that most risk-evaluation procedures are somewhat "esoteric." Usually, adustments for perceived risks are accommodated by changes in the expected returns on capital and cash flows, both in timings and in amounts.

Profitabilities of many existing products, however, are dependent on patent rights (more than 80 percent for agricultural products alone). The strategic moves toward more proprietary and high-technology products will increase such dependencies. Consequently, managers are required to protect patent rights. For this and other reasons, investments in most lesser-developed countries (LDCs) usually are considered high risks. Many LDCs offer little or no patent protection. Some others (notably Red China, Malaysia, and Indonesia) are drafting legislation to increase patent protection to encourage desirable foreign investment and technology.

Performance Evaluations. As with most multinational enterprises (MNEs), Monsanto attempts to apply the same criteria to evaluate domestic and ex – U. S. operations wherever practicable and realistic. As with most MNEs, however, adjustments must be made for international phenomena, both inherent and created. Two created dilemmas are (1) shared responsibilities for ex – U. S. profitabilities of product lines, and (2) inter-area transfers and sales.

Criteria employed. Measures and benchmarks applied to ex – U. S. activities tend to be as varied as their mission statements.

Earnings and related financial measures of efficiency (sales, asset management, product costs, return on capital, cash flow, and so on) are applied to subsidiaries and other free-standing operations. For more dependent activities, less comprehensive financial measures, from operating incomes to simply gross margins, are used. For support units, operating costs tend to be the only practicable financial measures. All of these are monitored monthly, evaluated annually.

Benchmarks and nonfinancial measures consist of approved operating budgets, standard costs, MBR programs, and local economic and market data (where available), among others.

Criteria for evaluations of ex – U. S. managers parallel those used in the United States wherever appropriate. Here again, measurements and benchmarks will be as agreed on by the individual and his or her superior. Normally, for most top managers of former U. S. operations, primary emphasis will be placed on the U. S. dollar – equivalent financial results of the related activities. Measurements established within MBR programs are usually considered supplementary for top managers and primary for lower-level decision makers.

Goals established by approved budgets and MBR programs serve as benchmarks for top managers and subordinates, respectively.

Currencies used to measure criteria. Financial performances of all free-standing units, domestic and ex – U. S., are made in U. S. dollars. Standard reasonings apply: investors contribute U. S. dollars and expect returns in U.S. dollars, in the form of dividends and stock appreciation affected by consolidated financial results.

Managers of ex – U.S. operations have a shared responsibility for exchange rate fluctuations. Forecast rates (and projected local prices) are used in approved budgets. Actual rates (and actual local prices) are used in tracking and evaluating financial performances. This approach involves local managers in exchange-rate fluctuations and encourages them to adjust selling prices in line with changes in exchange rates, as well as local inflation wherever possible.[3] Also, ex-post variance analyses can address not only the effects of changes in the quantities/mixes of goods sold, but also those of changes in the prices of goods *and* monies.

Treatments of exchange-rate fluctuations differ. Total variances are ascribed to activities. For manager evaluations, primary emphasis is placed on the management responses through changes in local market prices.

In the past, Monsanto was not overly concerned with exchange rate exposures or fluctuations. Operating with more than 100 currencies, Monsanto considered itself hedged internally. After the implementation of *SFAS-8*[4] in 1976, the resulting "paper, or accounting gains and losses" had significant adverse effects on reported earnings per share. In May 1970, Monsanto established a multilateral (intracorporate) netting facility in Switzerland (Monsanto Finance) monitored from Brussels (by Monsanto Europe). At least one-half of all European transactions were intracorporate and, given that volume, annual savings in conversion costs alone exceeded 1.5 percent per million dollars. Better controls over liquidity and exchange exposure proved to be additional intangible benefits. (Results would have even been better had some countries — notably France — permitted netting procedures.) Given this success, Monsanto is considering the establishment of a similar netting facility in the Asia-Pacific area where an adequate volume of intracorporate transactions now makes this possible.

In 1982, Monsanto adopted *SFAS-52*[5] for financial reporting purposes. This and other changes in financial reporting requirements have minimal impact upon activity evaluations, however, and are not used to evaluate managers.

Transfer prices and inter-area sales. Inter-unit transfers in 1983 were $297 million, or a 25 percent decline from the 1981 level — undoubtedly the result of the reorganization. Conversely, inter-area sales totalled $452 million in 1983: nearly a 50 percent increase over 1981 — the result of serving worldwide customer needs from the lowest cost production unit wherever located.

In the main, market prices are used for intracorporate transfers regardless of location. Where unavailable or otherwise impractical, transfer prices are negotiated by the units involved. In certain cases where transfer prices must be "managed" for whatever reason, ex-post adjustments are made to the activity and manager evaluations concerned.

Monsanto normally records inter-area sales on an "area basis" whereby sales and the related incomes are attributed to the customer locations; that is, a sale from a U.S. activity to Mexico is reflected as a Mexican sale and profit. This not only avoids any double-counting but also furnishes management with data concerning consumption locations, considered to be more valuable than information relating to sources of supply. (In recent annual reports, Monsanto disclosed world area segment data both on the area basis, cited above, and on the "entity basis" as required by financial reporting standards.)

Corporate charges. Wherever practicable, corporate, company, divisional, and area charges are made directly to the using organizations. Residual charges are assigned to units by means of an elaborate allocation system.

As might be expected, both types of charges produce complaints from the field units regarding the absolute amounts of the charges, their determination, and their non-controllability by field managers.

Income taxes. Foreign income taxes are used in evaluations of activities and their managers. Provisions for U.S. income taxes on foreign earnings are *not* so considered. The latter policy is followed for two reasons. First, Monsanto normally intends to use ex – U.S. earnings to finance ex – U.S. growth as opposed to repatriations in the near term. When and from where repatriations are to be made are corporate decisions rather than those of local managements. (As of the close of 1983, no tax provisions had been made for $741 million of undistributed foreign earnings.)

2.5 Role of Internal Auditing

Upwards of three hundred locations are subject to routine visits by Monsanto's internal auditing staff. The audit cycle varies from twenty-four to forty months, depending on the perceived risks, with an average of about thirty-six months.

Monsanto has relied historically on internal audit visits as assurances of compliance and strong internal control.

Today, an increased concern for the internal auditing function surrounds the security of data processing and information systems.

3. Conclusions

On the cover of Monsanto's 1983 *Annual Report* is the statement "Monsanto intends to be the best in whatever we choose to do — it's that simple."

This paper has touched on the evolution of Monsanto from a leading, old-line chemical company to a multinational enterprise building on its existing strengths and "creating windows on new technology." In the process, the corporation has restructured its organization, as well as its managerial accounting system, to minimize interdependencies and enable its several parts to function as strategic units – all to serve its customers better. As new technologies create new opportunities, the organization and its systems will undoubtedly change as well. As an old adage suggests, resources are not – but becoming!

The writer is indebted to several officials of the Monsanto Company. Permission and cooperation of Francis J. Fitzgerald, Executive Vice President, and Francis A. Stroble, Senior Vice President and Chief Financial Officer, enabled this paper to be constructed. Assistant Controllers, Don R. Daues and Rodney L. Bishop, contributed valuable time responding to questions and provided useful insights. Finally, Mr. Bishop gratefully agreed to review the draft of the paper and correct errors of omission and commission. Any that remain must be attributed to the author.

Notes

[1] Much of this section pertaining to Monsanto's situation and data prior to 1982 represent an updating of "Monsanto Company — Management by Results," appearing as Appendix B, in the writer's *Responsibility Accounting and Performance Evaluations* (New York: Van Nostrand Reinhold Company, 1982). Materials were extracted by permission of the publisher.

[2] In 1979, Harvard Business School developed a case study regarding PRB in concert with

Monsanto. The case, No. 9-380-048, was entitled "Monsanto Company: The Queeny Division — parts A and B."

[3] Monsanto experimented with managerial uses of current cost accounting but found the benefits were not worth their costs. Uses of projected market prices for inputs and outputs make managers aware of changing price levels without costly revisions of systems.

[4] Financial Accounting Standards Board, *Statement of Financial Accounting Standards No. 8*, "Accounting for the Translation of Foreign Currency Transactions and Foreign Currency Financial Statements" (Stamford, Conn.: FASB, 1975).

[5] Financial Accounting Standards Board, *Statement of Financial Accounting Standards No. 52*, "Foreign Currency Translation" (Stamford, Conn.: FASB, 1981).

GoldStar Electronics

K. Won Kang and Soong H. Park

1. Introduction

GoldStar is the flagship company of Lucky-GoldStar Group, the fiftieth largest non – U.S. industrial corporation in the world. The GoldStar electronics firm was founded in 1959 with the modest aim to provide basic consumer electronic items to the people of Korea who were still trying to recover from the devastating effects to Japanese occupation and the conflict with the North. In June 1959, the company produced Korea's first vacuum tube radios in regular production line, rapidly moving to transistor radios in 1960, telephones in 1961, black and white television sets in 1966, color television sets in 1977, and microcomputers in 1982.[1] Since the company went public in 1970, it has grown in size, market diversification, and technical sophistication. Its international operations not only grew in absolute size but also became a significant part of the total business. Establishment in 1982 of Goldstar of America's (GSAI) consumer electronics factory in Huntsville, Alabama, opened a new chapter in the history of the Korean electronics industry. See Figures 1 and 2 for overviews of the electronics industry. As of May 1984, the company's overseas network consisted of fifteen sales offices and three production/technical centers. (See Table 1.)

GoldStar first adopted a divisionalized operational system in 1967, along the product lines of consumer electronics, communications, and electrical wires. Only in 1983, however, did the company adopt true decentralization of authority and responsibility of operation. Diversity of GoldStar's operations and the vast geographical area covered by the company's operations made it virtually impossible for the central management to react in a timely fashion, and the extremely keen competition in consumer electronics, both in domestic and international markets, probably influenced the company greatly in adopting the decentralization of

Table 1. Lucky-Goldstar Companies

Field	Company	Main products or activities
Chemicals	Lucky, Ltd.	Chemical products
	Lucky Continental Carbon	Carbon black
	Gold Star Co., Ltd.	Electric & electronic products, mini-computers, mainframes
	GoldStar Cable	Electric wire & communication cable, heavy machinery
	Gold Star Tele-Electric	Telecommunication equipment, computer peripherals, automatic control systems, medical equipment
Electricity, electronics & communi-cations	Gold Star Electric	Telecommunication products
	Gold Star Instrument & Electric	Electric & electronic equipment for industrial process control system
	Gold Star Precision	Precision electronic equipment
	Shinyeong Electric	Electrical equipment
	Gold Star Semiconductor	Trs, ICs, LSIs, ESSs, computers, CAD/CAM
	Gold Star-Alps Electronics	Electronic equipment
Energy & resources	Honam Oil Refinery	Refined petroleum products
	Korea Mining & Smelting	Nonferrous metal smelting
Construction & engineering	Lucky Development	General construction
	Lucky Engineering	Technical services
Securities, insurance & finance	Lucky Securities	Brokerage, dealing and underwriting
	Pan Korea Insurance	Insurance
	Pusan Investment & Finance	Short-term finance

Table 1. Continued.

Field	Company	Main products or activities
	Gold Star Investment & Finance	Short-term finance
Trade & distribution	Lucky-Goldstar International Corp.	Exporting, importing, manufacturing
	Hee Sung Co., Ltd.	Advertising & supermarket retailing
Public services	Yonam Foundation	Scholarships
	Yonam Educational Institute	Education

decision making. In short, the company had all of the classical conditions of decentralization: need for technical expertise, necessity for timely decision making, vast size, and geographical diversification. The purpose of this paper is to describe and examine GoldStar's planning and evaluation system, with emphasis on the missions and evaluation of the overseas subsidiaries.

The paper will first present the company's management philosophy and the organizational structure. Next, the company's overall strategy is briefly discussed to provide background information for the discussion of the strategic/long-term planning system. Then the system of results reporting and evaluation of managerial performance is decsribed. The paper concludes with a discussion of the company's future plans in operations and administrative structure.

2. Organization of the Company

The key concept in the management philosophy of the Lucky-GoldStar companies is "inhwa" or harmony among people. Since the company's inception, its goal has been to achieve a synergetic effect through harmonious relationships among the employees, as well as with the suppliers and customers. The "inhwa" philosophy is almost opposite that of the

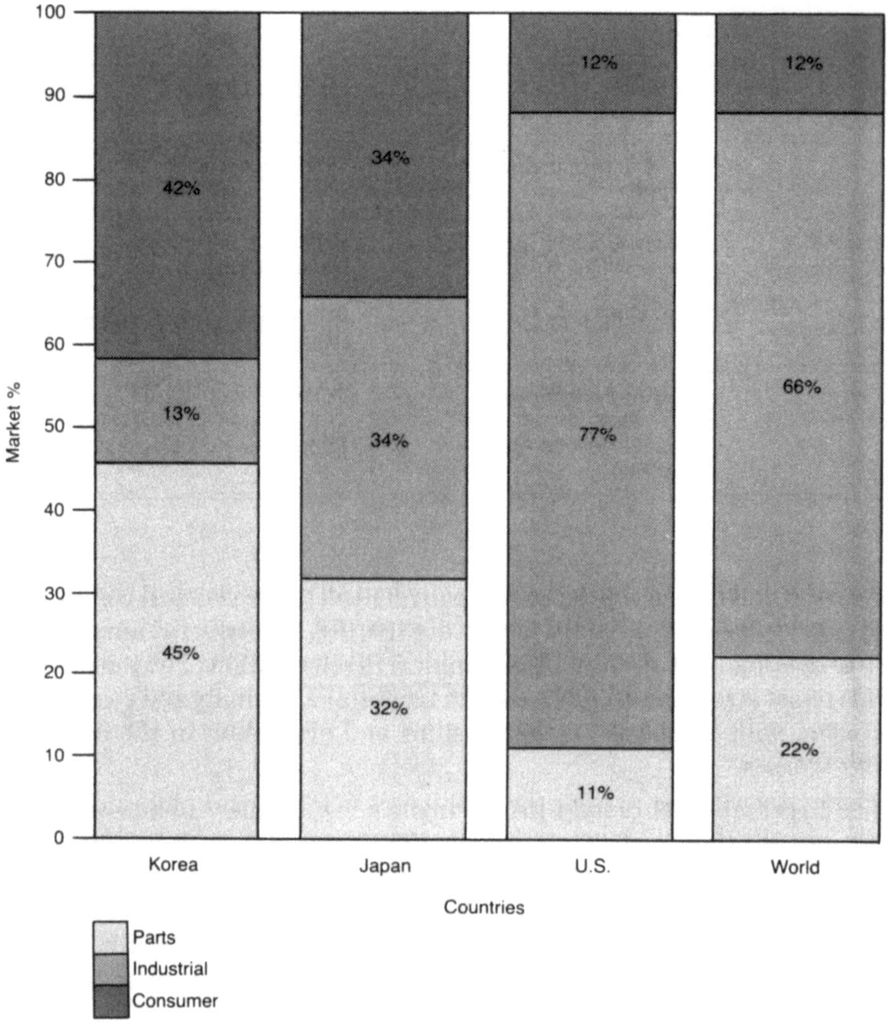

Figure 1. Electronics Market by Industry

uncooperative principal/agent relationship described in "agency theory." While the agency theory concentrates on the moral hazard issues and the need for monitoring in noncooperative game settings, "inhwa" investigates the opportunity costs of noncooperative gaming itself and seeks to maximize the fruits of cooperation with larger returns for everyone. The Lucky-GoldStar Group has been well known for good cooperation among the companies in sharing management talents, technology, and

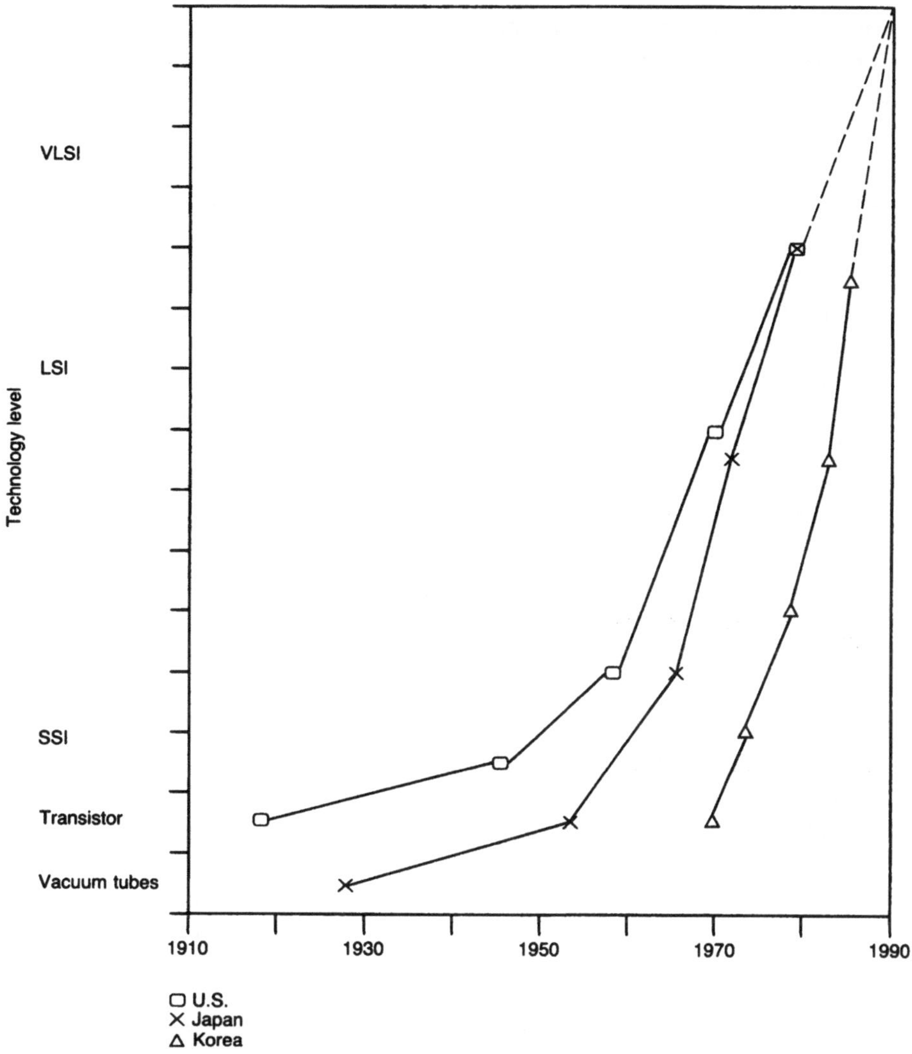

Figure 2. Technology Levels in Electronics

financial resources, and the formal organizational structure of the group also reflects the "inhwa" philosophy.

The executive decision-making body for GoldStar, as well as other companies in the Lucky-GoldStar Group, is the Executive Policy Committee led by Chairman J.K. Koo, and the presidents of key companies in the group comprise the committee members. Major investment decisions, as well as the assignment of the projects within the group, including joint ventures, are made by this committee.[2] Funding for major investments is also discussed here along with top-level executive appointments and the evaluations of their performance.

Shin-Koo Huh, president of GoldStar, directs the operations of GoldStar in three major divisions: marketing, manufacturing and finance, and administration, each under the direction of an executive vice president. Mr. Huh and the executive vice presidents form the Executive Operations Committee responsible for implementing the major policy decisions made by the Executive Policy Committee. Marketing efforts are again divided into domestic and export sales, while the manufacturing units are divided along the product lines. Industrial products, such as elevators and large electric motors and the products that require special knowledge (computers), are managed as special units. The manufacturing division is responsible for technology and product development, as well as the production in factories and related activities such as procurement and recruiting and training of factory workers. The organizational structure below this executive level is primarily based on product-line and geographical considerations. Each product line is considered as a profit center, as are sales units.

GoldStar has three subsidiaries in the United States: GSAI, the manufacturing plant in Huntsville, Alabama; GSEI, the sales division in New York; and GoldStar Microtech in Sunnyvail, California. GSEI's role is very clear; it is responsible for all marketing efforts in the United States, Canada, and South America. GSAI's role is to manufacture quality products in the United States with the techniques well tested in Korean facilities. Its contribution is mainly to develop brand recognition in the United States and to alleviate the impact of trade protectionism movements in this country. GoldStar Microtech, however, has long-run strategic responsibility to obtain information on new electronics technology and to evaluate it for commercial value. GS Microtech is essentially a sentry post for the technical information, although a moderate amount of product development research is conducted on the premises. In addition to the U.S. corporations, GoldStar maintains numerous branch offices in the United States. Figure 3 presents a more detailed description of the company's organization.

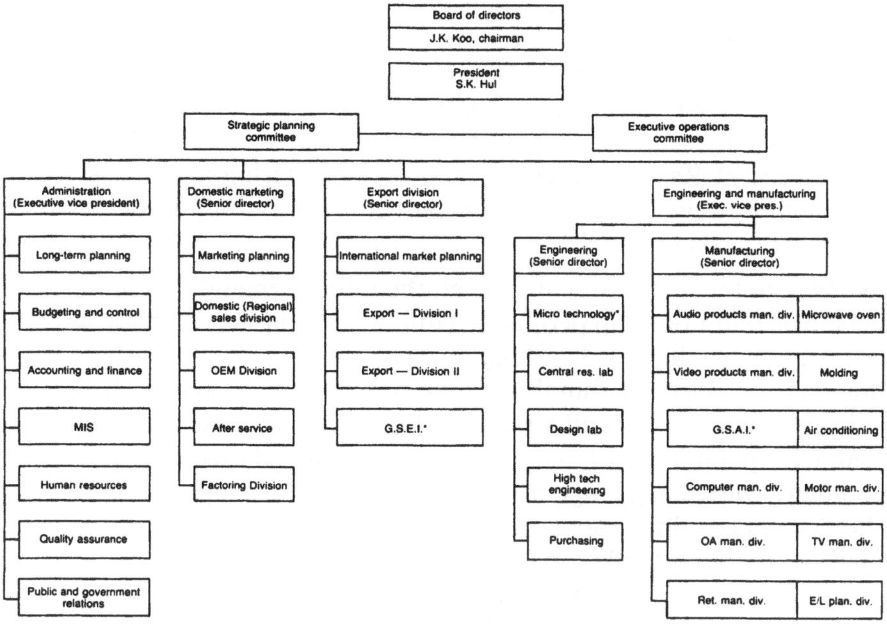

* US incorporated subsidiaries
Figure 3.

3. The Planning System

What should the name GoldStar represent, in the minds of consumers, five years from now? Should it represent good quality, inexpensive television sets in discount stores, or should the vision be in high fidelity audio/video systems, or in microcomputers in professional offices? GoldStar has settled on the latter.[3] This does not mean that the company will abandon color television and audio/video cassette recorder (VCR) production. It does mean, however, the company will invest heavily in the development of integrated circuitry technology, and that marketing will be geared to a more expensive, professional environment rather than a family-oriented electronic entertainment market, at least internationally.

Domestically, GoldStar enjoys the reputation of a technological leader and quality manufacturer. Therefore, the company will definitely utilize its good reputation in the domestic consumer market and continue to produce and sell consumer electronic goods. In Korea, however, what used to be the most prestigious and profitable color television market is rapidly reaching the saturation point with the average age of the sets being less than four years. That is, the ownership of color sets has spread so rapidly, it may reach the saturation point before the demand for replacement is generated. The industry is attempting to generate new demand for second sets by selling home computers and for new related products, notably the VCRs. To maintain the reputation of technological leadership in Korea, however, it is very important to do very well in the personal computer market as well.[4]

In short, in the international market, the future demand and profit lie in personal computers and peripheral equipment, and domestically, success in computers will provide a long coattail for television and other more mundane products. Within this overall company-wide goal, each division is to set its own goals and strategies. Operationally, each division has a long-term planning team reporting to the divisional executive and to the company-wide, long-range planning committee. Each profit center unit should prepare three categories of projects: long-term plan, investment plan, and operating plan.

3.1 Long-Term Plan Development

Long-term planning includes both the development of new future projects and the review of current projects with respect to their long-term profitability. Thus, the projects to be considered in the long-term plan can be classified into three categories: (1) existing projects; (2) new projects; and (3) Project X, as described in Table 2.

Plans for the existing projects include specific volume and profit goals and means to accomplish those goals, including financial and human resource requirements. The plans for the new projects are initially developed by project task force teams (TFTs) concentrating on the technical and capital investment requirements; then the long-range planning team examines the profitability using computerized simulation models. The Project X plans are long-term strategic items that have not been evaluated sufficiently to be classified as "new projects." The Project X items lack specific plans and relevant information, but the future of the company depends on these items, and the ability of top management to evaluate properly divisions' efforts in this area is very important. The format and content of proposals for Project X items are presented in Table 3.

A detailed description of the documents and contents used by profit cen-

Table 2. Classification of Projects for Planning Purposes

Projects	Existing	New	Project X
Definition	Items currently in production or being marketed that can be produced with the technology currently within the company.	Items that are not currently manufactured or marketed by the company at the present time. But these items can be produced with new technology available in the company.	Products that should be developed for long-term contribution to revenue and profits. Includes projects that have been approved, but have not been developed sufficiently to be classified as a "new" project.
Predictability of demand	Prediction of the quantity of demand and market share target is possible based on past experiences.	While the past experience is not directly relevant, prediction of sales quantity and market share is possible.	Reasonable prediction of demand quantity and market share is not possible at present.
Profitability determination	Possible to determine profitability based on current knowledge.	Some extra effort is necessary to determine profitability of these projects.	Not possible to determine profitability with some confidence.
Decisions	Expansion, contraction, or withdrawl of a product or product line.	Introduction of a new product.	Need more time and information to make decisions.
Examples	Ref.-Micro Computer Control TV-HiFi TV, LCD-TV	Personal computer network	Laser equipment

Table 3. Project Planning Process

Procedural steps		Contents
I. Environmental	1. Characteristics	Purpose of the project. Use of the product. User of the product. Technology needed for production. Related products.
	2. Market conditions	Product's market position – new to saturated. Potential market demand. Current/future competition. Who is the market leader?
	3. Competitors	When did they start? What markets are they in? (Geographical, price range) What are their future plans?
II. Developmental targets	1. Product development	Product introduction date. What technology is needed? How will the technology be acquired?
	2. Marketing targets	Sales target (Quanitity and price) Distribution channel and the market location.
III. Implementation plans	1. Developmental budget	Manpower requirements. Financial resource requirements.
	2. Production budget	Manpower requirement. Investment in facilities. Analysis of manufacturing costs.
	3. Marketing plans	Marketing channel. Manpower requirements. Customer service methods. Profitability.
	4. Overall evaluation	What is the greatest weakness in GoldStar in carrying out this project? What is the crucial support needed to carry out this project successfully?
IV. Simulation of the project		Profitability of the project. Financial resource requirements.

ters is too situation specific to be presented here. A close follow-up of progress in these projects is necessary since the firm is traveling on an uncharted course.

4. Reporting System

The reporting system collects all the input data for performance evaluation, as well as the data necessary for day-to-day operating decisions and coordination among various units. Selected items, such as sales and accounts receivable information, is summarized daily and made available for on-line retrieval by the executives. Production information is summarized weekly and on exceptional bases when the deviation from the budgeted volume or cost is substantial. Table 4 presents the reporting system used by GoldStar. The measures for performance evaluation are developed based on the reported data for semiannual evaluation and ad hoc reviews where needed.

5. Evaluation System

The core of the evaluation system is the profit center concept used in organization of the company. While all the divisions are evaluated based on a unique set of multiple criteria, a large classification of revenue-generating divisions (internal or external sales) versus administrative and research and development units can be made.

Some key considerations given to selection of the evaluation criteria used for the profit centers are the following:

1. Due to the different impact of environmental factors and market conditions, unit-to-unit comparison will not be emphasized. The primary comparison is between the plan and the actual rather than between profit centers.
2. To discourage the short-term maximizing behavior, short-and long-term objectives will be evaluated simultaneously.
3. To recognize the uniqueness of each profit center, a unique set of evaluation criteria will be selected for each profit center.
4. To assure balanced growth, balanced satisfaction of all of the selected criteria will also be evaluated.

Table 4. Reporting system

Activity	Reports	Frequency
Manufacturing		
Product cost	Analyses of companywide manufacturing costs	Quarterly*
	Actual vs. std. cost	Monthly
Product quality	Product inspection pass rate	Monthly
	Product quality analyses (Companywide)	Quarterly
	Consumer suggestions	Quarterly
Productivity	Value-added rate	Quarterly*
	Cost recovery rate	Monthly
Product movement		
Manufacturing	Act. vs. target qty. by product and market	Daily+, Biweekly
	Daily production problems	Weekly, as needed
	Act. vs. target qty. by plant & product line	Monthly
	Monthly target and actual with respect to moving quarterly target	Monthly
Sales	Act. vs. target qty. by product and market	Daily, Biweekly
	Sales by office	Daily, Biweekly
	Analyses of sales by product and market	Quarterly*
	Monthly target and actual with respect to moving quarterly target	Monthly
Collection	Sales, A/R, collection avg. A/R age by office	Weekly+
	Company level cash mgmt.	Monthly
Marketing		
Market share	Market share analyses by product line	Quarterly*
Sales promotion	Promotion programs	As needed
	Sales personnel development	As needed

Table 4. Continued.

Activity	Reports	Frequency
Purchasing		
Materials inventory control	Analyses of inventory control	Monthly
Materials requirements	Materials status	Monthly
Investment		
Investments	Actual investments	Quarterly*
	Evaluation of investments	Quarterly
R & D		
Development	Project status	Monthly+
	Development: Actual vs. plan	Monthly
	Development status and technology news	Weekly
R & D		
Expenditure	Actual investments in R & D	Quarterly*
Environment		
External issues	Economic outlook, government policy New products in the market Competitors' activities	Quarterly, As needed
Internal issues	Long-term objective/ guidelines Long-term priority outlook	
Profit		
Performance	Net income/Cost by plant	Monthly#
	Marketing division income	Monthly#

* Also reported to the Lucky-GoldStar headquarters.

+ All daily reports and some updates are reported through on-line computer terminals.

\# Current period actual compared to the prior year's actual and the plan for the current period.

5. In addition to the evaluation based on the plan versus actual within each profit center, each center's contribution to the company's revenue and profit will be evaluated.

Each profit center selects six performance measurement indexes, in consultation with the Planning and Evaluation Office, and classifies them into key, primary, and general indexes to reflect the priorities of each profit center. Table 5 presents the measurement indexes selected for various profit centers for 1984. The computation methods of each index are presented in Table 6.

In addition to the structured measurement indexes, each profit center reports the contributions made to other profit center units in the areas of administration, technology, facilities and machineries, and man power.

The overall performance evaluation is not rigidly structured, and the chief executive is expected to evaluate the performance with these indexes as a major input. Due to the rapid changes in the electronics industry, both in terms of technology and market conditions, any rigid system of performance evaluation was deemed impractical. To encourage the future-oriented outlook and the awareness of the changing environment, it was decided to leave a certain amount of flexibility, or ambiguity, in the evaluation of profit centers and the responsible executive. Obviously, this type of ambiguity can interject another item of uncertainty into the division manager's decisions. In an uncooperative game setting, that is, agency theory, this setting may be termed as transferring some risk from the principal to the managers (agents), but within "inhwa" philosophy, the same setting can be seen as a case of risk reduction on the part of managers. That is, the effect of an evaluation rule can be exactly opposite, depending on the basic premise regarding the relationship between the superior and the subordinate.

6. Evaluation of Overseas Subsidiaries

Of the three subsidaries in the United States, GoldStar Microtech, as indicated earlier, serves as the listening post for technical and market developments in electronics. Due to the nature of its responsibility and newness (established June 1984), no formal performance measurement system has been developed.

Table 5. Performance Measurement Indexes for Profit Centers

Activity group	Profit centers	Evaluation indexes
Manufac-turing	Television Electric appliances Audio equipments Electric motors	K: Net income, Production quantity P: Product development Product quality G: Product cost, Investment
	Office automation Video recorder Microwave oven	K: Production quantity Product development P: Net income, Product quality G: Product cost, investment
Product manufac-turing & sales	Elevators	K: Sales, Net income P: Market share, A|R collection G: Product development, Investment
	Air conditioner Heater Gas range	K: Sales, Net income P: A/R collection, Product development G: Gas range market share product quality
	Molds	K: Sales, on-time delivery P: Production quantity, Net income G: Product cost, Investment
Marketing	Domestic sales	K: Sales, market share (old) P: A/R collection, market share (new) G: Net income, Bad debts
	Sales of product obtained through OEM agreement	K: Purchases, New product sales P: Purchase price, Product quality G: Net income, New product development
	Export Sales	See Overseas section on page 64.
	Office automation and computers Domestic sales	K: Sales, Product development P: Market share (personal computers) A/R collection G: Net income, User education
	Office automation and computers Export sales	K: Sales, Product development P: Net income, Per capita sales G: Net income, Investment

K: Key Indexes P: Primary Indexes G: General Indexes

Table 6. Performance Indexes – Justification and Computation

Index	Computation formula	Notes
Net income (ALL)	Period NI + Period sales*.2 / Budgeted NI + Period sales*.2	NI is the unit's operating income less allocated homeoffice cost. 20% of sales is used to stabilize the ratio when the budget NI is small or near zero.
Production quantity	Actual production quantity / Budget production quantity	Applies to all manufacturing units except for computers.
Product cost	Actual production cost / Budget production cost	Can be modified to make high index measures represent good performance.
Per capita sales	Per capita actual sales / Per capita budgeted sales	Per capita sales = *Unit sales* / Average # of personnel
Product development	Project completion index / Scheduled project completion	Project unit: New product, new model. Project completion: Date of mass production. Index: on time = 1 delay = −.2/month ahead = +.2/month.
Investment	Actual period investment / Budgeted period investment	Penalizes both over and under the budget.
Export price	Act. Price/Budg. cost / Budg. price/Budg. cost	Weighing the importance of different products.
Sales	Actual sales / Budgeted sales	
A/R collection	Actual avg. coll. days / Target avg. coll. days	
Mold delivery	Actual deliveries / Budgeted deliveries	Running total of the delay days per mold model is used.
Bad debts	Total collateral / Total A/R balance	This ratio is compared to the target rate set by management.
Product quality	# of lots passing / # of lots inspected	This ratio is compared to the target rate set by management.

Table 6. Continued.

Index	Computation formula	Notes
Market share (old)	Actual market share / Target market share	The index is a weighted average of each product line M/S % weighted by the sales % of each line within GS.
Market share (new)	Actual market share / Target market share	New products are evaluated separately, so that these products would not be shadowed by large sales of old products.
Market diversification	Export to North America / Total exports	This index is compared to the target ratio. Management wishes to reduce dependency on U.S.
Product diversification	New product export sales / Total exports	Compared to target ratio. Stereo, electric appliances.
Purchases (OEM)	Actual purchases / Budgeted purchases	Good purchase is same as good production in this case.
Purchase cost (OEM)	Actual cost/Price / Budgeted cost/Price	Equivalent to manufactured product cost to price.
Product quality (OEM)	Returns and claims / Total OEM sales	Compared to target ratio.
User education	Total education days / Budgeted education days	Considered an important index of future market demand.
Contribution to the company		
Sales	Actual division sales / Actual company sales	Compared to the past period actual and current plan rates.
Income	Actual division NI / Actual company NI b/4 Tax	
*Growth	Export sales increase / Total sales increase	Measure of export division's contribution to the growth of the company as a whole.
*Product development	Sale of export model in domestic market / Total domestic sales of new models	

* Applies only to the Export Sales Division.

6.1 GoldStar Electronics, Inc.

GSEI, the marketing unit, reports to the managing director of export sales, and to some extent is evaluated like other sales units. The managing director has set the following as the desirable attitude of the export division, as well as each individual in the division: concern for colleagues, substance over form, thinking ahead, and working as a group. Based on these, the following four major objectives were set for 1984.

1. Prompt delivery
   a. Ability to predict market demand and plan ahead;
   b. Ability to consult with customers; and
   c. Ability to plan production.
2. After sales service
   a. Ability to provide replacement parts;
   b. Ability to assist in retail sales; and
   c. Ability to assist customers to achieve their objectives.
3. Product development
   a. Ability to assist in product design;
   b. Ability to assist in function and quality development; and
   c. Ability to assist in development of high margin products.
4. Productive management
   a. Rational decision making;
   b. Information management to support decision making; and
   c. Efficient utilization of office computers.

These objectives were selected as of primary importance if the company were to remain strong in the dynamic and hostile market environment. Given these objectives, the Export Sales Division has chosen the following indexes as the performance measures:

1. Key indexes
   a. Sales growth, absolute and relative to the target; and
   b. New market development.
2. Primary indexes
   a. Per capita sales ratio; and
   b. Export sales price ratio.
3. General indexes
   a. Product mix ratio; and
   b. Market diversification ratio

4. Companywide contribution indexes
   a. Sales growth;
   b. Profitability; and
   c. Development.

In addition to these, additional GSEI objectives are to increase brand recognition of GoldStar in the U.S. market and to upgrade its image to a level above its Korean and Tai competitors. Therefore, two additional indexes are used: (1) ratio of GoldStar sales to private label sales, and (2) new nondiscount store sales developed.

To the management of GSEI, some of these indexes conflict with one another. In a short run, most efficient use of marketing efforts would be to sell the proven products through well-established channels, but for long-term growth, it is necessary to develop new markets and introduce new products which may require more effort in the beginning.

The potentially harmful effect of the conflicting criteria is lessened by the trust that the home office executives will consider these factors in evaluation of GSEI's performance.

6.2 GoldStar of America, Inc.

GSAI is a manufacturing division and is evaluated based on the same criteria used for other manufacturing facilities. The decision to establish GSAI was primarily due, however, to the opportunity it provided to learn about the U.S. market, rather than immediate profitability of the venture.[5]

Therefore, an additional responsibility of GSAI is to provide a forum for managers to learn about doing business in the United States and working with Americans. In 1984, the U.S. government imposed several barriers which made the import sales of Korean-manufactured color television sets more difficult, and the GSEI became more dependent on GSAI as the primary supplier.[6] Thus, the current key index for GSAI is its ability to produce sufficient quantities of sets on time.

7. Summary

GoldStar began as a family business based on the philosophy of "inhwa," every worker working together as a member of the GoldStar family. It grew in size and in product and market diversification to require divisionalized operation. The management of GoldStar has chosen to adopt profit-center concept and formalized performance evaluation methods, but emphasized the need to recognize unique contributions made by each division by selecting different indexes for each division. Furthermore, the management recognized the potential danger of rigid performance measurement system, and tried to build in a "trust" factor in the minds of divisional managers that they will be fairly evaluated in addition to the applicable index scores. In contrast to the American style of using the monitoring and evaluation of performance as a tool to control basically uncooperative workers, GoldStar management decided to take the risk of moral hazard possibilities in order to take advantage of the cooperative gaming formulation, which they labeled "inhwa."

The U.S. subsidiaries carry unique responsibilities that cannot be measured by traditional accounting numbers, in addition to normal responsibilities of sales and manufacturing units. Unlike many of the foreign units of U.S. – based companies, GSAI and GSEI are to serve as the public relations office, technology and product information agency, and the management training location for not only themselves but also all of GoldStar. Management of GoldStar recognizes this fact.

Notes

[1] The strategy of beginning with technology developed elsewhere and quickly adopting it for the consumer market basically has remained the same to date.

[2] An example of an important decision to be made in the committee is whether GoldStar or another of the electronic companies in the group should be primarily responsible for development, manufacturing, and marketing of computers and peripheral equipments.

[3] President Huh of GoldStar explained the decision: "For the next ten years, it is obvious that we should move into computer-based intelligence equipment, laser telecommunications, and semiconductors. All of these new businesses, however, require extensive technology. Unlike the United States and Japan where private firms can easily tap well-educated human resources, we have an extra burden of educating our own people within the company in order to learn and utilize the technology. Therefore, this decision affects every facet of the company, and we must move quickly to find promising talents and educate them."

[4] The Lucky-GoldStar Group used the mechanism of international joint ventures to acquire advanced technology quickly. In fact, GoldStar is the only non – joint venture electronics firm in the group. One important role of the company is to acquire and accumulate technology of its own. GoldStar currently operates under six separate technology licensing agreements, but it also draws technical know-how from seven electronics related sister companies which are joint venture firms such as AT&T, Honeywell, NEC, Fuji, and others.

[5] The management team was sharply divided concerning the wisdom of manufacturing in the United States. Some thought the company did not have the experience to deal with American workers. They also showed skepticism toward the ability to build quality products at low cost. Others argued for the need to have operations inside the trade barriers, and the long-term learning benefits of such an operation. The long-term strategic argument won.

[6] At the end of 1984, the U.S. International Trade Commission ruled that the buyers of Korean-made GoldStar color television sets must pay an additional 7.5 percent. This ruling has put GSAI and GSEI in a difficult situation again. The sets manufactured in Korea enjoy approximately a 9 percent cost advantage over the units produced by GSAI. Should GSAI continue to produce at capacity or should it be put into the reserve role? What about the evaluation criterion of production quantity?

FMC Corporation: Inflation-Adjusted Performance Evaluation

Eric S. Evans

1. Overview of FMC

FMC Corporation is a diversified manufacturer of machinery and chemicals for industry, agriculture, and government. In 1984, FMC had sales of $ 3.3 billion. FMC's seven operating groups participate in five major segments. Industrial Chemicals consists of commodity products such as soda ash, phosphates, hydrogen peroxide, lithium compounds, and gold. Performance Chemicals consists of proprietary products such as agricultural pesticides, pharmaceuticals and food additives. Defense Systems produces armored tracked vehicles for the United States and other free-world armies, and naval missile launching and gun mount systems. In the Petroleum Equipment sector, FMC produces wellhead equipment and other fluid handling devices. The Specialized Machinery segment includes such products as fire engines, street sweepers, material handling equipment, and machinery for food production and processing.

FMC employs over 21,000 people with 107 manufacturing facilities in twenty-six states and fourteen foreign countries. Approximately 25 percent of FMC's revenues are earned from exports and foreign subsidiaries. FMC's operating groups function as autonomous business units, each controlling its own domestic and foreign operations.

In establishing performance goals for the eighties, FMC's management focused on the concept of maximizing shareholder wealth. The need arose for a financial framework that would best relate the firm's stock price to its financial performance. The Q-Ratio was considered an excellent way to measure the value of the firm. The Q-Ratio is an inflation-adjusted price/book multiple which relates the firm's market value to the inflation-adjusted book value of the firm's assets. If investors anticipate that cash returns on a firm's assets will be greater than today's discount rate, the

"Q" would be greater than 1. If the market anticipates returns lower than today's discount rate, "Q" would be less than 1. The question then becomes how best to capture this relationship in an operating performance measure.

Using scatter diagrams and regression analysis, FMC, in conjunction with a consulting firm, tested the effectiveness of historical cost accounting returns, price-earnings multiples, earnings per share (EPS), and an inflation-adjusted cash flow return on investment (CFROI) as means to explain how the market values stocks. Using ten years of returns for the Standard and Poor's (S & P) 400 companies adjusted for risk (risk is eliminated to make the companies comparable), it was demonstrated that inflation-adjusted CFROI had the highest correlation ($R^2 = .827$) to the Q-Ratio. The relationship was validated for shorter and longer-term periods as well.

CFROI, which can be considered as a firm's internal rate of return, is, however, not part of the traditional accounting model. Therefore, further testing was done to link CFROI to a traditional current cost accounting return. It was demonstrated that inflation-adjusted CFROI is highly correlated ($R^2 = .905$) to an inflation-adjusted return on capital employed, which FMC designates current cost ROCE. Finally, a test was made to validate the direct relationship between current cost ROCE and the Q-Ratio. The resulting correlation was an R^2 of .821.

These relationships are the foundation for using inflation-adjusted measures as tools for managing FMC's businesses. Furthermore, FMC established as its goal to be in the upper quartile of stock performance in the S & P 400. That threshold, in terms of the "Q"/CFROI framework, is 9 percent. This 9 percent goal is a base for FMC performance measurement when used in the process of strategic evaluation and assessment. The modified accounting model (CC ROCE) which measures *real* returns has a 6 percent threshold to the upper quartile of the S & P 400. That target is embodied in the inflation-adjusted operating measurement system and is fully consistent with FMC's strategic assessments and corporate objectives.

With this background in mind, this paper will describe FMC's reporting structure, its current cost accounting system, benefits of the system, FMC's incentive plan, and international reporting at FMC.

2. Reporting Structure

FMC is divided into eight operating groups, which are then divided into divisions and further subdivided into operating plants. The plant, the lowest reporting level, represents a cost center dedicated to the production of a number of products. They are not totally responsible for activity levels; instead, local management is charged with efficiently and effectively meeting externally determined demand. Efficiency is measured in terms of units of input required to produce a unit of output. Effectiveness is evaluated by whether the production schedule is achieved at the requisite quality and timeliness. Local management is limited to control over inputs as critical variables.

Greater control is afforded the division level, representing product-line profit centers which have responsibility for both production and sales. The division controls the trade-offs between price, volume, quality, and costs in an effort to create value from resources at their disposal.

The primary periodic reporting vehicle is a worldwide computer-based financial reporting system (FRS) which collects and consolidates actual operating results from over 250 operating locations. FRS compares actual monthly results with quarterly forecasts and annual budgets to generate performance variances for key operating variables. This management by exception highlights performance irregularities on which management should focus its attention.

FRS generates information for operating locations throughout the company, both foreign and domestic. In addition to FRS data, however, the locations are required to provide supplementary information to supply top management with a complete picture of the business operations and environment at each FMC location.

3. Inflation Accounting

Historical cost accounting, founded on the premise that an asset should be stated at the actual amount paid less depreciation and amortization, does not reflect changing prices due to inflation until assets are actually replaced at higher prices. Accountants have preferred to rely on the objectivity of historical cost statements rather than trust the judgment of managers and analysts to estimate asset replacement value or risk the introduction of inconsistency in public financial reporting. When the rate of inflation is small, the effect of price increases is rarely significant. As the inflation rate increases, however, it becomes apparent that the distortions cannot be ignored. At FMC, concern arose over the adequacy of historical cost accounting in an inflationary environment. Over the long term, regardless of whether the rate of inflation in any one year is low or high, inflation values build in the asset base and begin to distort reality.

Under historical cost, assets purchased today, as well as assets purchased ten years ago, are valued at their depreciated original cost. Profits are traditionally measured, taxed, and reported to shareholders by matching lower past costs against revenues from prices that have been forced upward by rising costs. In attempting to account for changing costs, the LIFO inventory valuation method provides a better match between current costs and revenues; however, LIFO can significantly understate inventory levels during periods of increasing prices. Ideally, FIFO costs should be used to value inventories, while LIFO should be used to measure income. This dichotomy of using one accounting principle to measure income and another to measure financial condition is typical of the difficulties that users of historical cost operating statements face in judging a company's actual financial position and distinguishing between real and inflated profits.

3.1 Constant Dollar versus Current Cost Accounting

General price-level adusted, or constant dollar, accounting uses conventional historical costs adjusted for the general purchasing power of the dollar. Constant dollar accounting does not change the accounting principles used to develop financial information and is analogous to restating financial statements from one currency to another: constant dollar disclosures change the measuring unit used in the disclosures from the nominal dollar to the general purchasing power dollar.

Advocates of constant dollar accounting argue that investors desire to earn a return on their investment which will sooner or later be distributed in the form of cash which they may use to buy goods at their current prices. They are concerned not only with the nominal amount of dollars they receive but also with the purchasing power of those dollars. The investors' need for this type of information is met by the use of a constant dollar measuring unit. The analysis of Q-Ratio and inflation-adjusted ROI utilizes constant dollar indexation.

Businesses, however, do not experience "general" inflation as measured by the consumer price index (CPI); they are affected by particular increases in operating costs and plant expenditures. Constant dollar accounting, while accurately representing changes in value arising from changes in the value of money, ignores changes in the value of goods and services relative to each other. Consequently, general price-level adjustments do not result in balance sheet valuations which can be interpreted as current values except for the unusual case of a firm which owns assets whose costs are increasing at the same rate as general inflation.

In contrast to constant dollar accounting, current cost accounting views income as those resources in excess of those required to maintain a company's productive capacity or earning power. Current costs are defined as "the cost of acquiring the same service potential as embodied by the assets owned." Unlike constant dollar information, current costs are not translated from historical cost statements, and, therefore, they depart from historical costs. Instead of restating historical costs, current cost accounting replaces these figures with current costs. Current costs are not equivalent to costs in the usual sense; they do not represent money spent or obligations incurred by the firm, but rather they represent hypothetical transactions based on estimates of what the company would have to spend currently.

Constant dollar information is based on the premise that prices in general are rising, whereas current costs are based on the fact that prices of specific goods are changing, independent of the rise in the general price level. While overall inflation is primarily related to an increase in the supply of money in excess of the increase in available goods, the prices of specific goods may rise more or less than general inflation due to other changes in supply and demand factors in the specific product area. Current cost accounting methods recognize *all* changes in value without distinguishing those attributable to changes in the purchasing power of the dollar from those attributable to changes in supply and demand conditions of the assets owned. It should be noted that current cost accounting could be applied and yield different results from historical cost/nominal dollar accounting, even if there were no general inflation, because relative prices of individual assets would still change.

Advocates of the current cost accounting framework argue that current cost statements are easier to interpret and provide a closer approximation to real income. Investors, as a result, are provided a better basis with which to evaluate the firm's current position and project its future potential. Additionally, because current costs, not historical costs, are reflected in asset valuations, management is effectively prohibited from trying to maintain unrealistically high book returns by "milking the business" and shying away from necessary replacements with new and better equipment and facilities. A company will typically find that some of its divisions have higher return on book investment than others. This performance criterion is one factor considered in allocating capital resources. The difference in returns on book assets between units, however, may be just a reflection of the age of their fixed assets. The unit that acquired its assets some time ago at deflated dollars can look very good in today's terms compared with a unit that acquired its fixed assets recently. It may be that the converse relationship is actually true in terms of economic returns on new investments. Then, too, the high-return units may be inhibited from making necessary new investments, because the investments will depress the historic return on book assets. Current cost accounting provides better incentives for management to make economic capital investment decisions.

In addition to ensuring proper incentives for investment decisions, current cost accounting motivates mangers to make desired operating decisions. Consider, for example, two plants of identical sales and physical capacity that differ only in dates of construction. Under historical cost accounting, the older plant enjoys greater net income, since it is charged a lower depreciation rate against sales revenues. The older plant's net income includes a component of holding gains on fixed assets. Under current cost accounting, however, managers running plants of identical physical capacity are charged the same amount of depreciation; any difference in their operating profits is due to the effectiveness of their decisions. By incorporating the holding gain into asset valuation, the reported net income reflects true operating profit generated by the business in the normal course of operations.

The primary practical difficulty of current cost accounting is the derivation of asset values. Most firms using current cost measurements at present derive their figures by using indices. This presents some practical difficulties, in that an appropriate index or some other measure must be "chosen," and this index must allow for the asset mix of the enterprise. Indexing measurements are subjective and may be open to manipulation, thereby creating potential problems for the public accounting profession if required to audit current cost data. Indexes do, however, represent a programmatic method to approximate current cost. Whatever better information is available is incorporated into the system.

3.2 FMC Current Cost Accounting

FMC adopted a current cost accounting system for internal measurement in 1983 for all domestic and overseas locations. Except for land, which is appraised at its current market value, FMC's current costs for fixed assets are determined by externally generated indices for specific categories of items which measure the change in cost from the time of acquisition to a specified present year-end date.

In addition to fixed assets, inventories were required to be restated at current values. Since FMC's objective is to stay in business and replace the inventory sold, realized inventory holding gains must be eliminated because they also overstate operating profit. Inventories are valued and charged against revenue at prospective standard manufacturing cost, rather than historical cost. Finally, monetary holding gains and losses are calculated and included in income but only for FMC operations in highly inflationary economies, that is, those economies having cumulative average annual inflation of 100 percent or more over a three-year period (for FMC, this is primarily Brazil, Costa Rica, Mexico, and Argentina). Hyperinflation seriously distorts all financial information in these countries. While the total distortion is reduced by fixed asset and inventory current cost adjustments, substantial misrepresentation of the true financial picture persists if monetary holding gains and losses are unrecognized. Monetary gains and losses are included in operating income because high inflation and, consequently, sizeable monetary gains and losses are part of the normal course of business in these countries. In short, modifications to FMC's historical cost system to account for current costs involve restating fixed assets and inventories and the related depreciation expense and cost of goods for all operations and, in addition, monetary gains and losses for the operations in hyperinflationary countries.

Although the inflation-adjusted results are used for internal measurement and supplements to financial statements, historical cost accounting results are retained for legal and external reporting requirements. The financial reporting system reflects current costs in the operating portion of the financial statements and provides offsetting entries in the non-operating section to return statements to historical cost.

4. Accounting/Reporting Systems

FMC's reporting cycle consists of a monthly closing for virtually all of its reporting locations. Some very small foreign operations are closed on a quarterly basis. Monthly results are submitted by computer to the corporate controller on the sixth workday after the end of the month. On the seventh workday, a financial report is issued to top management. This report contains key figures for each operating group such as sales, operating profit before and after tax, net income, funds flow, orders and backlogs, and working capital. In addition, consolidated corporate figures for operating profits, net income, and EPS are available. Variances versus the budget and latest forecast are presented for all reported numbers on a monthly and year-to-date basis.

One to two weeks after the "performance" report is issued, the finalized monthly results are presented to the chairman and president for the purpose of addressing key variances and identifying trends and their implications for the ability of the business unit to perform to the budget or forecast.

The principal control document is the budget. The budget is constructed in a bottom-up fashion. The process begins in July with the issuance of budget instructions and economic assumptions for the forthcoming year. Budgets are then submitted at the end of October, and individual reviews are conducted during November with the president at the divisional level. The final budget is resubmitted at the end of November and consists of a complete balance sheet and profit and loss (P & L) statement for all locations on a monthly basis. The budget is then presented to the chairman and board of directors in the first half of December. During the course of the year, new full-year forecasts are produced in a similar but slightly abbreviated fashion. These forecasts are assembled in April, July, and October. The presentation of each new forecast concentrates on the reasons for the changes versus the prior forecast and budget.

The primary measure of performance is called *net contribution*, which is defined as current operating profit after tax less an earnings target based on the working capital and net current cost of the assets employed by the business (capital employed). The earnings target used is 6 percent. Because of differences in asset life and FMC's use of specific indices as opposed to the gross national product (GNP) price deflator, it has been demonstrated that a current cost ROCE of 6 percent corresponds to a CFROI of 9 percent, the target discussed earlier. In order for the corporation to use a 6 percent target, the operating units must be charged an additional 2 percent, an 8 percent total, to cover corporate expenses. FMC utilizes this 8 percent target for all its operating units by multiplying the factor by the current cost capital employed and subtracting that amount from the after-tax operating profit to derive net contribution.

4.1 Mechanics of FMC's Current Cost Reporting System

For internal purposes, FMC uses a financial statement format that separates accounts into operating and non-operating segments. The purpose of this format is to place those accounts which the operating manager controls into the operating section and to place accounts influenced by decisions beyond the control of operating management into the non-operating section of the financial statements. In addition to format differences, FMC's system requires specific adjustments to the financial statements for inflation.

4.1.1 Profit and Loss Adjustments

- Depreciation — Using the specific indices previously mentioned, a current cost adjustment for depreciation is added to cost of sales. This reflects the amount by which the gross current value of an asset exceeds its gross historical cost, divided by the lives of the assets.
- Inventory Adjustment — One of the major problems with LIFO and FIFO inventory methodologies is that neither can properly state both the balance sheet and income statement in current cost terms. FMC overcomes this problem by combining its use of a standard cost system with its operating/non-operating format for internal statements. Standard cost inventories are adjusted to reflect the anticipated cost of inventories during the year. At the start of each year, the operations write up their inventory to its expected standard cost for the coming year. Thus, as inventory is used, current cost is charged to cost of sales. The offset to this write-up goes into the non-operating section of the balance sheet and is amortized in the non-operating section of the P & L as the inventory turns. Therefore, on an operating basis, managers are held responsible for current cost inventories and current cost of sales. The reversals in the non-operating section return the P & L statement and balance sheet to historical cost.

- Monetary Holding Gain/Loss — As mentioned, in hyperinflationary countries, a monetary holding gain or loss is charged to each affected location. Should domestic inflation return to significant levels, a monetary holding gain or loss would be introduced on a broader scale.
- In accounting for taxes, a reversal must be made for the benefit obtained from the current cost depreciation adjustment, which is not deductible for tax purposes.

All of these current cost adjustments are reversed in the non-operating section of each location's P & L statement to obtain the historical cost net income figure needed to compute overall corporate net income for reporting purposes.

4.1.2 Balance Sheet

- Inventories — As mentioned before, inventories are written up to the expected standard costs for the next year. This is offset by establishing a liability "reserve for standard inventory adjustments" that is credited to non-operating income as inventory flows through the income statement. The expected standard costs for a year can, of course, be less than the preceding year, in which case the inventory write-down would be charged to non-operating profit over the following year.
- Property, Plant, and Equipment — All plant and equipment is written up to its estimated current value. As mentioned, with the exception of land, which is appraised, the current value is determined by the use of specific indices. Overseas locations use local indices where available, but many propose alternate valuation methods they believe are appropriate.

As previously mentioned, the reporting system is divided into operating and non-operating segments. In the case of the balance sheet, operating managers are not held responsible for the investment of marketable securities. This is handled by the corporate treasury function, as is the capital structure and amount of debt. Therefore, these items are considered non-operating and are not included in the operating capital employed. Likewise, the interest income and expense generated from non-operating assets and liabilities do not impact operating results.

Balance sheets for various entities, especially foreign locations, also include intercompany accounts. As with debt and marketable securities, decisions on the use of these intercompany accounts often fall outside the scope of the operating manager. Because of this, they are not included in operating capital. Intercompany interest income and expense and intercompany dividends, as well as the amortization of non-operating intangible assets, such as goodwill, are also included in the non-operating section of the income statement.

4.2 Benefits of the System

The current cost accounting and control system at FMC is viewed not only as a method of conveying information but also as a means of keeping the goals of the corporation in focus at all levels of operating management. Advantages of current cost accounting include the ability to emphasize the importance of managing capital utilization, both fixed and working, and current cost accounting gives the managers a perspective on what returns they would achieve if the competitive environment or economic reality required them to replace the assets employed in the business. The use of current cost return measures allows management to focus not only on increasing profits to improve returns, but also to emphasize how effective working capital control, through actions like "just-in-time" inventory methods, can increase returns through improved asset utilization.

The use of real returns which result from current cost accounting is directly linked to the strategic evaluation of the businesses and encourages managers to seek ways to optimize returns consistent with their longer-term objectives. For instance, if a manger is currently being charged depreciation as if he had a new machine, he will be more aggressive in investigating the productivity gains available if he actually invested in a new machine. Likewise, asset values found in nonproductive or excess assets, which are hidden using historical costs, become quantified and can be targeted for liquidation.

Current cost accounting also aids in comparing different businesses, as well as different parts of the same business. This also helps the comparison of domestic and international businesses. For example, imagine that FMC had two plants producing hydrogen peroxide. One plant was built fifteen years ago at a cost of $ 30 million, the second five years ago at a cost of $45 million. The plants are identical in capacity and process technology and should last thirty years. Historical cost accounting would indicate that the product that comes from the second plant is more expensive than the one from the first because depreciation is $500,000 per year higher. Should FMC charge more for peroxide from the second plant? Obviously, it cannot, because peroxide is a commodity, and prices are set by competition in the market place. With current cost accounting there is no distortion of the operating results of the plants because of the age of their assets.

In addition, FMC believes that historical cost accounting does not offer any information on whether hydrogen peroxide is a good business for FMC's portfolio. Would the current prices pay for a new plant? If not, does historical accounting provide the proper incentives to reduce costs and increase utilization so that pressure on margins is eased?

5. International Reporting

FMC treats its foreign operations in an identical manner to its treatment of domestic operations. Both are measured on their ability to provide an adequate return in dollars based on the current value of dollars invested. FMC also employs current cost accounting at all its foreign subsidiaries. In hyperinflationary countries such as Brazil, Argentina, and Mexico, measuring returns based on the current cost of the capital required to generate those returns becomes even more important.

Unlike domestic operations, the foreign operations in hyperinflationary countries are required to compute a monetary holding gain or loss on their net monetary position. This is considered an operating charge, since it is computed on the net position of current operating assets and liabilities, such as accounts receivable and accounts payable. Because operating managers control their working capital utilization, it is reasonable to expect them to be able to control their inventory turns, receivables collection, and other monetary items to minimize the impacts of inflation.

Since historical cost accounting does not recognize monetary holding gains or losses resulting from the impact of inflation on monetary assets and liabilities, this account is reversed into the non-operating section of the income statement. Included in the non-operating section of the income statement, however, are gains or losses from translation. FASB *Statement 52* requires the use of FASB *Statement 8* to recognize gains and losses from the translation of foreign subsidiary accounts in hyperinflationary countries in the P&L.

As long as inflation and devaluation move together, the combination of the current cost adjustments to plant, property and equipment (PP & E), inventory, and the monetary holding gain or loss approximates the translation gain or loss. When devaluation and inflation do not move together as a result of government interventions, such as the 1983 maxi-devaluation in Brazil, the incremental translation gain or loss is appropriately in the non-operating section of the P & L, since local managers cannot be held responsible for such currency fluctuations. Hedging strategies to prevent losses due to asset or liability exposure to such actions are handled through the corporate treasurer's function. Therefore, just as domestic operating managers are held responsible for only those elements under their control, so, too, are the foreign operating managers.

Because capital allocation is a corporate function, the operations have the same earnings target for their operating capital, rather than being held accountable for actual interest expense. Like the domestic operations, the foreign operations are charged an 8 percent earnings target on their current cost operating capital employed. FMC applies one earnings target to all foreign operations regardless of the type of business or the risk. Although each operation is charged 8 percent on its operating capital, each operation is not required to earn an 8 percent return. What is deemed to be adequate short-term performance for a given business can be more or less than 8 percent, but the target for the corporation is to manage its businesses such that, in the aggregate, they earn a long-term real return of 8 percent.

6. Incentive System

Two main components are used in establishing bonus targets for FMC operating managers. First is the strategic performance factor (SPF). SPFs are derived from the operting unit's strategic plan. The strategic objectives to be achieved in any given year are negotiated by the operating manager, the vice president of corporate development, and the president. The second factor is the business performance factor (BPF). FMC had been using a weighting of pretax current cost operating profit (OPBT) and working capital cents per dollar of sales to derive its BPF. Beginning in 1985, FMC uses net contribution for its BPF. The operating unit's budget serves as the "1.0 target." Around that target, ranges are set to establish what would be outstanding or "2.0 performance," and what performance would not merit a bonus, "0.0." Numbers falling in the 0.0 to 2.0 range correspond to a salary factor that determines bonus compensation.

Similar 0.0, 1.0, 2.0 targets are established for the SPFs. The BPF and SPF are weighted to focus the managers' attention on the proper "mix" between the near-term performance and long-term strategic aspects of the business. Adjustments are made to the results so that varying such strategically important expenditures as R & D and fixed asset additions cannot be used to improve bonus performance. The most important element of the incentive system is that it is consistent with the reporting system in that a manager is held responsible only for those things under his control and it is directly measured against the strategies and objectives for the business over the long-term.

7. Summary

FMC believes its current cost system offers managers incentives to increase returns, not only by increasing profits but also by properly managing the operating capital employed. The system encourages refitting or disposing of idle capacity, increasing inventory turns, increasing payables, improving accounts receivable collections, and selling in hard currencies and purchasing in soft currencies. The system also encourages the use of new production techniques, such as "just-in-time" manufacturing methodologies, to maximize asset utilization. Finally, it is a flexible system that accounts for changes in a business' total environment, not just for increasing prices, and that serves both the short- and long-term planning needs of the corporation.

Management Control and the Internal Auditor: The Borg-Warner Case

John C. Fletcher

The term "management control" has been such a part of the internal audit profession that few would suspect that agreement on definitions would be a problem. In the 1981 Symposium on Internal Control at the University of Florida, however, participants found enthusiastic support for a wide range of definitions.

The fact that internal auditors do not agree on the meaning of management control has led to a significant change in the way that internal auditing is practiced at Borg-Warner Corporation. In this Fortune 200 company with worldwide operations in manufacturing, financial, and protective services, the role of the internal auditor has become a more important element in monitoring and implementing managerial accounting policies and procedures. Borg-Warner has adopted the philosophy of decentralization in both its U.S. operations and all of its international operations. A key element in the structure of management control in this firm has been the realization that Borg-Warner is in a global market with each unit needing to understand and respond to business and political conditions in all of the company's markets.

Underlying Borg-Warner's management philosophy is the belief that the company hires capable and dedicated managers who exercise their responsibilities to the best of their abilities without the "policeman type" monitoring of a traditional corporate headquarters. It is felt that these managers, with clearly defined responsibilities and objectives, will reach higher levels of success if they are allowed to make as many of their own decisions as possible without corporate influence. This philosophy permeates the entire organization worldwide. This paper is designed to explore the nature of the innovations which underly the new approaches to management control and their impact on the further evolution of managerial accounting and internal auditing.

Must the internal auditor be viewed as an adversary to the operations manager? At least one company says "No!" In a dramatic move, it has transformed the internal audit group into an effective force for evaluating and improving management control systems. The firm has implemented action programs for improving manufacturing controls in more than fifty manufacturing plants and operating divisions in seven foreign countries and the United States.

1. Control Evaluation Review Technique (CERT)

The keystone of this change is a diagnostic technique founded on the identification and management of critical success factors. A team of external consultants and internal management control analysts (formerly called internal auditors) developed the Control Evaluation Review Technique (CERT), which is the tool applied by the Control Evaluation Department to work with operating management. CERT spotlights control deficiencies and provides the basis for formulating practical action plans for implementing improvements. These action plans are practical in that they reflect the priorities of needed improvements and then consider the ability and resources of the operating organization to implement the necessary changes.

A fundamental element of the CERT process is the elimination of the traditional internal audit report. It has been replaced by a documented action plan developed by the operating management, with the support of the control analysts and data gathered using CERT. Thus, the role of the internal auditor has turned 180 degrees from that of adversary to that of adviser.

The benefits of the new program have been many:

- The firm has documented substantial improvements in the manufacturing control process in its production facilities around the world.
- The program has improved the effectiveness and efficiency of the control evaluation staff greatly and has improved relations in the workplace. Operating management now sees the staff as professional internal consultants rather than as a police squad dedicated to finding faults.
- Operating management has adopted CERT as an ongoing, self-assessment tool to maintain operations at or above the requirements of the corporation.

- The control evaluation department attracts a higher caliber staff, and it also serves as the corporate "training ground" for manufacturing line managers.
- The nature of the CERT program allows the control analyst to focus quickly on problem areas, to assure complete coverage of the analytic effort, and to analyze many more production facilities than was possible under the former program which used more traditional audit approaches.
- The CERT approach has been applied outside the manufacturing realm to evaluate management controls in other corporate areas such as accounting, marketing, information systems, and distribution.

2. Traditional Audit Approach

Until 1975, the internal audit function at this company was performed in a traditional manner. Audit programs were written to analyze specific functions within the company, with particular attention to the adequacy of internal accounting controls. The audit programs were a kind of checklist against which the auditor could test compliance with company policies and procedures. Often the audit disclosed a number of instances where procedures were not followed to the letter. In such cases, a report was prepared and distributed to senior management.

These audit reports were designed to expose management practices which were less than ideal. Because the auditor was expected to gain evidence of noncompliance, the audit tests were associated with activities which could be measured. When the auditor found policies or procedures which were not being followed, the report tended to communicate, whether intended or not, that the manager was not performing effectively. The report did not necessarily address the question of whether the primary performance objectives of the unit were being achieved.

When necessary, corrective measures were recommended to avoid the recurrence of such "weaknesses." Most often these recommendations would be "intuitive" — fix the problem by performing assigned tasks. Usually, the auditor did not have sufficient time to investigate the underlying cause of the problem.

Certainly, some of the most creative writing has been seen in internal audit reports which exaggerate the impact of findings and of the auditee's noncommittal responses to these reports. After reading a typical report, a manager could justifiably question the original motivation behind performing the audit and writing the report. Too often serious disagreement exists as to the validity of what the auditors test when compared to what managers believe is important in the operation of their unit.

In this more traditional approach to internal auditing, the objective of the function is to serve as the eyes and ears of top management, giving them frequent written reports on management practices in audited divisions. This approach often fails to put conditions in correct perspective, however, and it frequently concentrates on functions which are not critical to the success of the audited unit. The likely cause of this weakness in the audit process is that the auditors find it very difficult to measure success relative to the most important functions of a manager. It is much easier to collect evidence by testing administrative or task-oriented activities than to measure progress in achieving primary accountabilities.

A major failing of the traditional approach to auditing has been the frequent absence of improvements in critical areas. The distribution of written audit reports cloaked in the most negative terms and concentrating on the less important activities of a department understandably lead to defensive and nonresponsive behavior. The recommendations in these reports do not consider the conditions in other functions in the same system or overall unit. Hence, they often recommend an action that overrides the manager's own priority list. This traditional practice of internal auditing results in the development of an adversary relationship between auditor and audited management.

The reaction of auditees to this process is no surprise. Recognizing the usual response to personal criticism, auditors should expect auditees to be guarded and even defensive. This would be especially true if a young auditor were auditing in a technical area without adequate work experience. Few senior managers welcome the opportunity to have a junior auditor tell the president of the company about all the administrative shortcomings of the unit, especially when the report does everything possible to state the problem in the most uncomplimentary light. The Institute of Internal Auditors recognized this condition ten years ago when it published its research study on behavioral relationships between auditors and auditees.[1] Many audit staffs have not yet responded to the conclusions of that valuable study.

Traditional reports have been viewed as noncompliance exposés concentrating on areas important to the auditor. They have not been developed as change agents to the extent needed today.

James Hooper, 1983/84 chairman of the board of the Institutė of Internal Auditors, concluded in his acceptance speech that "historically, internal auditing has been perceived as a critical disclosure-oriented activity. Disclosure and criticism were central elements of our professional style."[2] In practice, the traditional audit process, combined with the deficiency-oriented reporting structure, has been seen as a painful physical examination where auditors report symptoms rather than problems. Many operating managers feel this condition exists because the auditors lack the depth of knowledge to investigate problems fully and develop meaningful alternatives. Reports whose recommendations say little more than "fix it" can be seen to support this conclusion. Whether intentional or not, the traditional audit process is perceived as geared to discredit management. The auditee's reaction is often dysfunctional. Either the process is passively tolerated or challenged. Some managers try to please the auditors by telling them what they want to hear. Others inadvertently misdirect the scope of the review, while still others intentionally mislead or misinform the auditor (or withhold information). The great joy seems to occur when audit findings are challenged in a meeting with higher officials. This meeting is often seen as a field of competition rather than a time for consideration of constructive improvements to fundamental management control systems.

Hooper concluded:

> We are learning by recent experience that our effectiveness in dealing with management is greatest when we concentrate on problem solving and is weakest when we view our mission exclusively in terms of problem disclosure.... The idea is now emerging that we may contribute much more to the welfare of our organizations as partners than as critics.[3]

3. Evolution: From Traditional to CERT

In 1975, the audit department in the case study firm recognized the need for change in the internal audit process.[4] Operating under a philosophy which views operating managers as responsible for control,[5] the department determined to design a corporate program which would fully support managers who needed help in designing and implementing effective management control systems. It was felt that operating managers should monitor the extent to which their subordinates achieve or fail to achieve their objectives. The audit task would better serve the firm by testing the accuracy, relevance, and timeliness of the data being collected and used by the decision makers in managing the enterprise. In short, it would be the manager's job to make sure the staff is doing its job. It would no longer be the auditor's job to tell management once a year (or even less frequently) which subordinates fail to complete their assignments as directed.

The audit function began to resemble an internal consulting group with the goal to undertake needed improvements in the firm's management control systems. The external auditors were to concentrate on accounting controls while the internal auditors concentrated on underlying operating controls. Efforts of both units would be fully coordinated to provide the company with a comprehensive appraisal of the effectiveness of its management control systems in all areas.

Most important in the new program was the elimination of deficiency-oriented audit reports which were distributed to top management, and a move toward more professional staff to provide operating management with a consulting service in the area of automated information and management control systems. Action plans developed and distributed by operating managers would provide top management with feedback on the conditions in each division.

As mentioned, the renovation began in 1975. The audit staff was renamed Control Evaluation Department (CED). The decision was made to staff the department with persons capable of providing a higher-level consulting service. The staff was to be well educated, preferably with master's degrees in business-related subjects, and with effective interpersonal skills to support their new "change agent" status. The adversary relationship had to be eliminated. Reports of studies were not to be issued until operating management had fully responded to the analysis presented by CED. Action plan distribution was to be limited to operating managers and the corporate controller who has overall responsibility for internal control in the company. The results of these reviews were not to be used to punish field managers.

All of this may have worked very well had the Foreign Corrupt Practices Act (FCPA) not been passed. It was passed, however, and, as a result, many public accounting firms began encouraging internal audit staffs to adopt external audit approaches for their reviews. The documentation of internal accounting control systems became a primary task for internal auditors. This change certainly aided the public accounting profession and would have aided operating managers had they been committed to the administrative task of defining and documenting their policies, procedures, and related control systems. Unfortunately, many managers were not committed to the task, especially where it required continual update of the documentation to reflect current operating conditions and practices.

Many CPA firms had not previously documented the accounting control systems. They had, rather, concluded that it was more cost effective for the client if substantive audit procedures were used. In effect, they had ignored the condition of the control systems because they were often ill defined and too dynamic to be reliable. With the threat that the Securities and Exchange Commission would require public companies to report the condition of their internal control systems and require CPAs to validate these assertions, the internal auditors were used in many cases as extensions of the external audit process. In many cases, a major change in audit approach occurred. A wide variety of audit programs, each tied closely to the objectives of the annual financial audit, was developed by the internal audit staff.

The threat of public reporting was reduced in 1981, and the impact of the FCPA was effectively lessened. Because the CED staff had fallen victim to the FCPA, it had become difficult to recruit the high-caliber staff desired. Few people chose to spend their time documenting control systems and applying the financial audit programs. The final evaluation of nearly three years' work was that the renovation begun in 1975 had been sidetracked.

As this evolution was occurring, others were becoming acutely aware that many manufacturing facilities in the United States were simply not working efficiently. Both internal and external management consultants had been an integral part of the development for industry of materials requirement planning (MRP) in the late sixties and then manufacturing resources planning (MRP II) in the seventies. By 1980, the great American pilgrimages to Japan had begun. Many people were asking, "What is really wrong?" There seemed to be nothing technically new in Japanese methods of industrial development. It could be concluded that the Japanese were pursuing simplicity and discipline in systems and procedures, and good old-fashioned (American?) hard work in application.

Much literature has been written on these basic management subjects, and it has been available to American management for years. The words of Fayol, Grant, Taylor, et al. discuss the basic issues regarding effective management. These are not new ideas! For example, as far back as 1912, a consulting management engineer, Harrison Emerson, outlined his twelve principles of effective management: clearly defined ideals; common sense; competent counsel; discipline; the fair deal; reliable, immediate, and adequate records; standardized operations; written standard practice instructions; efficiency reward; dispatching; standards and scheduling; and standardized conditions.

Why, with all of this management thinking recorded in our literature and taught in our educational programs, are our systems not working? For example, why do we often not have all of the parts needed to finish an assembly run? Is it because we do not have "just-in-time" inventory systems? Is it because we do not employ the participative human systems such as quality circles? The author's conclusion was no — we simply have forgotten or ignored the basics which apply to managing our businesses.

4. Technique for Evaluating Manufacturing Performance

In 1980, work began on an improved Technique for Evaluating Manufacturing Performance (TEMP). It was felt that an approach was needed to assess where operations were out of balance measured against a basic set of principles similar to those set forth by Emerson and the others around the turn of the century. TEMP was developed as a two-phase diagnostic tool. Phase I is a quantitative study designed to identify symptoms of management problems while Phase II, using the symptomatic evidence diagnosed in Phase I, identifies the root causes of management problems. Phase I consists of diagnostic ratios designed to indicate the effectiveness of key controls and disciplines.

In Phase I, inventory, production, and planning disciplines are measured using historical data through such quantitative measures as inventory record accuracy, bill of material accuracy, level of expediting in purchasing and on the shop floor, level of incomplete production runs, as well as several other traditional performance measures. In addition to establishing the symptoms of the immediate problem (for example, inventory record accuracy measures show 64 percent of the inventory line items were adjusted at the last physical). Phase I measures establish a performance baseline against which action plans for improvement can be measured.

Phase II through structured interviews with representatives of all levels of employees, as well as the use of information checklists, leads the analyst to the cause of the problem. Continuing the previous example, in several situations it was found that stock clerks were never told that their primary responsibility was to transmit accurate transactions. They thought they were employed to help the supervisors and operators move material to and from the stockroom shelves. Thus, Phase II is designed to pinpoint where the knowledge of goals and objectives fades in the organization, who is not trained adequately, where procedures are ill defined, and how the informal organization works (or does not work). Thus, the stage was set for an effective collaboration between manufacturing clients and consultants with the development and testing of the TEMP diagnostic process.

In 1982, our case firm rekindled its efforts to redirect the control evaluation function. The first action taken was to change the thinking of the existing staff and to begin recruiting a staff to fill each proposed role. The greatest effort was placed on building a positive attitude for the staff and in attracting staff who could apply their academic training to the task of assessing the effectiveness of management control systems in areas such as manufacturing, accounting, marketing, and information systems. Awareness of the difficulty facing operating managers was key in molding a more effective CED function.

With staff attitude toward helping operating managers gain better control over their operations changing, the staff began to develop a more effective approach to completing management reviews. Management knew that the staff wanted a review program which would concentrate on the most important functions in a business unit. It also knew that pressures were mounting to reduce corporate overhead. This need supported a program to make control evaluation more efficient as well as more effective. Because the company was heavily involved in the manufacture of a wide variety of products, it was concluded that the initial efforts should be directed toward manufacturing. It was also perceived by some that the United States was falling behind its competitors in many areas of manufacturing. It was becoming painfully obvious that improvements were needed in the area of inventory management, productivity improvements, cost of quality measurement, and improved processes for management. It was also clear that more traditional financial measures of success were inadequate in the quest for motivating managers toward achievement of long-term objectives.[6]

The control evaluation staff was faced with several obstacles to quick success. While recruiting staff was difficult, the more challenging task was developing a more effective approach to evaluating management control systems. The staff had worked closely with its external auditors in implementation of more effective techniques for documenting controls in an established system. Since a diagnostic approach for evaluating manufacturing performance (TEMP) had already been designed by the external audit firm and successfully tested with other clients, it was decided that a joint effort could produce not only a more effective process for manufacturing control evaluation but could also speed the development of similar evaluation processes for other systems.

The combined effort was begun in the spring of 1982. It was the desire to develop a control evaluation review technique (CERT) which could be effectively applied by management control analysts in any control system in the company.[7] The technique would be based on the belief that certain performance objectives must be achieved by each functional element of a major system if the total system were to be effective. From a personnel administration standpoint, these objectives are at the heart of any system. Performance must be monitored through these controls. Measurement devices must be developed to allow managers to measure their and others' success.

The pilot reviews, applied in West Germany and in the United States, were initiated in March and completed about eleven weeks later in May. The analysis of operating conditions was presented to plant management and a list of potential improvements, in order of importance, was prepared by management. The areas lending themselves to significant improvement included physical management of material, scrap control, wage incentive programs, management team building, computer system development, cost of quality measurement, bill of material maintenance, and productivity measurements. It was concluded that the pilot CERT reviews were not only successful for the manufacturing review, but that the basic approach would be applicable for evaluating any business control system.

The process highlighted the significant interrelationships between key functions in the manufacturing process. It also allowed the operating managers to quantify better the benefits gained from changes that could be implemented. Since the time that this review was completed, many improvements have been experienced by the plant management at the locations. The CED analysts have been asked to revisit the locations for the purpose of measuring the degree of improvement and to study in more depth those areas where improvement was more difficult. After these pilot reviews were completed, their application was critiqued, and the control evaluation review technique was refined for future reviews by Borg-Warner. Since that time, more than eighty reviews have been completed in nine countries by a staff of nine analysts. Each review takes about eight staff weeks, requiring approximately two weeks on site by two analysts to screen the entire manufacturing control process.

The mechanics of the CERT process are not complex and can be completed by analysts with relatively little experience in manufacturing.[8] The key to using the technique is competent supervision provided during the reviews and thorough analysis provided afterward by a person skilled in assessing the needs of a manufacturing process. The evaluation staff provides an operating unit with a basic review package tailored to its location. It is then asked to provide the data relative to each selected control. While operating management completes the CERT package, the analysts develop a complete understanding of the system(s) under study. The flow of information, job functions, automated systems, and existing control characteristics are defined and documented.

When the analysts have completed their work and operating management has indentified the control measurements currently available, the analysts combine this information for presentation to management in the form of a system model highlighting the interdependencies of key elements of the system. Through this presentation, analysts have been successful in helping management to recognize important trouble spots and opportunities for improving controls. If the manager recognizes the need for change and is committed to implementing effective improvement, an action plan is begun. The role of the analyst becomes one of the consultant in the development of effective action plans and in the evaluation of the effect of the changes. The original quantitative information gathered provides a baseline from which to measure improvements.

Written study results are provided to operating management only. The action plan, complete with dates, actions, and people involved, is provided to the corporate controller sixty days after the review is completed. If a division has begun to implement appropriate changes, it is usually apparent at this time. If a unit does not recognize a needed improvement or fails to take necessary action, it is asked to present the study results to the next higher level of management. Significant control weaknesses are not allowed to persist without higher-level attention being directed to the problem.

This approach to reporting results has great potential for many audit staffs. It is not unusual for an audit department to spend 30 to 40 percent of its available hours on the report preparation and discussion process. By making the auditee responsible for the preparation of the action plan as the basic report of the audit process, possible audit bias is removed from the communication process. Management perspective is assured. The auditee has the burden of explanation to upper management. The reporting process therefore concentrates on positive actions being taken rather than deficiencies which support the need for change. As a result, the audit staff has the option to reduce its cost to the organization or to increase the audit coverage at no additional cost. The benefits of using a control system screening approach, in contrast to a functional compliance process, include an improved understanding of the business decision process for the auditor, and a much more comprehensive evaluation of control conditions in the unit for operating management.

5. Summary and Conclusion

The implementation of the new approach has had significant results in this case study firm. Every plant reviewed has committed to implementing the identified major impovements. Some of the plant managers have decided to adopt the CERT as an ongoing management monitoring technique. In West Germany, the division is automating the collection and analysis of the key indicators and is routinely providing the results to CED for use in improving the technique. In the interim period, a software program has been developed to support the review process. It has the benefit of providing an ongoing operations-performance-analysis program which can be used to supplement existing information systems. Managers are now exploring the desirability of supplying this software program to plant and division management as an integral part of the action plan monitoring process, and as a continuing control performance monitoring system.

Thus far, CERT programs have been developed and implemented for manufacturing control systems, accounting control systems, and management information systems effectiveness. A CERT package for administrative control systems has also been developed. The use of CERT may ultimately result in the development of a more systematic approach to holding functional managers accountable for their performance objectives. An improved set of performance standards should also result from the adoption of this approach.

The use of this approach has had significant results for audit management in terms of audit efficiency. The technique enables the analyst to make an assessment of an entire system, investigating in-depth only those areas which indicate a problem and which have a significant influence on the overall system. Implications for staff development are also indicated. Staff analysts are charged with assessing the overall effectiveness of a management control system, giving them unique exposure to the normal accountabilities of a general manager. They do not become involved in a detailed study of single functional areas unless an area is found to have serious problems. At that time they become problem solvers for the unit management.

The most important result of this change in the audit process is that the internal auditor has been transformed from an adversary of management to an adviser without losing the corporate monitoring benefit of having a corporate audit staff. The external auditor and the audit committee are better served in that all underlying control systems are systematically evaluated as an integral part of the coordinated audit process. The synergism gained through these cooperative efforts between internal audit and various divisions of the external firm provide an improved basis for the evaluation of internal accounting controls and of the operating controls which underlie the financial statements audited each year.

Notes

[1] Research Committee Report 17: "Behavioral Patterns in Internal Audit Relationships", *The Institute of Internal Auditors* (1972).

[2] James A. Hooper: "Internal Auditing: Professional on the Move", *Internal Auditor* (August 1983): 18.

[3] Ibid.

[4] J.R. Deters: "Renovation and Innovation in Internal Auditing", *Internal Auditor* (May/June 1975): 28–35.

[5] Terry L. Campbell, Christopher R. Narvaez and Linda T. Savage: "Implementing External Reviews Six Years Later", *Internal Auditor* (August 1983): 27.

[6] Bazil T. van Taggerenberg and Stephen T. Cucchiaro: "Productivity Measurements and the Bottom Line", *National Productivity Review* (Winter 1981/2): 87–99 and Robert S.

Kaplan: "Manufacturing Performance: A New Challenge for Accounting Management Research" (Graduate School of Industrial Administration, Carnegie-Mellon University, Pittsburgh, Pa., 1983).

[7] This need was recommended by Fletcher in: "In Search of the Elusive Definition of 'Internal Control'", *The Internal Auditor* (June 1981): 39–45.

[8] J.C. Fletcher, and C.C. Verschoor: "Managing Innovation: The Internal Auditor Challenge", *Internal Auditor* (August 1984): 29–32.

Performance Evaluation in Multinational Companies: Two European Examples

Hanns-Martin W. Schoenfeld

1. General Observations

The following two cases of European corporations presented here are part of a larger research project analyzing the systems used by European multinationals to evaluate subsidiary performance. All together, fourteen major multinationals based in Germany, the Netherlands, and Switzerland were interviewed. The two cases were selected for inclusion because the material represents a detailed description of the evaluation system and, at the same time, allows some of the basic differences which seem to exist between the European and the U.S. approaches to emerge. Both companies have reviewed and approved the material for discussion and publication. In both cases, top management and staff specialists working with the system on a day-to-day basis have generously given their time to assure the accuracy of presentation.

Based on the findings of the larger study, the two cases can be regarded as state-of-the-art descriptions of this part of management accounting, but each case represents a different approach. The Philips case describes a system based on the German/Dutch type of replacement cost thinking, which uses up-to-date prices in a high technology environment, whereas the Nixdorf case, showing the efforts of a newer, smaller company, by and large uses accounting data without direct attempts to integrate replacement costing and is, due to the type of subsidiaries operated, strongly marketing and service oriented. Both companies have developed their own systems, although in the Philips case, the basic ideas from headquarters in the Netherlands are clearly present. Nixdorf, on the other hand, has developed its systems in a relatively short time period, in an attempt to match the rapid growth of the company. Details concerning size, operations, and development of the companies are presented at the beginning of each case.

Both cases are noteworthy because they do not use only accounting data but also go beyond these by including other quantitative information and make an attempt to improve evaluation through ratio analysis. The ratios employed differ from the usual financial ratios because they are based on data important for performance measurements in the managerial accounting context. Nixdorf extends its attempt even beyond that by using some of the data explicitly for motivational purposes by instituting annual contests between its subsidiaries; performance for this purpose is measured in terms of previously announced results of the reports.

Another feature common to all multinational systems of performance evaluation is the use of a multistep procedure which consists of (1) development of long-range strategic plans (usually summarized in a few pages which briefly address the areas to be emphasized in future periods; the Philips case includes well-developed attempts to quantify even some qualitative issues by assigning previously determined weights to ranking scale of particular issues. Specific actions to be taken are stated with dates of completion and expected results); (2) pursuance of a policy of establishing a market presence and of long-term goals. This permits, even requires, use of objectives other than immediate profitability; the latter may, even if used, not represent a desirable short-term objective; (3) summary and detailed budget schedules extending over two or three years express the expected outcome in terms of accounting data and also in percent changes from previous results; and (4) reporting schedules, used to inform headquarters on a monthly and quarterly basis on specifically selected data which may assist in determining necessary countermeasures. These data include such non-accounting information as deemed necessary to adjust operations (deviation in accumulated orders, liquidity changes, and other ratios). In both cases, managerial and financial accounting data are reported at the same time.

2. Comments on the Philips Case

Although it is not necessary to note all of the specific schedules and their purposes, it might be helpful to the reader to discuss some of the features unique to this company. As already mentioned, Philips uses replacement costing throughout its system. This permits an assessment as close as possible to the actual market situation. It also requires, however, a continuous adjustment to new prices with the aid of indexing. To avoid a continuous adjustment of budgets, the company utilizes throughout the period a stable budget and (usually in the last column of the reporting forms) a prognosis for the remainder of the budgeting period. This approach permits continuous adjustment and a measurement of expected deviations without the need for expensive revision of all budget data. It therefore permits management action whenever necessary. In addition to the individual schedules, explanatory (verbal) reports are required to show reasons for the deviation from the initial budget. In addition to the replacement cost-oriented reports for each unit, quarterly reconciliations with financial accounting data are submitted to measure the impact on financial statements in a particular country. The subsequent reconciliation with the consolidated data for the entire multinational is achieved by also reporting data which are in accordance with the Securities and Exchange Commission (SEC) requirements, thus permitting adjustments for purposes of worldwide consolidation.

Since interest costs are subject to the financing procedures either required locally or imposed by headquarters, a uniform imputed interest rate is used for the entire company; interest calculations are based on replacement values (7 percent on revalued assets; 11 percent on all other assets not subject to revaluation during 1982). To permit elimination of imputed items, actual and imputed interest costs are both included in the reports. To avoid the problems of changing values due to currency fluctuations, all reports are in local currency. For shipments across borders, the company uses a basic exchange rate for budgeting purposes, which — as all other budget values — remains unchanged throughout the year. This enables headquarters to use basically market prices and calculate currency fluctuations from a stable basis.

For the entire system, standard costs are used (which are adjusted at least quarterly to facilitate a trend analysis — see factory sales price development at standard cost, p. 111). This permits price and quantity variances to be isolated at any point in time. The company, being strongly production oriented, places particular emphasis on the capacity utilization factor as shown in utilization hours and volume variances. This approach in turn requires separate budgeting for market-oriented production and major individual projects (for which projections over several years are prepared).

In keeping with standard cost policy, development cost (so-called technical cost) for specific projects or products is budgeted separately, totaled at completion, and then absorbed over the life span of the product (which for managerial accounting purposes can be regarded as a treatment similar to capitalization; see 4.3.11, p. 117). For every period, the projected and actual absorptions (= charge to each completed unit) are tracked, and deviations (or adjustments when necessary) are shown. In a similar detailed fashion, quality cost records (in the form of deficiency reports, service calls, and other relevant information) are kept to trace product and manufacturing performance (see 4.3.6, p. 116).

To complete the systems, a set of ratios is presently under development and partially in use. This system is designed to capture as early as possible all changes in performance and provide the company with a shortcut in reporting because these ratios will eventually permit management to follow subsidiary performance within the framework of an abbreviated flash report system. (For details, see Performance Indicators, pp. 135).

3. Comments on the Nixdorf Case

Similar to the Philips case, Nixdorf begins its performance reporting and evaluation system with a strategic plan, thus allowing each subsidiary in conjunction with headquarters personnel to define its own progress. The outcome of this analysis is summarized in the table of key indices (see p. 146). The reliance on this planning process is necessary due to the different stages in the development of each subsidiary and the fact that the missions assigned shift over time from market development goals to profit goals. Budgetary data for this purpose are based on market prices during the budget year. Since the company has only computer or computer-related inventories, conversion to a replacement cost system was not deemed necessary because all items are subject to rapid depreciation and have a relatively short life span. This philosophy carries over into the use of interest cost. Subsidiaries are subject to the application of an imputed interest rate on total assets; however, this rate is determined on a per-country basis to reflect prevailing financing cost in a particular environment.

Because of its marketing and service orientation in a highly competitive environment, activity class results (hardware, software, customer services) are separately analyzed, and items such as sales per employee, profit per employee, cost recovery from order backlogs, fluctuations in the ratio of new orders (bookings) versus completed orders (billings) receive a great deal of attention.

In the process of determining the position of an individual subsidiary, basic economic indicators are analyzed, as well as the portfolio of activities (see p. 147) with special attention to similar data concerning the main competitor (to the extent available). Similar attention is given to the advertising activities (see p. 151), which is typical for a company attempting to increase its market share. In the area of rental policy — typical for a computer company — an "as if" analysis comparing the rental situation with a situation of straight sales clearly reflects the attempts to analyze actual results and policies at the same time.

Nixdorf also has a well-defined set of indicators used for annual evaluation purposes (see pp. 154–59) which at the beginning of the period discloses all items to be used for this purpose. This approach differs distinctly from procedures used in many other companies; although objectifying this procedure, the company states clearly that this by no means removes all subjective elements from the process. It connects evaluation very closely to the budgeting process, because it permits comparison of actual results with identifiable budget projections. As indicated in this schedule, only actual performance of a given subsidiary is counted after elimination of all transfers or the impact of joint actions, in which a subsidiary only participated peripherally. Finaly, the motivational impact of the performance evaluation procedures is strenghthened through annual contests (which do not carry monetary rewards) but permit publication of results by announcing winners and rankings of individual subsidiaries. The fact that all contests and measurement criteria utilized are announced at the beginning of the period seems to improve the effectiveness of this process.

Alldelphi Germany (A Subsidiary of N. V. Philips Gloelampenfabrieken-Eindhoven / The Netherlands)

Hanns-Martin W. Schoenfeld

1. Description of Worldwide Philips Group (1982)

	Million Fl.		
	Netherlands	*Foreign*	*Total*
Sales	2,842	40,149	42,991
Trading profit (Deliveries less costs excluding financing costs, miscellaneous income, charges, and tax)	−52	2,182	2,130
Net profit percentage of equity			3.4
Net profit percentage of sales			1.0
Total assets	10,300	33,000	43,300
Number of employees	73,000	263,000	336,000
Cost of sales			32,150
Selling and general expenses			8,711
Depreciation			1,904
Capital expenditures (Investment)			2,082

Operating Segments	Sales	Investments in property, plant and equipment
Lighting and batteries	4,661	186
Home electronics for sound and vision	11,725	398
Domestic appliances and personal care products	5,151	103

Products and systems (for professional applications)	13,721	540
Industrial supplies	5,512	699
Miscellaneous activities	2,221	177

Trading profit is determined on the basis of current values.
All majority-owned subsidiaries are consolidated. Investments in non-consolidated associated companies are valued at net asset value under the current cost principles.

Geographical distribution of sales

	Sales million Fl.	Growth %
Netherlands	2,842	0
European Common Market (EC) excl. Netherlands	16,728	0
Europe, excl. EC	4,492	2
United States and Canada	9,803	4
Latin America	3,452	2
Africa	1,274	−3
Asia	2,874	2
Australia and New Zealand	1,526	−1

Geographical distribution

	Sales %	Factories %	Capital %	Employees %
Western Europe	56	50	50	66
United States and Canada	23	33	16	15
Latin America	8	8	7	8
Rest of the world	13	9	9	11

2. Description of Alldelphi

The German operations of Philips are combined in the German Alldelphi GmbH which controls, directly or indirectly, forty business units, organized in eighteen separate companies. The production program includes lighting and batteries, home electronics for sound and vision, domestic appliances and personal products, products and systems for professional application (telecommunications, cables, defense systems, traffic control, office automation, medical systems, security systems, scientific and industrial equipment, and industrial supplies).

The German subsidiaries employed 32,300 people as of April 4, 1983, in the following activities:

Production	17,200
Research and development (R & D)	4,600
Distribution and administration	9,500
Trainees	1,000

In 1983, empolyment was reduced by 1,300 (4 percent).

Sales by groups (in Mill DM or percent)

	1981/82	1982/83
Consumer products	30%	31%
Industrial consumer products	19%	19%
Investment goods	51%	50%
Total	DM 6,065	DM 6,262

Key data (in Mill DM)	1981/82	1982/83
Capital expenditures	261	252
Depreciation	231	244
Personnel expenses	1,734	1,787
Total assets	2,964	2,845
Annual loss/gain	−39	+66

3. General Remarks Concerning the Control and Evaluation System

The German subsidiary is subject to German accounting system requirements as far as financial statements are concerned; however, for reporting to and consolidation into the worldwide system, *replacement costing* is used. For reporting, control, and evaluation purposes, the group utilizes the economic grouping principle rather than the legal entity concept; the latter must be used for financial accounting purposes.

Philips uses thirteen main industrial groups (divisions) on a worldwide reporting basis, which in turn are further divided into industry groups, major product groups, and article groups. The national analysis is performed quarterly on several levels; however, the details to be submitted differ (for example, balance sheets are to be submitted by industry groups, income statements for each major product group or even article groups). For managing country segments (national organizations, NO), the national management acts jointly with the major industrial groups (international segments of Philips NV), which internationally guide the segments of the whole entity. The German NO applies the general reporting and evaluation system of Philips and is presently in the process of upgrading its performance indicator (PI) system to improve the control function.

4. Parts of the System

4.1 Strategic Planning Information

The strategic planning period extends normally over a period of three years; during the first year of this period the budget for the upcoming year is formed. The second and third years must be stated partially in quantitative terms; however, most information is given verbally in the budget. Whenever needed, strategic planning considerations are extended beyond the three-year horizon. The approach is basically marketing oriented and develops the important criteria for performance assessment in several steps. The entire planning process initially uses exchange rates predetermined by headquarters; these are adjusted for future years as the need arises.

Strategic background data for all business units are prepared for the same periods; they are to be categorized by industry groups. The quantitative and qualitative information shown on the following forms is required for this planning step. Forms are to be prepared for each major product group, industry group, and major product as required for coordination and control. The entire analysis consists of summaries for market attractiveness, competitiveness, strategic framework, and basic information about expected results.

The entire strategy is summarized by showing the impact on operating data for future years. The company uses comprehensive survey data for this purpose, as shown in Figures 1–7.

Business unit ________

Market Attractiveness Analysis						
Quantitative factors	Evaluation (check appropriate cell)					
	1	2	3	4	5	Weight
1. Market volume — normal year in Mill LC	0–100	101–300	301–500	501–750	750	10
2. Market growth in % average for 3 years	negative	0–3	3–8	8–12	12	20
3. Market profitability in % average for 3 years	negative	0–1.5	1.5–2.5	2.5–5.0	5	30
Qualitative facors — Market structure*	very negative	negative	neutral	positive	positive	
4. Entrance/Exit business						
5. Supply concentration						
6. Demand concentration						
7. Price sensitivity						
8. Internationality of competition						

Figure 1.

Figure 1. (continued).

9. Economies of scale						
10. Capacity utilization						
11. (Other factors)						
12. (Other factors)						
Market structure summary (Overall assessment)						30
Qualitative factors — Risks/Changes			(Describe elements)			
13. Sudden demand changes						
14. Swings in economic cycles						
15. Legal changes						
16. Exchange rate developments						
17. (Other factors)						
18. (Other factors)						
Risk/Change summary						10
						100

* Comments on five most important factors required.

4.2 Capital Expenditures Budget

Capital expenditures are grouped into (1) normal investments (without technology changes and capacity adjustment); these are subject to approval at the national level, within the limits originally authorized for the

NO; and (2) special investments (all others); these are subject to special approval by the international product division. For each project, a summary sheet (see figure 8) and supporting documents containing additional details (impact on market, capacity), employment, subsidies, development of profitability, and so on) are to be submitted. All prices are to be based on future market prices.

4.3 Annual Budget

Basic budgeting information (internal delivery requirements, coordination with other subsidiaries, projected exchange rates, and so on) are distributed to individual subsidiaries before the beginning of the budgeting period.

The annual budget consists of a standard set of forms which must be submitted at predetermined dates (between early September and end of November). The essential features of these forms are briefly described here.

4.3.1 *Factory Sales Price Development at Standard Cost*

These data begin with prices as of January 1 and show expected changes for all external costs and all internal influences (change in efficiency, capacity usage, and allocation of R & D cost). This analysis is translated into standard prices as follows:

	Current price	External influ-ences	Internal influ-ences	Others	Next year's price
	LC	LC	LC	LC	LC
Materials					
from third parties	80	+2	−5	–	77
from subsidiaries	160	+5	−10	–	155
Personnel	280	+20	−25	+8	283
Other cost	160	+8	−10	–	158
R & D cost allocation change	120	–	–	–	120
	800	+35	−50	+8	793
Changes in % of current price		= 4.4%	= (6.2%)	= 1%	

Since these changes assume the same output quantity at new prices, an additional computation, which translates the total expected change into index adjustments (giving proper weight to the new quantities) is necessary. This is accomplished with the following equation:

$$\frac{\text{new output quantity} \times \text{new prices}}{\text{new output quantity} \times \text{old prices}} = \text{index of price changes}$$

Business unit ____________

Competitiveness						
Quantitative factors	Evaluation (Check appropriate cell)					Weight
	1	2	3	4	5	
1. Market share, in %, current year	0–5	5–10	10–20	20–30	>30	20
2. Profitability % of market segment (ϕ of 2 previous years)	negative	0–2.5	2.5–6	6–10	>10	20
Qualitative factors* (major product — comparison; comparison with main competitor)	much weaker	weaker	same	better	much better	
3. Assortment range and depth						
4. Level of innovation						
5. R & D flexibility and effectiveness						
6. Price/value relationship						
7. Quality						
8. Product image						

Figure 2.

Figure 2. (continued).

9. User software						
10. Application know-how						
11. (Other factors)						
12. (Other factors)						
13. (Other factors)						
14. (Other factors)						
Product strength summary						30
Organization						
15. Positioning						
16. Personnel/ Qualifications						
17. Performance capabilities						
18. Distribution channels/ Market coverage						
19. Delivery service/ Logistics						
20. Technical service						
21. Customer contacts						
22. Customer support and advice						
23. Advertising/PR						
24. (Other factors)						
Organizational strength summary						30
						100

* Comments on five most important factors required.

Strategic Framework
The data of the previous two forms must be evaluated; the resulting major strategic goals must be stated briefly. Specific strategic measures have to be mentioned including their date/dates of completion. For all major capital expenditure projects, separate analyses are to be prepared (see Figure 8).

Figure 3.

Basic Information as to Expected Results
Each national organization (NO) must show expected results on the attached summary forms (only two such forms are shown; separate forms for the supply sector are used which require similar information). In addition, each NO must submit a statement of net assets (based on replacement cost).

Figure 4.

4.3.2 *Sales budget.* a) The budget contains annual data of past and future sales by product groups showing all variances (past and expected). These are separated into (1) quantity variance and (2) variances for other causes. b) Monthly sales

4.3.3 *Order portfolio.* Data consist of orders on hand January 1, past year

+ order intake
− cancellation and corrections, past year
= orders on hand, current year

expected monthly distribution of orders for budget year.

4.3.4 *Investment budgets* (as shown in Figure 8 by individual projects).

4.3.5 *Movement of inventories.* This schedule consists of (1) inventory changes past year (by source and destinations), (2) revaluation of inventories on hand, and (3) shipment values at standard and actual prices (past year).

4.3.6 *Quality cost.* Data are divided into cost for (1) prevention, (2) inspection, and (3) correction of quality deficiencies (total amounts and in percent of output value). These are allocated to own production and purchased parts.

4.3.7 *Personnel budget.* Data consist of (1) projected personnel levels and cost (including fringe benefit cost), and (2) breakdown of personnel (in full-time equivalent) by function and work classification (matrix).

4.3.8 *Distribution cost budget.* Selling expenses are budgeted by major product groups and distribution channel (changes require specific explanation).

4.3.9 *Results from sales activities.* Results are subdivided into sales activity (intercompany, domestic, exports) and product groups. Past periods are shown in terms of the following:

actual gross revenues (amounts billed)
− cost of sales at predetermined prices (×) applicable index
− selling expenses

---

net results

and compared with monthly budgeted sales quantities for the budget year.

4.3.10 *Financial statement projections.* All other financial statement items not covered in previous schedules are included in this budget segment (using uniform system of accounts classifications). All values are at replacement cost; depreciation items are reported in accordance with imputed depreciation values (replacement value depreciation).

All items impacting on the liquidity are projected in separate detailed forms (monthly distribution); internal settlements are to be treated as cash payments. For all accounts payable, the average number of days outstanding and the turnover period (in days) are included.

4.3.11 *Cost projections for support activities.* Activities such as R & D, innovation, engineering support for factories, equipment development, marketing assistance, repairs, and maintenance are charged to user departments. Information is shown as period cost data by activity. For each item, the scheduled cost recovery (through charges to products or departments) is clearly shown.

NO ____________ Industrial group ____________ Date ____________

National Strategy Basic Information — Commercial Sector Survey Data — Page 1 Totals[1]		Actual year t		Expected year t + 1		Strategy year t + 2	
		Amount/ number LC	% of prev. Year	Amount/ number LC	% of prev. Year	Amount/ number LC	% of prev. Year
Sales	1. Sales to third parties at current prices						
	1a. Export sales included in 1						
	2a. Annual net price change[2]						
	2b. Annual volume change						
	3. Export supplies						
Results			% of sales		% of sales		% of sales
	4. Gross margin 5. Selling expenses						
	6. Result on sales 7. Other commercial results						
	8. Results market sector						
	9. Imputed interest (to be eliminated later)[3]						

Figure 5.

			% of prev. year		% of prev. year		% of prev. year
	10. Corporate cost of financing						
	11. Misc. corporate income and charges						
Personnel 12/31	12. Total personnel (market sector — full-time equivalent)						
Investments	13a. Normal investments (to be approved) 13b. Special investments (to be approved) 14. Investment cash expenditures 15. Depreciation 16. Disinvestments						
Inventories 12/31	17. Gross commercial inventories 31.12.[4]		number of month		number of month		number of month
Receivables 12/31	18. Accounts receivable						

[1] Information to be classified by major products on separate forms.
[2] Defined as current quantities × current prices − current quantities × last year's prices.
[3] These amounts arise from the inclusion of total cost for capital via imputed interest charges.
[4] The number of months covered by inventories is to be computed as inventories divided by 1/12 of expected annual consumption.

Figure 5. (continued).

National Strategy Basic Information — Commercial Sector Survey Data — Page 2 Totals		Actual year t		Expected year t + 1		Strategy year t + 2	
		Amount/ number LC	% of prev. year	Amount/ number LC	% of prev. year	Amount/ number LC	% of prev. year
Market and market share	1. Total market at net prices						
	2. Market share in %						
	of which: internal deliveries						
	3. Total market in quantities						
	4. Market share in %						
	of which: internal deliveries						
Sales	5a. Sales to third parties at current prices						
	5b. Of which export sales						
	6a. Annual net price changes						
	6b. Annual volume changes						
	7. Export supplies						
	8. Sales to third parties in quantities						

Figure 5. (Continued)

Results	9. Gross margin		% of sales		% of sales		% of sales
	10. Selling expenses						
	11. Result of sales						
	12. Other commercial results						
	13. Result of market sectors						
	14. Refunded interest						
			number of month		number of month		number of month
Inventories	15. Gross inventories 31.12						
Receivables	16. Receivables 31.12						

Figure 5. (Continued)

NO ______ Industrial group ______ Date ______

National Strategy Basic Information — Manufacturing Sector Survey Data (This form is supplemented by product specific data)		Actual year t		Expected year t + 1		Strategy year t + 2	
		Amount/ number LC	% of prev. year	Amount/ number LC	% of prev. year	Amount/ number LC	% of prev. year
Production	1. Total production value at current factory sales prices[1]						
	2. Annual consumer cost price increase/decrease:						
	of which due to internal factors						
Results			% of produc- tion value		% of produc- tion value		% of produc- tion value
	3. Results technical sector of which: a) capacity results b) results on product subsidies						
	4. Results development sector of which: results on initial costs[2]						
	5. Imputed interest (to be eliminated later)						

Figure 6.

	6. Corporate cost of financing						
	7. Misc. income and charges						
			% of prev. year		% of prev. year		% of prev. year
Personnel	8. Direct technical personnel 9. Indirect technical personnel of which: a) product development b) product process development						
	10. Total technical personnel						
Equipment	11a. Normal investments (to be approved) 11b. Special investments (to be approved) 12. Investment expenditures 13. Depreciation 14. Disinvestments						
			number of month		number of month		number of month
Inventories 12/31	15. Gross factory inventories						

[1] See discussion of pricing p. 125.
[2] Initial R & D costs are capitalized and later allocated to endproduct in accordance with internal guidelines.

Figure 6. (continued).

NO ______ Industrial group ______ Date ______		
National Strategy Basic Information Net assets employed[1] beginning of budget period	Totals in LC	
1. Fixed assets 2. Intangible assets 3. Nonconsolidated companies (incl. loans to such companies) 4. Securities not readily marketable 5. Inventories 6. Accounts receivable (incl. prepaid expenses) 7. Liquid assets 8. Intercompany current account – debts abroad 9. Intercompany current account – debts abroad 9a. of which not interest bearing 10. Creditors, other short-term liabilities 10a. of which not interest bearing 11. Provisions (excl. provisions based on present value) 12. Long-term equalization accounts 13. Expenses payable and advance receipts 14. Advance payments from customers 14a. of which not interest bearing		
Total net assets employed		
15. Intercompany current account – claims abroad 15a. of which interest bearing 16. Intercompany current account – debts abroad 16a. of which interest bearing 17. Provisions based on present value 18. Intercompany long-term liabilities 18a. of which interest bearing 19. Intercompany short-term liabilities 19a. of which interest bearing		

[1] All values at replacement cost.

Figure 7.

The system works in the following manner. All initial technical costs are budgeted in the department where such costs are incurred; total costs are grouped and allocated to activities (subsidiaries) which incurred these costs. Projected recovery charges are then determined. Amounts not recovered during the current period are shown as "remaining items" at the end of the period. These will be charged to products during later periods. Over or under amounts for specific projects are separately identified.

Special forms are used for budgeting *consumer service activities* classified as warranties, chargeable services, presale tests, etc.; projected charges are used to determine cost recovery. For purchased services, estimated cost will be used. Services to be performed by company personnel are priced in accordance with current hourly rates (including overhead) for such activities.

Individual budget schedules are reported through the computerized system and consolidated by the national organization (NO) and submitted to headquarters. The worldwide budget is classified by NOs and industry groups.

4.4 Reporting System

For reporting purpose, essentially the same forms are used as for the budget. Reports are submitted monthly or quarterly. For all critical reports, comments are required to explain major deviations. Special emphasis in all reports is placed on

result control-sales,
inventory development,
order backlog,
liquidity-related transactions, and
personnel development.

The company-wide application of standard cost permits the determination of differences between actual and budgeted cost (standards), as well as the differences between actual cost accrued and standard cost charged to other departments. This is of particular importance in all departments concerned with technical development or support services, since these basically render services to other segments of the company.

All data containing price information are initially based on budgeted prices (as of January). These are compared with actual prices monthly.

NO ____________ Industrial group ____________ Date ____________

Capital Expenditure Request

Normal investment ☐ Special investment ☐

Country ____________ Company ____________ Project no ____________

I. Project description: Total value in LC ____________

If investment in other subsidiaries required, give project No. ____________

	Total at current price	Expenditure distribution at future prices			
		Total	Year 1	Year 2	Following years
II. Amounts requested Fixtures Equipment Minus revenues from sale of old property, etc. Minus subsidiaries (if applicable)					
Total to be capitalized (in LC)					
Other related expenses Chargeable to provisions Chargeable to P & L Management expenses Start-up cost All others Total not to be capitalized					
Grand total					

Figure 8.

III. Changes in current inventories, receivables, etc.				
	Discounted cash value	Annual payments	End of contract	
IV. Leasing Project description				
V. Profitability Discounted cumulative surplus Economic lifetime (number years to recoup investment) Payoff period (number years)				

Figure 8. (continued).

For price adjustment purposes, a so-called index is computed. It compares actual prices with the January basis and identifies

material price changes,
labor cost changes,
allocation changes of technical cost (due to adjustments in output expectations), and
changes due to construction or technical changes.

Of these line-by-line assessments, a new index is developed for future periods and applied to all production values (internal prices).

Separate reporting is required for all major orders requiring individual project planning. The information given for each project consists of

expected sales value, expected results (absolute and percent of sales), degree of completion, and expected completion date.	both actual and budget

These data require a separate analysis of the following factors (budgeted and actual) for each project:

net sales,
inputs (materials, total overhead, inputs from third parties, services of technical departments, and price differences).

In addition, order backlog reports are used to show (at estimated sales prices)

total project orders on hand,
expected completion (in terms of sales value) for year t, $t + 1$, $t + 2$, and $t + n$.

The utilization of assets must be reported four times annually. All asset positions are to be combined into groups by account numbers and shown at current values.

In this context, reports of revaluation of assets and resulting changes in depreciation by major product groups are submitted, including the allocation of revaluation amounts to respective reserves.

In monthly intervals, a report on product gross margins is submitted which utilizes the following classification:

$$\text{Total variance in margin} = \text{gross margin actual} - \text{gross margin budgeted}$$

(both in percent and absolute values)

This total is to be divided into

$$\text{net sales price variance} = \Sigma\left(\text{actual quantity} \times \text{actual price}\right) - \Sigma\left(\text{actual quantity} \times \text{budgeted price}\right)$$

$$\text{materials input price variance} = \Sigma\left(\text{actual quantity} \times \text{actual price}\right) - \Sigma\left(\text{actual quantity} \times \text{budgeted price}\right)$$

$$\text{quantity variance} = \Sigma\,\text{budgeted price}\left(\text{actual quantity} - \text{budgeted quantity}\right)$$

$$\text{input structural variance} = \Sigma\,\text{budgeted input price}\left(\text{actual quantity} - \text{budgeted quantity}\right)$$

If products not contained in the initial budget are included in the actual output, they must be treated as if a budget value had been computed at the beginning of the planning period; items not manufactured at the beginning of the period are to be inserted with actual quantity 0.

The foreign exchange position is assessed monthly by analyzing

old order backlog ± new orders/deliveries new order backlog	foreign currency orders only

The new foreign exchange position is allocated over twelve months for expected payment dates and separated into internal and external payments. These are shown at the expected currency exchange rates – internal/external hedging amounts.

Prognosis/budget adjustments. The annual budget is computed at the beginning of the period. Since changes are likely to occur, all subsidiaries are required to submit updated prognosis data on a monthly basis to their NOs which in turn report these data to headquarters on a quarterly basis. Prognosis data are required specifically for

inventories (expected values, price adjustment for end of year),
sales, value of production, results (expected values, price adjustments for end of year),
personnel,
all other balance sheet positions (expected values, price adjustments for end of year), and

all headquarters charges, imputed interest items, etc., which lead to internal adjustments.

Comments must be provided for all items differing substantially from the initial budget.

For *financial statement purposes*, the relevant information is submitted monthly, quarterly, and annually to permit data collection for interim and final financial statements. Special reports permitting adjustments from company-internal valuation to national financial statement requirements and SEC requirements are included.

Summary reports for management. To minimize delays in informing management, a set of summary reports is used. The reports are shown in Figures 9a–9d.

The results (as shown in totals for the NO) are reported separately for all major product groups. *Inventories* are reported as a summary for the NO using the following form:

Inventories Report

Month:

	Actual current month	Changes/Variances			Activity level vs. budget*	Budgeted for 12/31	Expected variance for 12/31
		Preceding month	Budget				
	Mill DM	Mill DM	Mill DM	%	%	Mill DM	Mill DM
Market sector Supply sector Technical sector							
Total							

* These percentages show sales/deliveries/production value changes between actual and budget as a measure to evaluate appropriateness of inventory changes.

The same data are also required for each major product group.

Personnel data are reported monthly by subsidiary units and/or functions. The form used is shown below. The same form is used for results of each major product group.

Personnel Report

Month:

Units functions	Actual end of current month	Variance from budget	Variance actual/budget		Expected variance until end of year	Budgeted for 12/31	Expected variance from budget 12/31
			previous month	end of previous year			
⋮	⋮	⋮	⋮	⋮	⋮	⋮	⋮
Total							

The monthly *sales data* report for major product groups shows the development by using the following information:

Sales Report

Month:

Major product groups	Current month		Year-to-date			Budget		Expected change from budget
	Mill DM	% Var. from budget	Mill DM	% Var. from budget	% Var. from previous year	Mill DM	% Var. from previous year	
⋮	⋮	⋮	⋮	⋮	⋮	⋮	⋮	⋮

In addition, an overview of all relevant data must be provided for each subsidiary; for this, the form in Figure 10 is used. For all manufacturing units, production values (at standard cost) are used instead of sales values.

Finally, control data are reported for orders received in the following format.

Subsidiaries	Orders received			Orders on hand at end of current month		Sales expec-tation current year Mill DM	% of expected annual sales covered by orders
	Current month Mill DM	Year-to-date					
		Mill DM	% of previous year	Mill DM	% of previous year		
⋮	⋮	⋮	⋮	⋮	⋮	⋮	⋮

In addition, detailed analysis of production values and a liquidity analysis (commercial receivables) are required on a monthly basis. The entire set of *cost data* (in substantial detail) is reported by the various production units directly to the NO and to the product divisions at international headquarters.

4.5 Performance Indicators (PI)

In addition to the regular financial/cost accounting data (all adjusted to current replacement cost), Alldelphi is in the process of developing a performance indicator system for immediate control of operations and development of an early warning system. The following PI are in use:

$$\text{cost index} = \frac{\text{actual cost}}{\text{budgeted cost}} \text{ (for selected items)}$$

$$\text{absenteeism quota} = \frac{\text{hours lost}}{\text{total hours}} \text{ (by employee groups)}$$

$$\text{cost business quota} = \frac{\text{possible sales} - \text{actual sales}}{\text{actual sales}} \text{ (for specific products)}$$

$$\text{customer profitability} = \frac{\text{profit from actual sales per customer}}{\text{actual sales to customer}}$$

$$\text{product contribution} = \text{product sales} - \text{product direct cost (for specific costs)}$$

$$\text{quality index} = \frac{\text{number of product units without deficiency}}{\text{total number of product units manufactured}}$$

The quality analysis also requires the reporting of

$$\text{quality performance fall-off} = \frac{\text{number of repairs (for any reason)}}{\text{number of end products produced}}$$

outgoing quality = percent of major defects (which are likely to materially reduce usability) reliability = number of service calls received during stated time period

$$\text{productivity} = \frac{\text{production value}}{\text{number of direct employees}}$$

$$\text{production speed} = \frac{\text{output quantity (or value)}}{\text{direct labor hours}}$$

$$\text{sales realization} = \frac{\text{actual sales}}{\text{budgeted sales}}$$

$$\text{sales development} = \frac{\text{budgeted sales increases}}{\text{actual sales increases}}$$

$$\text{distribution cost quotas} = \frac{\text{distribution cost}}{\text{actual sales}}$$

$$\text{product margin} = \frac{\text{sales} - \text{allocated corporate overhead} - \text{factory sales price} - \text{delivery cost}}{\text{sales}}$$

$$\text{sales profitability} = \frac{\text{profit}}{\text{sales}}$$

$$\text{factory price development} = \frac{\text{factory price(t)} - \text{factory price(t-1)}}{\text{factory price(t-1)}}$$

$$\text{inventory coverage} = \frac{\text{inventory value (given date)}}{\text{sales (given period)}}$$

The following performance indicators are presently tested in several units:

$$\text{consumer service level} = \frac{\text{number of orders filled immediately (for selected products)}}{\text{total number of orders}}$$

$$\text{committed volume performance} = \frac{\text{(actual production quantity in month n)}}{\text{(budgeted production as committed in month n} - 4)} \times 100$$

$$\text{committed volume performance} = \frac{\text{budgeted production} - \text{absolute variance of production}}{\text{budgeted production (as committed in month n} - 2)} \times 100$$

$$\text{committed line item performance} = \frac{\text{number of internal order lines completed}}{\text{total number of internal order lines}}$$

$$\text{inventory performance} = \frac{\text{stock on hand (month n)}}{\text{planned consumption per day (month n} + 1)}$$

$$\text{throughput time performance} = \frac{\text{materials value of factory inventory}}{\text{materials value of daily shipments}}$$

$$\text{record accuracy} = \frac{\text{number of correct data}}{\text{number of audited data}}$$

$$\text{deviation measurement} = \frac{\text{deviation in single item}}{\text{monthly value of consumption (same group of items)}}$$

Additional performance indicators are presently under study for purposes of enlargement of the PI System.

5. Summary

The Philips system has some unique features which include the following:

1. Utilization of replacement values which permit an integration of financial accounting and managerial accounting data even under inflationary conditions.
2. Utilization of imputed interest charges for the entire capital used to keep price levels is realistic; for financial accounting purposes, these changes are eventually eliminated.
3. The system reflects the European cost accounting concept of physical quantity-based resource consumption measurement and — at the same time — permits the use of traditional financial indicators.
4. The resource utilization measurement idea also surfaces in the adoption of performance indicators (cost or physical quantity-based ratio), which permit early measurement of performance fluctuation unhampered by inflationary influences.

	Sales		Value of production		Profits						
					Market sector		Technical sector	Development sector	Profit adjustments	Total profits before Taxes
	Mill DM	% of plan	Mill DM	% of plan	Mill DM	% of total sales	Mill DM	Mill DM	Mill DM	Mill DM
Previous year monthly data										
Total previous year										
Current year monthly data										
Total current year										
Budget[1]										
Prognosis[2]										

[1] Budget data are not adjusted during operating period.
[2] Prognosis data represent adjusted expectations.

Figure 9a. Summary data (Sales and Profits)

	Inventories								Personnel			
	Market sector		Technical sector		Supply sector		Total		Distribution and adminestration	Factories		Total
	Mill DM	Variances in %	Mill DM	Var. in %	Mill DM	Var. in %	Mill DM	Var. in %		Indirect	Direct	
Previous year monthly data												
Year end												
Current year monthly data												
Year end												
Budget												
Prognosis												

Figure 9b. Summary data (Inventories and Personnel)

Items	Current month	Year to date	Budget	Prognosis
Sales Mill DM % change over previous years % budget target				
Production value Mill DM % change over previous years % budget target				
Investment expenditures				
Inventories in Mill DM Market sector Supply sector Technical sector				
Total				
Receivables In Mill DM ϕ credit extended (in month)				
Personnel Distrib. & adm. Factory direct Factory indirect				

Figure 9c. Summary data — NO

In summary, this system may be classified as highly developed and adaptive to problems of multinational enterprises, since it permits — at the same time — local evaluations and cross-border aggregation of data with minimal distortion.

	Current month		Year-to-date		Budget		Prognosis	
	Mill DM	% of sales	Mill DM	% of sales	Mill DM	% of sales	Mill DM	% of sales
A. Market sector Budgeted sales % of budget attainment Actual sales								
Gross margin − distribution cost ± other revenues								
Total results market sector								
B. Production Technical sector output at market prices Developmental sector								
Total results from production								
C. Results supply sector D. Results general sector E. Results from internal deliveries								
Total results A–E								
F. Imputed interest cost to be eliminated ≈7% on net revalued assets) ≈11% on other assets								
Operating results								
G. Financing adjustment (interest due to shareholders; 7% on equity) H. Interest and exchange adjustment I. Other results								
Total results before taxes								

Figure 9d. Summary data – NO

Month ________

	Total		Subsidiaries	
	Current month	Year-to-date	Current month	Year-to-date
Sales Actual in Mill DM Prognosis, rest of year, Mill DM Annual prognosis in Mill DM Annual budget in Mill DM Actual in % of budget Prognosis, rest of year, in % of budget Annual-prognosis, in % of budget Actual in % of previous year Prognosis, rest of year, in % of prev. year Annual prognosis, in % of prev. year				
Results Actual in Mill DM Prognosis, rest of year, in Mill DM Annual prognosis, in Mill DM Annual budget, in Mill DM Actual in % of sales Prognosis, rest of year, in % of sales Annual prognosis in % of sales Annual budget in % of sales				
Inventories Actual end of month in Mill DM Variance vis-à-vis budget Expected variance on 12/31				
Receivables Actual end of month Mill DM Actual credit in month Budgeted credit in month				
Personnel Actual number end of month Change vis-à-vis prev. month Change vis-à-vis budget Expected change by year end				

Figure 10. Monthly Overview

Nixdorf Computer AG Paderborn / Germany

Hanns-Martin W. Schoenfeld

1. Description of Company

Nixdorf has been the fastest growing computer company in Germany; it has expanded rapidly during the last decade and at the same time internationalized its operations. As a relatively small computer company — compared to some international giants — it has specialized in providing computer systems for the needs of selected customers. These systems — among others — are geared to its large number of customers in the banking and commercial industries.

Some key data are shown here.

	1976	1977	1978	1979	1980	1981	1982
Sales worldwide (in Mill DM)	686	839	1,013	1,250	1,557	1,934	2,287
Domestic (Mill DM)	–	–	525	637	744	834	1,041
Growth rate in %	11	22	21	23	25	24	18
Sales per employee (in 1,000 DM)	94	101	111	120	126	136	157
Value added (Mill DM)	369	438	570	732	883	1,082	1,204
Value added growth rate %	18	19	30	28	21	23	11
Value added per employee (1,000 DM)	51	53	62	70	71	76	79
Wages and fringe benefits (Mill DM)	285	342	402	481	609	783	892
Wages and fringe benefits per employee (1,000 DM)	39	41	44	46	49	55	59
Wages and fringe benefits in % of sales	41	41	40	39	39	40	39
Employees domestic	5,508	5,749	6,253	7,042	8,468	9,249	9,956
Employees abroad	2,034	2,919	3,603	4,213	5,182	5,511	6,061
Employees total	7,542	8,668	9,856	11,255	13,650	14,760	16,017
Equity (in Mill DM)	212	238	262	460	497	582	624
R & D expenditures (Mill DM)	–	–	82	95	120	156	197

	1976	1977	1978	1979	1980	1981	1982
Investment expenditures (Mill DM) (not including rental equip.)	–	–	87	165	186	258	283
Depreciation (Mill DM)	–	–	–	–	–	129	176
Rental equip. (Mill DM)	–	–	–	–	–	248	307
Total assets (Mill DM)	–	–	–	–	–	2,307	2,478

The company included in its worldwide consolidated financial statement these subsidiaries:

	Equity in 1,000 LC		% of ownership
United States Nixdorf Computer Corporation, Burlington	US $	45,609,8	100
United States Nixdorf Computer Software Company, Richmond	US $	12,6	100

Twenty-four other foreign subsidiaries are not included in the financial statement because they are presently insignificant in size.

	Equity in 1000 LC	% of ownership
Domestic		
Nixdorf Computer Miete GmbH & Co., Salzkotten	20,000	100
Nixdorf Gesellschaft für Computer-Vermietung mbH, Salzkotten	10,000	100
Nixdorf Computer Miete GmbH, Berlin	10,000	100
BOG-Nixdorf Computer GmbH, Münster	10,000	50
Nixdorf Computer GmbH & Co. Datenverarbeitungssysteme, Berlin	10,000	100
Nixdorf Computer GmbH, Berlin	8,000	100
Nixdorf Computer Haus GmbH & Co, Paderborn	8,000	100
Nixdorf Beteiligungsgesellschaft mbH, Paderborn	1,000	100
Nixdorf Computer Miete Verwaltung GmbH, Berlin	500	100
Nixdorf Microprocessor Engineering GmbH & Co. Systemtechnik, Berlin	500	100
Nixdorf Grundstücksgesellschaft mbH, Paderborn	100	100
WESTFALIA Assekuranz Versicherungsvermittlungen GmbH, Paderborn	50	100

Foreign			Equity in 1000 LC	% of ownership
Australia	Nixdorf Computer Pty. Ltd., Sydney	A $	1,640	100
Australia	Nixdorf Computer Rental Pty. Ltd., Sydney	A $	300	100
Belgium	Nixdorf Computer SA, Brussels	bfr	170,000	100
Belgium	Nixdorf Computer Rent SA, Brussels	bfr	20,000	100
Brazil	Nixdorf Computer Equipamentos Eletronicos Ltda., Sao Paulo	Cr $	257,170	100
Denmark	Nixdorf Computer A/S, Copenhagen	dkr	5,500	100
England	Nixdorf Computer Ltd., London	£	1,500	100
Finland	OY Nixdorf Computer AB, Helsinki	Fmk	15,000	100
France	Nixdorf Computer SA, Paris	FF	70,500	100
France	Nixdorf Computer Lyon SA, Lyon	FF	37,000	100
France	Nixdorf Computer Locations SA, Paris	FF	9,000	100
Greece	Nixdorf Computer AE, Athens	Dr	75,032	100
Ireland	Nixdorf Computer International Ltd., Bray/Dublin	Ir £	2,600	100
Ireland	Nixdorf Computer Ltd., Dublin	Ir £	250	100
Ireland	Nixdorf Computer Software Ltd., Dublin	Ir £	10	100
Italy	Nixdorf Computer S.p.A., Mailand	Lit	2,500,000	100
Italy	Nixdorf Computer Leasing S.p.A., Mailand	Lit	500,000	100
Canada	Nixdorf Canada Ltd., Toronto	US $	1,001	100
Luxemburg	Nixdorf Computer Finanz AG, Luxemburg		4,000	100
Luxemburg	Nixdorf Computer SA, Luxemburg	lfr	10,000	100
Morocco	Nixdorf Computer SA, Casablanca	DH	1,800	50
Netherlands	Nixdorf Computer BV, Rotterdam	hfl	7,500	100
Norway	Nixdorf Computer A/S, Oslo	nkr	510	100

		Equity in 1000 LC		% of ownership
Austria	Nixdorf Computer Ges. mbH, Vienna	öS	50,000	100
Austria	Nixdorf Computer Miete Ges. mbH, Vienna	öS	10,000	100
Sweden	Nixdorf Computer AB, Stockholm	skr	3,000	100
Sweden	Nixdorf Datasystem AB, Stockholm	skr	500	100
Switzerland	Nixdorf Computer AG, Zürich	sfr	8,000	100
Switzerland	Nixdorf Computer Miete AG, Zürich	sfr	1,000	100
Switzerland	Nixdorf Computer Software Company AG, Zürich	sfr	50	100
Singapore	Nixdorf Computer International Singapore Pte. Ltd., Singapore	S $	25	100
Spain	Nixdorf Computer SA, Madrid	Pta	660,000	100
Spain	Nixdorf Computer Rent SA, Madrid	Pta	200,000	100
South Africa	Nixdorf Computer (Pty) Ltd., Johannesburg	Rand	1,100	51

2. General Remarks on the Planning and Evaluation System

The company is marketing- and growth-oriented without neglecting the strong emphasis needed on research and development (R & D) and quality improvements in this particular industry. Since all marketing efforts are concentrated on providing problem solutions for the customers together with the required software and hardware (50 percent of all sales are in software and customer services), the planning and evaluation system strongly reflects this emphasis. The planning emphasis, consequently, must allow the local manager in foreign markets the necessary leeway to adapt to local conditions. The emphasis of the entire evaluation system is therefore placed on jointly assessing profitability, growth, productivity, and quality improvements. This is also reflected in the compensation plan for local managers.

Another reason for placing a strong emphasis on a properly functioning evaluation system is the fact that 90-92 percent of the operating costs must be regarded as fixed. Therefore, sales minus purchases from continuing contracts should result in cost coverage of ≥ 100 percent. The management information system (MIS) consequently is built around a regular reporting system, integrating planning and actual data on a monthly basis, preceded by so-called flash reports to the worldwide marketing manager.

3. Parts of the System

3.1 Planning and Budgeting System

The budget consists of a one-year plan and additional two-year planning data. The entire plan is basically revised in a regular two-year cycle. Detailed budget data are finalized between September and November for the next fiscal year. Corrections of plans will be undertaken in May of each year if conditions require adjustments. The emphasis on a one-year planning procedure is justified because the production system is strictly job order – oriented and the time elapsed between order and delivery is approximately eight months.

All subsidiaries are supplied by headquarters with information about (1) product availability, (2) prices, and (3) detailed targets for each subsidiary (including profitability, productivity, growth, and target financial structure).

Each plan to be submitted by the subsidiary consists of (1) a management report (analyzing market position, competition, etc.), and (2) a standardized set of analytical, financial, and cost data. All data are projected on an inflation-adjusted basis in local currency. Translation into German marks (DM) takes place at headquarters using estimated exchange rates. The foreign exchange risk will be borne by the subsidiary, however, since all billing is in German marks.

The required planning data to be submitted by each subsidiary consist of the schedules discussed here.

3.1.1 Key indices

The data shown in table 1 have to be reported.

Table 1.

Subsidiary:			
GROWTH (in %)	t	t+1	t+2
Incoming orders			
Total revenues			
Gross profits			
Total expenses			
Employees (year end)			
FINANCING			
Accounts receivable			
– Acc. rec. in % of total revenues			
Inventories			
– Inventories in % of total revenues			
Balance sheet total			
– Bal. sheel total in % of total revenues			
Indebtedness (including equity from headquarters)			
– Indebtedness in % of total revenues			
Imputed interest (X% of total assets)[1]			
Actual interest			

[1] X is selected to reflect the prevailing interest rate in the area in which the subsidiary conducts its business operations.

Table 1. Key Indices (continued)

Subsidiary:			
PRODUCTIVITY	t	t+1	t+2
Orders per salesman			
Total revenues per employee			
Gross profit per employee in % of total exp. per employee			
Cost coverage Software Department			
Software results (incl. licenses)			
(excl. licenses)			
Cost coverage Sales Department			
Cost coverage Sales + Software Department			
Cost coverage Technical Services			
Result of rental company			
SECURITY			
Booking and billing ratio (Hardware)[2]			
Gross profit from installed base as % of total cost[3]			
Excluding hardware backlog			
Including hardware backlog			
Gross profit from all services in % of total expenses			
Hardware revenues coverage by hardware backlog (%)			
Cash flow I. (net profit and depreciation)			

[2] Booking = revenues from existing contracts; billing = revenues from new contracts.
[3] Gross profit from continuing revenues of hardware, HW upgrades, software, licenses, rental, etc.

3.1.2 Economic data for country of operation

	t	t+1	t+2
Economic growth			
Inflation rate			
Unemployment			
Balance of payment			
Interest rates			

Comment on other general economic factors relevant for the development of your subsidiary in t, t + 1, and t + 2.

3.1.3 Portfolio analysis

Define your activities for year t, t + 1, and t + 2 regarding portfolio management. Provide separate diagrams for each individual activity. Past position and developments should be shown in these diagrams. Describe the overall perspective for your activities separately for each of the years and show results in table 2.

Subsidiary ____________

Portfolio Diagram

Activity (such as hardware rental, technical service, software, etc.)

Year ____________

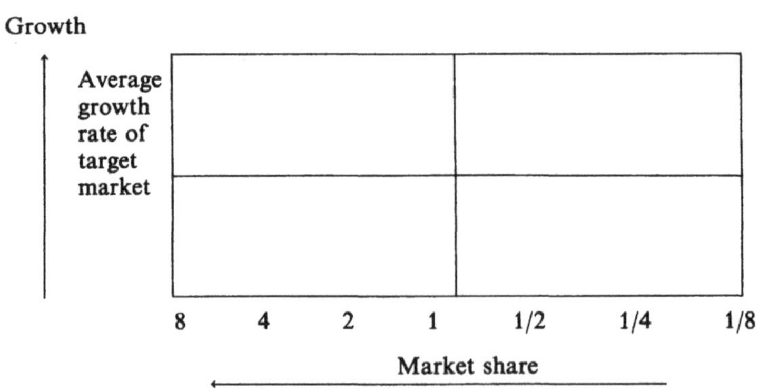

Table 2.

Volume of installations LC				Share of market		
	t	t+1	t+2	t	t+1	t+2
Main competitor (name)						
Own company						

3.1.4 Sales price analysis

Describe the development of the sales prices (for t to t+2) in each product line in local currency (LC). Sales price should be based on your *typical average configuration* of orders; give details for this configuration. The competitor(s)' sales price(s) should be based on a *comparative configuration*. For each configuration show expected gross margin.

3.1.5 Large-scale projects

Describe all large-scale projects not yet included in your planning figures. For each project, a separate investment profitability analysis must be submitted.

Project	System	Value	Probable decision date	Remarks

4.1.6 Investment planning

Enter all scheduled investments for years t and t + 1 in the table below. All investments with a value of > DM 10,000 are to be included.

Investment project	Value in LC	Planned date of purchase	Write-off period	1 = Replacement 2 = New invest.
Test machines				
Rental machines				
Technical custom/ service equipment				
Land				
Buildings (purchase/rent)				
Participations				
Automobiles				
Other investments				
Total				

3.1.7 Financing

Specify scheduled credit lines for t and t + 1 in LC.

Financing through credit lines (in LC).

Bank	Credit line	Estimated usage		Estimated interest	
		t	t + 1	t	t + 1

Financing from headquarters (in DM)

Account description	t	t + 1

At the same time, comment on the expected exchange rates as provided by headquarters.

3.1.8 Personnel

Explain scheduled increases in personnel by describing the jobs and justify the need for this increase.

No. of employees		Comments
t	t + 1	

3.1.9 Advertising

Scheduled advertising expenses for t and t + 1 by major categories:

	t	t + 1
Public relations activities		
Advertising		
Fairs		
Sales promotion		
Brochures		
Misc. (seminars)		
Others		
Total		

3.1.10 Rental policy

Rentals are made through a separate rental company or direct leases by subsidiary and are measured in local currency. Data to be reported are shown in Schedules 1–3.

Fixed assets (in TLC)	Rental company		Direct rentals	
	t	t+1	t	t+1
Leased equipment (at cost) as of 1.1. + Additions (at cost) − Disposals (at cost) = Balance as per 31.12.				
Depreciation on old equipment + Depreciation on additions − Disposals = Balance as per 31.12.				
Committed lease stream (installed mach.) as of 31.12. (Thereof sales leaseback) − Netbook value 31.12. − Sales leaseback payments 31.12. = reserve as per 31.12.				
Leasing rates				
1. Year contracts 2. Year contracts 3. Year contracts 4. Year contracts 5. Year contracts 6. Year contracts 7. Year contracts				

Schedule 1. Analysis of Asset Value

Systems designation	Total revenues (if sold)[1]		Thereof "Eigenver-mietung"[2]		Sales to own rental company[3]	
	t	t+1	t	t+1	t	t+1
Equipment group xxx						
Upgrades						
Total						
Equipment group yyy						
Upgrades						
Total						
Total systems						

Schedule 2. Analysis of "as if" sales values for rentals (in LC)

Total Upgrades						
Grand total						

[1] Enter price if sold to customer.
[2] Enter price if sold to third-party leasing company
[3] Enter price if sold to company-owned leasing company
In all cases, use the sales value of the contract year.

Schedule 2. (continued).

Systems designation	Revenues from direct leases		Revenues from rental company	
	t	t+1	t	t+1
xxx				
yyy				
zzz				
Other hardware				
Total				
60-month revenues				

Schedule 3. Revenues from leases

3.1.11 Others

Schedule 11 (consolidated balance sheet for operating and leasing companies in each country) and *Schedule 12* (breakdown of assets) show the details necessary to prepare financial statements according to German corporation law. *Schedule 13* shows all necessary details on intercompany transactions.

3.2 Reporting of Operations

The reporting practice follows the usual accounting-based approach. Monthly reports are a comparison with budget data and previous year's actuals, using a standard format shown on the next page.

Monthly actual data	Year-to-date		Budget for year t	Comparison with previous year	
	Actual	% of budget		Variance compared to year t-1	Year t-1 budget achievement as % of year t-1 total

The following schedules are in use:

(1) sales (hardware by groups, software, technical services, supplies), and order received;

(2) rentals and rental equipment inventories;

(3) detailed expense reports by sales categories (this includes imputed interest, price adjustments, additions and subtractions for various provisions, foreign exchange gains and losses);

(4) financial statements (balance sheet and income statement);

(5) reports on inventories, receivables, and payables; and

(6) in addition, selected key data are reported as shown in Table 3 (pp. 156–57).

3.3 Evaluation

For purposes of performance evaluation, the following strategic data are compared annually. All comparisons are based on years t and t-1; sometimes, the development is analyzed using several previous years.

3.3.1 General Data (comparison t and t-1)

1. Growth

   a) Incoming orders per country
   Incoming orders hardware in units and Mill. DM
   Incoming orders software in Mill. DM
   Incoming orders technical services in Mill. DM

b) Revenues per country
Consolidated revenues
Hardware revenues
Software revenues
Licenses
Supply revenues
Technical service revenues
Consolidated gross profit

c) Employees (average per period)
Total
Sales department
Salespersons
Software employees
Technical service employees
Administration

d) Expenses
Consolidated expenses
Personnel expenses
Consolidated interest expenses
} both in DM and % of consolidated profit

e) Backlog of hardware orders

2. Productivity
Incoming orders per salesman
Consolidated revenues per employee
Consolidated gross profit per employee
Total expenses per employee
Incoming orders per sales employee

3. Security
Booking/billing ratio
Planned hardware revenues covered by backlog
Cost coverage by gross profit from installed base

4. Financial statement figures (in Mill. DM and % of revenues)
Consolidated total assets
Consolidated accounts receivable
Inventories
Consolidated indebtedness (including capital received from headquarters)
Revenues per administrative employee

Table 3. Monthly Report

Monthly report Subsidiary: ______________ Month ________				
Item	Current year LC or %	% of budget LC or %	Variance from previous year LC or %	Previous year actual
Total sales				
Order per employee Sales per employee Labor cost per employee Other cost per employee Total cost per employee Net profit in % of sales				
Receivables, Inventories, Payables, Total assets } in % of 12-month moving sales average				
Labor cost, Other cost } in % of net profit				
Profit for services as % of total service cost				
Booking/billing ratio (new orders/total hardware sales)				
Hardware sales coverage $\frac{\text{actual hardware revenues + backlog current year}}{\text{budgeted hardware revenues}}$				
Sales activities only Orders per salesman Salesmen as % of total sales personnel Hardware sales per employee Other sales per employee Net profit per employee Labor cost per employee Other cost per employee Total cost per employee				

Table 3. (continued).

Item	Current year LC or %	% of budget LC or %	Variance from previous year LC or %	Previous year budget LC or %
Software				
Sales per employee				
Software employees as % of total sales personnel				
Net profit per employee				
Labor cost per employee				
Other cost per employee				
Total cost per employee				
Net profit (without license fees)[1]				
Net profit (including license fees)				
Cost coverage (without license fees)				
Cost coverage (with license fees)				
Coverage of personnel cost through software sales (%)				
Software sales in % of hard-ware sales				
Technical services (field engineering)				
Net sales per employee				
Net profit per employee				
Labor cost per employee				
Other cost per employee				
Total cost per employee				
Cost coverage in %				
Administration				
Labor cost per employee				
Net sales per employee				
Computer installations (entire area)				
Number				
Value in 1,000 DM				
Number of employees by service classification				

[1] License fees represent charges for the use of operating systems.

5. Economic results[1]/cash flow
   a) Economic results
      in Mill. DM
      in Mill. DM per subsidiary (if there is more than one in the area)
      in % of revenues
   b) Cash flow
      Total in Mill. DM
      per subsidiary in Mill. DM (if there is more than one in the area)

3.3.2 Data on a departmental basis (comparison t and t-1)

1. Sales
   Hardware margin total in % of total sales
   Hardware margin for specific items in %
   Cost coverage
   Supplies revenues in % of total revenues
2. Software
   Software gross profit (excluding licenses) per software employee
   Software licenses in % of hardware revenues
   Software licenses in % of technical service revenues
   Software employees paid by licenses
   Software employees paid by licenses in % of total software emolyees
   Cost coverage
      Including licenses
      Excluding licenses
   Software results
      Including licenses
      Excluding licenses
      In % of hardware revenue
3. Technical services (TS)
   Technical services gross profit per TS employee
   Cost coverage
   Technical services results (profit)

[1] Economic results are accounting profits after elimination of transactions (such as tax adjustments, non-essential capital transfers, orders required by other subsidiaries, etc.) which are not the result of a specific subsidiary's activity.

3.3.3 Comparison actual and budget

Incoming orders hardware in DM
Incoming orders by individual hardware items in units
Total revenues in DM
Hardware revenues in DM
Software revenues (excluding licenses) in DM
License revenues in DM
Supply revenues in DM
Technical service revenue in DM
Booking/billing ratio in %
Cost coverage in % of sales
Software results including licenses in DM
Software results excluding licenses in DM
Technical service results (excluding repairs) in DM
Total employees (average)

Additional comparisons are undertaken as needed. Similar subsidiaries are evaluated jointly. The accounting department also attempts to compare the results of each country/subsidiary with various non-accounting data for the annual budget.

3.4 Management Contest: Best Performing Subsidiary

3.4.1 General remarks

In addition, the company sponsors annual contests to stimulate further performance. The contests are described here.

For the contest in year t, the figures of t-1 and t-2 are employed. The best subsidiary for each criterion and year is awarded the place number 1 and the weakest subsidiary a higher place number according to the number of participating subsidiaries. The place numbers for each criterion and year are added without weighting. The winner of the contest "Best Performing Subsidiary" is the subsidiary which achieves the lowest total. Each winner receives a certificate. The Best Performing Subsidiary will also be awarded a challenge cup to be passed to the winner the following year. The criteria listed under the Sales, Software, Field Engineering, and Administration classes are used to determine the first, second, and third places for Best

Performing Sales Department, Best Performing Software Department, Best performing Engineering Department, and Best Performing Administration Department. The winner in each of the classes will also receive a challenge cup for the particular contest held each year.

3.4.2 Contest Criteria

Table 4. Contest criteria (comparison of years t and t-1)[1]

I. Hardware sales
1. % increase in orders received for hardware group x (value basis)
2. % increase in orders received for hardware group y (value basis)
3. Total orders received per salesman
4. Sales revenues/sales employee in each department
5. Booking/billing ratio in %
6. % increase in sales and stationery and supplies
7. % increase in booking/billing ratio
8. % increase in hardware order backlog
9. % coverage of sales + software costs [gross profit total cost (not including depreciation)]
10. License fees in % of field service revenues
11. Balance sheet total in % of revenues
12. Accounts receivable in % of revenues
13. Inventories in % of revenues
14. Capital and debts in % of revenues

II. Software
15. Software operating results (excluding license fees)
16. Increase in 15
17. Software operating results (including license fees)
18. Increase in 17
19. Software operating results (excluding license fees in % of gross profit)
20. Increase in 19
21. Software employee paid by license fees in % of total employees
22. Balance sheet total in % of revenues
23. Accounts receivable in % of revenues
24. Inventories in % of revenues
25. Capital and debts in % of revenues

III. Field engineering (Technical services)
26. % increase in field engineering profit
27. Field engineering profit as % of field engineering revenues
28. Increase in 27
29. Field engineering gross profit for employee
30. Increase in 29
31. Field engineering cost coverage in % (excluding repairs)
32. Increase in 31
33. Balance sheet total in % of revenues

[1] Criteria 24, 24, 32, and 35 are information only and will not be used for the contest.

34. Accounts receivable in % of revenues
35. Inventories in % of revenues
36. Capital and debts in % of revenues

IV. Administration
37. Punctuality of flash reports
38. Punctuality of management information systems reports
39. Punctuality of quarterly reports
40. Deviation of balance sheet totals from budget
41. Deviation of accounts receivable from budget
42. Deviation of inventories from budget

43. Reduction of balance sheet totals in % of revenues
44. Reduction of debts and capital in % of revenues
45. Reduction of accounts receivable in % of revenues
46. Reduction of inventories in % of revenues
47. Reduction of accounts receivable in days outstanding as of December 31
48. Revenues per administration employee

V. Others
49. Operating results of other services in % of other service revenues
50. Absolute value of other service revenues
51. % increase of other service revenue
52. % increase of gross profits for other services
53. Other service revenues in % of hardware revenues
54. Increase in 53
55. Other service revenues in % of field engineering revenues

VI. Profitability and security
56. Economic results in % of revenues[2]
57. % increase in 56
58. Cash flow in % of revenues
59. % increase in 58
60. Consolidated revenues for employee
61. Increase in 60
62. Planned hardware revenues covered by order backlog
63. % cost coverage by gross profits out of installed basis

[2] Annual results (sales and rental companies) ± result from rental business in sales company + depreciation/devaluation of inventories ± other internal measures = economic result.

3.5 Contest: Special Targets

3.5.1 Rules

The rules for the "Special Target Winner" contest are as follows. A winner is selected for each of the nine targets and receives a certificate. Selection criteria are either absolute figures for year t or changes between t and t-1. The targets in use are listed below.

3.5.2 Targets

Criteria	Calculation
1. Best economic results	Highest percent increase in revenues
2. Best balance sheet management	Highest percent reduction of balance sheet totals compared to revenues (increased in %)
3. Best cash management	Highest percent reduction of indebtedness + capital compared to revenues
4. Best cost coverage	Highest increase of cost coverage by gross profit of installed base
5. Best performing Sales + Software Department	Highest percent increase of cost coverage from Sales and Software
6. Best performing Field Engineering Department	Highest percent increase of field engineering profit compared to field engineering revenues
7. Best marketing performance in each region Northern Europe Central Europe Southern Europe Scandinavia Overseas	Judgment by regional managers Best achievement of marketing plans and highest increase in systems sold compared to previous year

4. Summary

The Nixdorf system is fairly typical for a company with mostly sales-oriented subsidiaries. It places particular emphasis on sales/personnel ratios and also employs "as-if" analysis in the area of rental policy to develop an accounting basis for policy analysis. A concentration on inflation-adjusted data appears unnecessary because the limited life span of high-technology products assures a quick turnover of assets. The system is highly developed and facilitates rapid management responses.

VIEW OF INDEPENDENT ACCOUNTANTS

Performance Evaluation Techniques for International Operations: Impacts on Managerial Incentives and Strategic Planning Considerations

Armin C. Tufer and Leisa B. Aiken

1. Introduction

Horngren defines control as the implementation of decisions and the use of feedback so that goals are attained.[1] The system of controls in any organization includes performance evaluation techniques which include gathering, summarizing, and analyzing information to determine whether goals are being achieved and to prescribe the actions required to further those goals. The process also encompasses evaluation of managers who are responsible for the resources being used to achieve these goals. Separation of the evaluation of operating units and the evaluation of their managers has been consistently advocated in the literature in order to evaluate managers on only those factors over which they exercise control. Studies have indicated, however, that in practice, performance evaluation for the manager is not separated from the evaluation of the operating unit for which he is responsible.[2]

In this discussion, an overview of the measures used to evaluate foreign operations will be presented and considered in light of the goals for establishing those operations, the choice of defining performance measures in local or parent currency will be discussed, and the potential effects of the performance measures and currencies selected on managerial inventives will be examined. Finally, some recommendations for performance evaluation will be made.

2. Strategic Considerations for Establishing Operating Units — The Initial Investment Decision

Performance evaluation systems should be constructed to consider the strategic objectives for which the operations were established. Companies establish foreign operating units for a variety of reasons. A 1979 study[3] in which more than one hundred manufacturing multinational corporations were surveyed reported that the general objectives most often mentioned were increased profits, increased growth, and increased market share. Specific reasons cited were, from the most frequently mentioned to the least frequently mentioned, to overcome tariff barriers, to gain economies of scale, to respond to government pressures to produce locally, to take advantage of government incentives, to follow the customer, to take advantage of market potential, fear of losing export markets, and to lower wage costs. Most respondents cited several reasons with even the least-cited factors being noted by 13.3 percent of the respondents. The study concluded that the profit motive was important, but that market share and potential were also weighty considerations. An additional observation was that lower wage costs seemed to increase in importance because they were mentioned in conjuction with the respondents' most recent investments more often than with the previous investments.

Additional information regarding the manner in which the decision was made was gathered. An absence of comparative decision making was noted; the majority of firms analyzed each investment proposal separately and a "go, no-go" decision was made. The financial criteria used to evaluate proposals in order of decreasing importance were return on investment (as measured by accounting return on investment or internal rate of return), payback period, and net present value. Although use of payback period is subject to theoretical drawbacks, its use was justified by the fact that rapid return of the investment was seen as a control against political risks. Clearly, this practice would favor projects with early cash flows over those with larger present value if the earnings were spread over many years.

Potential income was most often defined as earnings after taxes, cash inflows to parent after foreign and domestic taxes, cash inflows to parent plus reinvested earnings after taxes, or all after-tax earnings available for repatriation. The amount of investment required was usually measured as the parent's net contributions, including parent's share of equity plus loans and advances, followed by total capital employed. Most firms defined the cost of capital from the parent's viewpoint with the parent's weighted average cost of capital being mentioned most often. Approximately 23 percent of the respondents defined cost of capital as the subsidiary-weighted average cost of capital, however.

In most cases, business risk was evaluated subjectively or through sensitivity analyses, and then the rate of return, payback period, or cost of capital (for those firms using net present value) was adjusted subjectively according to the perceived level of risk. The most common method to evaluate political risk was to qualitatively describe the political environment and subjectively make adjustments similar to those made for business risk. A sizable number of respondents noted that proposals with a high degree of political risk were screened and never reached the formal evaluation stage.

Most often, income projections were made in local currencies and translated based on current or projected exchange rates so that the final decisions could be weighed with dollar-denominated measures. The most common definition of currency exposure was accounting translation exposure as defined by FASB Statement No. 8 followed by present and future cash flows to the parent in foreign currency.

As the author noted, the risk adjustments were not standardized, with the result that the techniques do not lend themselves to comparisons of risks among projects. Since all sources of risk were subjectively combined and summarized as a single required rate of return, payback period, or discount rate of estimated net present value, these evaluation techniques do not lend themselves to subsequent risk monitoring after the operations begin. Monitoring these risks on an on-going basis is required, however, if the company is to determine to what extent its goals are being achieved.

3. Monitoring Foreign Operations after the Initial Investment Decision — Common Measures for Evaluating Unit and Manager Performance

Studies have found that control systems for foreign operations are approximately the same as those for domestic operations. The most common measures by far are return-on-investment (ROI) and actual versus budgeted performance, with smaller companies emphasizing ROI and larger firms more likely to use comparisons of results to those budgeted. U.S. multinationals were almost totally dollar oriented in the 1960s; however, by the late 1970s, they were increasingly using local-currency figures to evaluate managers. One study found that almost one-half of the companies surveyed favored local-currency information for evaluating managers.[4]

The measure often recommended in the literature and used by large firms is some form of budgeted versus actual results. The budget is usually defined as some form of accounting earnings; however, other criteria including costs of production on a per unit basis, efficiency measures such as inputs per unit of production, or market-oriented measures such as number of orders or market share information may also be used. This flexibility with regard to the number and kinds of factors that can be incorporated is one of the clear advantages to using a budgetary system for control and evaluation. The information can be gathered and evaluated in light of the role played by the unit within the organization. The importance of this flexibility can be seen even more clearly when budgetary techniques are compared to condensed measures such as ROI. A clear disadvantage of using the budgetary approach is the potential for rewarding managers who are good forecasters or who successfully negotiate goals which are easily achieved in lieu of those which represent optimal performance. The budget must be determined subjectively, and interunit comparisons are difficult. The complexity involved in making comparisons among operating units makes resource allocation decisions difficult. Additionally, deviations from benchmarks are difficult to evaluate; what percentage deviation from the target is detrimental and what kinds of deviations are positive? Finally, a budgeting system may not promote or facilitate periodic evaluations of whether it would be preferable to sell or discontinue operations entirely in light of current company goals.

The second most commonly used measure to evaluate subsidiary performance is return on investment. Return on investment, the ratio of income to invested capital, can be defined in several ways. Possible definitions of income include accounting income or only those earnings which can be repatriated to the parent. Capital can also be defined as total net assets or parent equity; the valuation of capital is subject to various valuation techniques including book value (which is most often used for convenience), replacement cost, and disposal value.

The advantages of using ROI for evaluation purposes lie in its simplicity. If defined in the same manner for all operating units, it offers a succinct measure for comparing units. It is easy to determine benchmarks for this measure — the parent- or subsidiary-weighted average cost of capital, the hurdle rates used for the initial investment evaluation, or rates of return available for the proceeds of the potential disposal of the unit's assets — all are potential benchmarks. Use of ROI has several disadvantages, however. If used for manager evaluations, it will lead the manager to reject projects with a lower expected rate of return than the operating unit's current ROI, although their rates of return are higher than that of the company as a whole and, therefore, acceptable from the viewpoint of the enterprise taken as a whole. Similarly, it promotes a short-term focus, and capital outlays which are expected to produce large long-term returns, but which will increase the capital base and lower ROI in current periods, are likely to be rejected. Finally, this measure cannot encompass the complex objectives of establishing the operating unit.

4. Parent Versus Local Currency for Performance Evaluation

A 1979 study found that although almost two-thirds of the companies surveyed reported that they believed that local currency financial statements provide better information for evaluating international operations, the majority still used U.S. dollars for evaluation purposes. However, firms were increasingly using foreign currency information to supplement U.S. dollar statements to evaluate foreign managers.[5]

To examine how the choice of currency affects managerial incentives, it is first necessary to describe how currency fluctuations affect the financial results of foreign operating units. Currency fluctuations generally do not occur in a vacuum but in connection with other economic fluctuations which also affect revenues and expenses even as they are measured in local currency. Large devaluations are often accompanied by or preceded by local inflation, a downturn in the local economy, or both. When inflation is the major cause of devaluation, if local currency sales prices are not increased at the same rate as inflation, revenues will be lost.

Such price increases may be precluded by competitive pressures, however, or even by price controls imposed by the host government. Additionally, foreign subsidiaries may be encouraged by the host government to borrow hard currencies and convert them to local currencies in lieu of borrowing local currency to provide reserves to the host government. The host government usually promises to guarantee subsequent conversion of local currencies to the parent's currency at favorable rates; however, if conditions worsen, the host government may be unable to fulfill its promise. Such an offer would certainly be viewed more favorably by a manager who was being evaluated strictly on the basis of local currency results. In terms of local currency, there is almost no risk of loss; in terms of the parent currency, the risk is real and limited only by the ability of the host government to rebuild its international reserves.

Currency fluctuations affect the parent's financial statement results even if local operations seem unaffected. The fact that, in 1979, most companies defined currency exposure as accounting exposure as prescribed by FASB Statement No. 8 for purposes of evaluating the initial investment decision[6] is evidence that companies were indeed concerned not with subsequent cash flows but with how foreign operations would impact their consolidated financial statements.

Under the provisions of FASB Statement No. 52, which was effective for fiscal years beginning on or after December 15, 1982, the accounting exposure for foreign currency fluctuations depends on the functional currency of the branch or subsidiary. If the functional currency is the U.S. dollar, which is always the case for countries where there is hyperinflation, the prescribed process for converting local currency results of parent currency is remeasurement, the purpose of which is to produce the same results that would have arisen if the foreign entity's records had been kept in the currency of the parent company. In the remeasurement process, monetary assets and liabilities are translated at historical rates, revenues and expenses relating to assets translated at historical rates are translated at the same rates, and other revenues and expenses are translated at the rates in effect when they occurred or at the weighted average rate for the period. When local currency statements are subjected to remeasurement, currency gains and losses can arise from a net monetary asset or liability position or from fluctuations between rates used to value inventory and cost of goods sold and rates in effect when sales occur. These gains and losses are included in income for financial statement purposes.

When the functional currency is the local currency, the financial statements are converted to the currency of the parent company by a process denoted as translation. All assets and liabilities are translated at rates in effect when they occur or at the weighted average rate for the period covered. The translation adjustments which result from this process are not included in income but reported as a separate component of equity. In the event of disposal of the unit, the amount accumulated in the translation adjustment component of the equity is reported as part of the gain or loss on the disposal.[7]

Whether the manager is evaluated in local-currency or parent-company currency results, the conversion method used will probably impact on how he reacts to currency fluctuations. A brief example will be examined assuming the following:

- The manager is evaluated primarily on operating margin as determined by local currency historical financial statements.
- The local currency devalues during the period against the dollar which is the parent company's currency.
- The local market conditions are such that the manager believes that sales will drop significantly if prices are increased.
- The dollar is the functional currency, and the company converts local currency results to U.S. dollars using the remeasurement technique, and the company has concluded that currency risk should be defined as the FASB Statement No. 8 translation risk.

The manager has different price-setting incentives, depending on which currency the company has chosen for evaluating his performance; he will certainly be more likely to increase prices if the results are measured in U.S. dollars.

Another example will show that the currency selected may affect the manager's decisions regarding how to allocate resources among various assets. Suppose the parent's objectives for creating the foreign operations included generating cash flow to remit to the parent, not establishing a permanent presence in the host country. Again, the company deems the parent currency to be the functional currency and evaluates the subsidiary in terms of income remeasured into the parent company's currency. The management of the foreign operation is expecting steady devaluation of the local currency. If the manager perceives that his success is tied to the income results for his operations, he is likely to shift resources to fixed assets from monetary assets which will generate translation losses. He can do this by accelerating capital improvements of equipment replacements. This may be in conflict with parent goals, however, if — for example — the parent management had deemed it appropriate to maintain the minimum level of capital investment because of risk of appropriation or even destruction of capital assets. In such cases, the parent management could detect such behavior by carefully evaluating proposals for such capital improvements or replacements in light of its own goals and could encourage the repatriation of cash flows as soon as possible. Note also that in this situation, if given the authority to do so, the local management has incentives to incur debt denominated in the local currency to finance fixed assets. These debts could offset monetary assets and lower translation gains and losses even further. Should the movements in the values of the currencies reverse, however, the parent could find itself in the position of guarantor of substantial debts, even as measured in its own currency, in addition to having significant assets exposed in a country where it had intended only to establish more limited operations.

In one case, of two operating units in different countries, one, unit A, generated losses in circumstances precluding the use of net operating loss carry forwards for tax purposes and a second, unit B, generated income. For several years, because of discussions at intercompany meetings and in intercompany correspondence, the manager of B had been aware of the net operating loss carry forwards which could not be used by A. The manager of A became aware of a method to re-invoice goods through B and establish an additional cost of transhipment that would move the loss from A to B where it could be used to offset taxable income. The manager of B balked at the suggestion and stated that he had been aware of the possibility for some time but did not want such a policy implemented because his unit's operating profits would suffer. Finally, an agreement was made at top management level to incorporate a factor into the calculation of B unit's operating profit to compensate that unit for enabling such tax savings to be generated. Although corporate policy stated that managers were judged on several criteria, apparently this manager perceived that his fate hinged on operating profits and would not risk compromising his unit's results in terms of that measure without some compensation although the company as a whole clearly benefited.

Consider also the position of the local manager who is a local national and is responsible for developing long-run projections of the local environment. If the company does not offer him opportunities for employment on a worldwide basis, is he not likely to make more optimistic forecasts for the local situation than he would otherwise, and encourage commitment by the parent when it would be better off to invest available funds elsewhere? One study found that although most of the firms it surveyed subscribed to outside sources which rate or rank countries in terms of political factors, no attempt was made to incorporate these rankings into required performance for potential investments,[8] and it seems to be the case that they are often ignored in on-going evaluation when they could be compared with local management's assessment of the local situation. Local management's forecasts for the environment and the local unit's results should be viewed by the parent company in light of the position of the local manager within the company and compared with forecasts for the environment which are available from third-party sources. When third-party sources offer a more pessimistic view of the environment, the parent management should carefully consider how the unit's operating results are likely to be affected. For example, if the outside source predicts that currency restrictions will be imposed and the local manager has not considered this possibility in his forecast, the parent could require accelerated payment of intercompany obligations, dividends, or any other amounts denominated in other currencies owned by the unit before such restrictions were imposed.

Let us turn now to those countries where the parent company country has an established presence. These are the operations whose financial statement results were most affected by the implementation of FASB Statement No. 52, because in these countries, the local currency is more likely to be selected as the functional currency. As noted earlier, the parent currency income statement results for these countries will mirror the local currency results, but all assets and liabilities held in these countries will generate translation adjustments. These translation adjustments are recorded as a separate component of parent equity for reporting purposes. If, as in 1979, companies view currency exposure as income statement exposure, the only currency exposure in these countries arises from assets that the foreign unit holds which are denominated in currencies other than the local one. In periods when the parent company's currency is strengthening, however, serious erosion of equity which could distort debt/equity agreements and impact loan covenant agreements can occur. Some writers have suggested that the parent borrow funds in local currency and designate these borrowings as hedges of their net investment positions. The impact of currency fluctuations on these borrowings will be classified as equity impacts under FASB Statement No. 52.[9] Cross-currency hedges can also be so classified.

It has been anticipated that such parent-company borrowing will replace local currency financings that under FASB Statement No. 8 were used to hedge local monetary assets and will be integrated as part of a move to a more completely centralized management of foreign exchange exposure through parent-company level financing and policy setting for billing and invoicing strategies. Given the diversity of economic and legal situations across the world, the costs and benefits of such a centralized management must be carefully scrutinized.

If local management is relieved of all responsibility for foreign exchange exposure, performance will certainly be affected. Such a centralized policy may require tighter monitoring of operating decisions and forecasts of local operating results made by local managers. The latter is especially important since accurate forecasts of operating results and asset positions will be required for effective hedging.

In addition to tracking the results of foreign operations in terms of the objectives they were established to achieve, the evaluation system should prompt explicit periodic consideration of whether to continue such operations. This is especially important when the operations require continuing contribution of resources by the parent or in cases where the parent company's outlook has changed since establishing the foreign unit. For example, suppose that a foreign unit is generating losses that cannot provide benefits to the parent because the parent is also incurring tax losses. If the foreign unit is viewed only with consideration to continuing its operations, the possibility of selling the unit to a company that can benefit from the tax losses might not even be explored, while a transaction might provide much needed cash flows to the parent. The decision to continue, expand, or dispose of even profitable foreign operations should be considered periodically. Additional resources that the parent must provide to continue or expand such operations or the potential proceeds from disposal might provide funds for new projects or endeavors that are more congruent with current parent strategy.

In conclusion, the parent management should evaluate the system for rewarding managers of foreign units. Although the parent management may insist that local managers are not evaluated on factors they cannot control, the policy statements may not be credible in light of shrinking resource contributions to foreign units whose results do not measure up to the budget or other benchmarks. This is especially important for managers who are local nationals. One policy alternative would be to assure these local managers of employment outside the host country, or, if this is impractical, to provide some sort of compensation in the case of liquidation of the operating unit.

It is probably impossible to design a system for evaluating managers that completely separates their evaluations from those of the units they manage. Perhaps it is more practical to consider how evaluations impact the incentives of managers and design corporate procedures that explicity consider possible motivations of local managers when evaluating both the units and the forecasts and proposals made by their local managers. Procedures for periodically considering the disposal of foreign units should also be established to help encourage a better allocation of all the resources available to the parent. Finally, with the implementation of FASB Statement No. 52, companies should re-evaluate and re-establish the goals for their international operations in light of the new treatment available for hedging foreign investments through foreign-currency borrowing by the parent. The current strength of the dollar and the relatively high level of U.S. interest rates will undoubtedly offer U.S. multinationals some interesting opportunities.

Notes

1 Charles T., Horngren: *Cost Accounting* (Englewood Cliffs, N.J.: Prentice-Hall, 1977), 6.
2 Helen Gernon Morsicato: *Currency Translation and Performance Evaluation in Multinationals* (Ann Arbor, Mich.: UMI Research Press, 1980), 130–35.
3 Marie Wicks Kelly: *Foreign Investment Evaluation Practices of U.S. Multinational Corporations* (Ann Arbor, Mich.: UMI Research Press, 1981), 68–102.
4 Morsicato: *Currency Translation*, 136–41.
5 Ibid.
6 Kelly: *Foreign Investment*, 91–92.
7 Financial Accounting Standards Board: *Statement of Financial Accounting Standard No. 52* (Stanford, Conn.: FASB, 1981).
8 Kelly: *Foreign Investment*, 91–92.
9 Fredick C. Militello Jr.: "Statement No. 52: Changes in Financial Management Practices: *Financial Executive* (August 1983), 48–51.

Financial Reporting Systems of Multinational Companies — An External Auditor's Viewpoint

Lenz Neuhauser

1. Developments in the Past Year

In discussing the implications of the events of the last eighteen months on the way multinational companies keep their foreign subsidiaries' books and measure their results, the first observation relates to the continued strong rebounding of the U.S. economy in contrast to a still sluggish or mildly upturning economy in Europe. For most U.S. multinationals, that development has resulted in a larger proportion of their revenues and, even more importantly, their profits being generated domestically than three or five years ago.

The relative lethargy of the economies outside the U.S. has also contributed to the increase of a trend visible a year and a half ago, when this author last spoke on this campus: U.S. multinationals have become much more conservative in their foreign investment decisions and in monitoring the on-going performance of their foreign subsidiaries. Evaluation of country risk which ranked rather low on the list of priorities has risen on the agenda for evaluating a major investment decision in a foreign country or re-evaluating an ongoing financial commitment.

Similarly, the U.S. market continues to exert substantial attractiveness on foreign multinationals which not only reinvest their U.S. earnings but also continue to pour substantial sums into this economy. In terms of financial results, this means that U.S. dollar – based operations tend to increase their significance to all multinational companies around the world.

Of course, this trend receives an additional boost from the unexpected and continuing strength of the U.S. dollar vis à vis most major foreign currencies. Thus, revenues and profits generated in U.S. dollars add more and more strength to financial statements of multinational companies.

Apart from the strong U.S. economy and the strong dollar, a third development has occurred during the last two years or so that impacts significantly on measuring the results of foreign subsidiaries. This development is the almost unprecedented slowing in the rate of inflation in most industrialized nations. Concurrently, the already weak interest in inflation accounting has all but vanished during the last eighteen months, not only in the United States, but also in the United Kingdom and other European countries.

The Financial Accounting Standards Board (FASB) has recently admitted that the information generated as a result of its Statement No. 33 on inflation accounting has not been widely used. This author believes that even this is an exaggeration. Consequently, the FASB has agreed to eliminate the historical cost requirement for those companies reporting current cost information and has also asked its staff to consider further reductions and modifications in its inflation accounting requirements. Similarly, SSAP No. 16 (the British parallel to FASB No. 33) is all but being ignored in the United Kingdom. This writer regrets this development and continues to believe that efforts should be made by the preparers of financial information and members of the accounting profession to enhance the understanding and use of financial data adjusted for the results of inflation.

On the negative side, however, is the continued very high level of interest. This has forced more companies to focus sharply on the implications of interest expense and/or imputed interest costs, on the time value of money on investment decisions, and on evaluating domestic and foreign operations in countries with widely varying levels of interest.

A fifth development demanding more discussion in board rooms of multinational companies is certain foreign subsidiaries' strategic missions that stretch beyond direct measures of profitability. This holds particularly true for U.S. subsidiaries of foreign multinationals which view their U.S. bases as strategic outposts to fend off what they perceive as an increasing trend in the United States toward protectionist measures that might prevent or at least seriously impede their exports to this country. Continued unprofitability is widespread among many U.S. subsidiaries of foreign corporations. In many of these situations, profitability of their U.S. operations is being viewed on a corporate level, that is, losses generated by those U.S. operations are being offset against gross margins realized on sales to the United States by the parent company and/or other subsidiaries outside the United States.

Last, but not least, we have seen very little discussion on FASB Statement No. 52 dealing with translation of foreign currency financial statements. This seems to confirm a hope that we expressed a year and a half ago with respect to satisfaction in using the current rate method.

Clearly, though, while these developments have had an impact on the financial reporting systems of multinational companies, the fundamentals remain as follows:

1. A MIS of a multinational should closely reflect the philosophy and structure of the company. Centralization versus decentralization and the issue of organizing the system along product lines, or along geographic regions (or a combination of both) are key factors to be considered.

2. Even the best financial reporting system only partially reflects reality. At best, it will indicate whether the ship is sailing in the right direction but not whether it will arrive safely at the destination.

3. It is imperative that both corporate headquarters and the foreign managers understand the system thoroughly and that they agree and identify with it. A good design alone is far from doing the job adequately. Continued education and close communication between home office and foreign subsidiaries are indispensable ingredients in that process. This author repeatedly recommends the old and proven tool of periodic meetings of the multinational's worldwide subsidiary controllers to present budgets, discuss reporting systems, and exchange ideas and experiences.

4. Subsidiaries are always subject to erratic development and sudden change due to external forces, for example, exchange rate variances and uncontrollable price changes by the parent or other affiliates. This requires that an MIS not be cast in iron once it has been designed, but that it be flexible enough to adapt to change in the environment without abandoning the underlying principles.

5. As subsidiaries mature and become more independent of the head office, changes in information systems and in the organizational structure and reward systems become critical issues in the context of the ever-changing fabric of a multinational company, for example, with respect to local financing, local purchase decisions, and local hiring practices.

6. Beyond any MIS are many non-financial and intangible factors that may be more important than the numbers and should be considered in evaluating and measuring foreign subsidiaries: public relations in the host country, employee morale, and staff turnover.
7. An MIS for a multionational should not stress short-term profitability at the expense of longer-term goals. This is especially true in the case of foreign subsidiaries in which, as previously mentioned, strategic considerations such as market presence or protection against import curbs by the host country assume greater and greater importance.
8. External reporting considerations (both financial and tax) should not take precedence over the MIS because neither necessarily reflects company philosophy or structure, nor is either necessarily geared to measure actual economic performance.

2. Areas of International Environment

In attempting to isolate those areas unique to the international environment from those common to both domestic *and* multinational companies, the following six topics have been identified as being the most important: (1) foreign currencies; (2) transfer pricing; (3) foreign country risks; (4) interest cost; (5) foreign inflation; and (6) performance measures.

Other areas of importance include worldwide computerization and worldwide versus local accounting procedures. In this writer's opinion, each multinational should have only one set of worldwide accounting principles which need not necessarily mirror the ones generally accepted for external reporting purposes in the parent company's home country.

U.S. multinationals tend to match external and internal accounting rules, whereas non – U.S. multinationals more often than not use internal accounting instructions that differ from their external ones. In most cases, they contend that they are striving to design internal reporting that most clearly reflects economic reality while being sufficiently prudent.

2.1 Foreign Currencies

The first concern is foreign currencies. This topic is, of course, inseparable from inflationary concerns. It is curious to the writer that many U.S.

companies spend a great deal of time on the currency aspect and comparatively little on the inflationary aspect of this issue. Fortunately, Statement No. 52 has brought some relief in that area. The foreign currency issue also seems to be an exceedingly complex one as witnessed by the lack of uniformity throughout the world in dealing with it as it relates to both the multinational companies' MIS and the accounting professions. There are at least three dimensions to the problem: (1) the question of taking a headquarters' currency versus a foreign subsidiary's currency viewpoint; (2) setting predetermined rates of exchange and related responsibility; and (3) translation into home-office currency.

As to the first point, companies in favor of using headquarters' currency generally contend that because the owner (that is, the parent company) ultimately must measure risks and rewards in its own currency, this is the only one that counts. The other group believes a foreign currency viewpoint is more realistic, especially in measuring the subsidiary's performance because many of its business transactions are conducted in local currency and are beyond the parent company's control. Studies seem to indicate — and our experience would appear to confirm – that U.S. companies tend to take a dollar viewpoint for their subsidiaries, whereas European- and Japanese-based companies more often take a foreign subsidiary's currency viewpoint in measuring the financial performance of their subsidiaries. This observation is also in "agreement" with our experience that non – U.S. companies generally grant their foreign subsidiaries a greater degree of autonomy than their U.S. counterparts. This writer's position is that the foreign subsidiary's currency viewpoint makes increasingly more sense as it becomes more fully integrated into the host country economy and transacts an increasing amount of its business in local currency.

Next is the question of setting predetermined rates of exchange, including responsibility therefor, and of subsequent comparison to actual rates. As you know, this procedure may be applied in a number of ways, the details of which will not be discussed here. In almost all cases this writer has seen, multinationals attempt to use a projected rate for one year for budgeting purposes and a final actual rate at year-end or at period-end to compare to budget. The author has also seen some cases where budget rates are used for both budgeting purposes and for comparison to actual performance.

An alternative we have recommended is to recast the budget at the actual period-end rate and compare these numbers to those for period ends, also measured at actual exchange rates. That way, variances due to exchange rate fluctuations are eliminated while performance measurement takes place at real, up-to-date exchange rates.

In keeping with what appears to be the greater degree of autonomy granted by non – U.S. companies to their subsidiaries, an inconsistency seems to exist in that the actual exchange rate is generally beyond the control of the local unit and therefore should not be used to measure its performance. The writer believes, however, that most companies are aware that exchange rate fluctuations are controllable neither locally nor at headquarters and therefore are looked on as a budget "aberration" rather than an ingredient of actual performance.

From a practitioner's viewpoint, this whole question of assigning responsibility for differences between budgeted and actual rates of exchange and the related issue of allocating responsibility for exchange gains and losses is one that has not been resolved satisfactorily.

For example, one of this writer's local clients in the United States with a Spanish parent imports goods from Spain to sell in the United States. As the peseta loses value against the dollar, should the U.S. subsidiary not make a decision to change its selling prices? And should local management not be held accountable for the wisdom of that decision? Similarly, many foreign subsidiaries have the autonomy and ability to take loans in local currency. Thus, they are able to hedge, at least in part, assets denominated in local currency which should therefore be measured as to how successful they have been in their hedging efforts.

To the extent, however, that more and more companies operate on a truly global basis and so necessitate a global viewpoint on managing a variety of foreign currencies and related exposures in a centralized manner, it seems that the related responsibility should rest with the central controlling or treasury function at corporate headquarters.

2.2 Transfer Pricing

It could be argued that multinational companies should not spend so much time trying to determine how to measure their foreign subsidiaries' performance, because all those that supply goods or services in substantial amounts to their subsidiaries can influence their results quite easily by changing the prices charged for those goods or services. Obviously, this is an oversimplification because the area of transfer pricing in its widest sense has become one that tax authorities are increasingly emphasizing. Also, the extent to which multinational companies attempt to influence their taxable income through the vehicle of intercompany pricing is generally overestimated, despite some well publicized stories.

To be sure, a number of U.S. companies dealing abroad influence their subsidiaries' performance picture and respective tax liabilities by over- or undercharging for goods and services provided within the concern. According to a widely held view, however, it is primarily non – U.S. multinationals charging intercompany purchase prices that vary greatly from those charged to outsiders. It goes without saying that the price level for these intercompany purchases can — and usually does — have a significant impact on the results of the foreign subsidiary and on its performance evaluation.

Parent companies that change their intercompany pricing structure frequently find that their foreign managers become confused and demotivated. The foreign managers not only see their operating results influenced by factors beyond their control, but also find that intersubsidiary performance comparisons become impossible.

It is also worth noting that U.S. multinationals tend to charge their subsidiaries with corporate services such as management fees, corporate interest charges, data processing services, and research and development more often than do German multinationals, for example. This is particularly true for companies in a start-up phase. The result is often that substantial costs incurred in connection with the establishment of a foreign subsidiary are hidden in the corporate expense pool and thus not measured and evaluated in judging the overall appropriateness of the investment decision. An interesting observation in this context is that companies which "play around" with their transfer pricing tend to place less emphasis on performance measurement based strictly on numbers, rather than placing the emphasis on subjective criteria and non-financial measures. Surprising? Of course not! They know that the numbers are "relative," at best.

For those who do charge for these services, documentary support for the fairness of the price becomes more and more an issue to which foreign tax jurisdictions pay attention and have become more sophisticated and successful in challenging.

Multinationals that traditionally follow a philosophy of treating their foreign subsidiaries as independent third parties, charging for goods and services on arm's-length bases, generally have good experiences both in measuring and comparing subsidiary performance and in avoiding trouble with the tax authorities.

2.3 Foreign Country Risks

In the first two decades after the Second World War when many U.S. corporations began to go abroad, they did not place great emphasis on evaluating political and social risks inherent in the countries in which they invested. Nor did their European and Japanese counterparts when they followed suit. Perhaps there was no need to be concerned then. Unfortunately, the political, financial, and social stability of many countries on this globe has worsened significantly in the 1970s and into the '80s.

Examples include the Iranian debacle, the Falklands crisis and its impact on Argentina, more generally the Latin American debt crisis, the financial crisis in Poland, and the shaky financial and political conditions in most of Africa, to name a few. Regrettably, this trend is likely to persist and worsen for some years to come. In our experience, many companies have been slow in dealing appropriately with these increased risks.

Recently, however, we see a noticeable new conservative attitude taken especially by American investors, not only toward existing but especially toward any additional foreign expansion moves. The standards required of any new international investment have become much stricter and more selective. Also, existing investments are being more critically assessed as to their growth, performance, and future profit potential. Existing investments are being re-examined in the context of their fit into newly developed corporate strategic plans. This trend toward a stronger, more strategic orientation is particularly evident in corporations and has already led to a number of reorganizations and divestitures of U.S. subsidiaries abroad. In summary, it is fair to say that the assessment of foreign country risks attracts much more attention than it did a mere two or three years ago.

Quantitative measures of various risk levels are still hard to acquire. Also, the various firms providing information on foreign country risk have been blamed for concentrating too much on long-term exposure in a given country and for relying too heavily on government statistics which in certain regions lack a considerable degree of reliability. More recently, we have seen foreign country risk evaluation move in the direction of providing day-to-day intelligence on events in a country and more emphasizing areas other than raw economic data. These other areas include labor relations, exchange controls, tax environment, evaluation of the country's social system, level of political development, and quality of its economic management.

Despite those improvements, country risk evaluation will remain as much an art as a science. However, the point here is that the management of multinational companies should continuously endeavor to evaluate the risks involved in those countries in which they have invested. Also, when they set the performance standards for subsidiaries in those countries, higher rates of return should be demanded to counterbalance the higher risk.

2.4 Interest Cost

The introduction mentioned that the continued high level of interest rates coupled with the higher level of difference in interest rates from country to country compared to the past has forced more multinational companies which heretofore did not concentrate so much on the issue to emphasize interest costs in evaluating their foreign subsidiaries. Most multinational companies have treated interest expense incurred at the local level or through intercompany loans as an interest expense at the level of the foreign subsidiary. One trend, however, that seems to be gaining popularity is that more and more multinationals feel compelled to charge their subsidiaries interest on an imputed basis for the use of corporate funds. There are, of course, many variations to this theme such as a net asset charge based on a worldwide weighted average interest cost, or, which appears to make more sense, based on local interest cost, or on net current assets only. The latter version attempts to motivate the foreign subsidiary's management to make prudent use of its working capital by punishing or rewarding it with an imputed interest charge, while arguing that non-current assets and liabilities are generally beyond the control of local management and therefore the related interest costs should not be a determinate factor in measuring its performance.

Whatever the method, it is important to note that imputed interest charged to the subsidiary does gain in popularity; and, based on this writer's experience, it has proven to be a good management tool in times when interest expense could easily be the second or third largest item on the profit and loss statement, provided that the method is structured in such a way that local management is able actually to manage the amount of imputed interest charged to its subsidiary.

2.5 Foreign Inflation

It has been previously mentioned that with the worldwide decline in the rate of inflation, the interest in inflation accounting has also declined markedly from an already low level two or three years ago. This author continues to believe — even knowing that it is a minority view — that investors and companies making economic decisions on the basis of information that has not been adjusted for the effects of inflation do themselves a disservice.

Perhaps one of the reasons for thinking so highly of inflation accounting is the fact that the author saw it work so well in his first assignment as an internal auditor with Philips, the large Dutch multinational, and because he comes from a country that has been ravaged by very serious inflation in the past. He has seen only a few multinational companies utilize inflation accounting for MIS and for performance measurement purposes during his career after leaving Philips. None of these companies is U.S. based.

When reading annual reports with Statement No. 33 disclosure, one can hardly resist the idea that some large U.S. companies regard this as a nuisance imposed by the Financial Accounting Standards Board (FASB), designed primarily to increase accounting staffs and raise useless shareholders' questions. Such readers appear not to attach much significance to inflation-adjusted data.

Looking abroad, one can detect a much wider use of inflation-adjusted financial data in measuring performance and making investment decisions. This is not just a reference to the United Kingdom and Holland, but also to such countries as Germany, where a number of companies find it beneficial to adjust their financial statements for inflation and to discuss with their owners and shareholders the related impact on dividend policy and capital requirements.

Certainly no clear trend exists yet as to which method of inflation accounting is preferred in foreign countries. Most financial managers this writer has talked with over the years seem to believe, however, that current cost accounting is perceived to be a more exact measure of inflation than constant dollars. This preference has now also been shared by the FASB, as previously mentioned.

In the final analysis, the method being used may not be all that crucial. However, if there is one area where the reporting practices of multinational companies could be improved, it is inflation accounting. Although everyone says the opposite, many top managers of multinational companies do not realize that they are decapitalizing their companies by not considering the impact of inflation on the asset base and the profitability of their company.

In line with previous observations on autonomy, which is also reflected by the non – U.S. multinationals' "local currency" viewpoint, it seems only logical that those who adjust for inflation do so on a local basis, and, after adjusting, translate into home office currency, again, at the current rate. This procedure generally also enables management to evaluate performance of the foreign unit separately from inflation and separately from currency changes.

2.6 Performance Measures

Before summarizing these remarks, a few comments on performance measures are necessary. The most common approach clearly is to measure actual performance against a predetermined budget. This is almost universally true for the more developed multinational company that has been dealing abroad for years. In a surprisingly large number of cases, however, particularly in medium-sized European companies that have begun to invest abroad — especially in the United States within the last five to ten years — we observe a lack of budget data. Instead, these companies attempt to rely on past results to make comparisons with current ones. Also, in cases where budgets are set, they are often restricted to income statement items without consideration for working capital requirements, especially cash, or for long-term capital requirements to finance fixed asset acquisitions. As a result, many of the smaller non – U.S. companies are finding themselves caught off guard when having to satisfy short-term cash needs of the subsidiary. We have found that for these smaller companies in start-up phases which more often than not are coupled with loss phases, cash flow and working capital budgets frequently are more important than, or at least equally important as, bottom-line budgets. Certainly they should go hand in hand.

Generally, U.S. companies enjoy a lead in budgeting and controlling systems over many of their non – U.S. counterparts. Similarly, one observes that intersubsidiary comparisons are more common in the United States than they are abroad.

Key actual and budget numbers typically compared include profit (before or after tax), return on investment (most often measured as total assets), actual sales, and return of sales. This writer continues to be amazed by how few companies use *return on equity* as a performance criterion.

Given the strategic nature of many foreign subsidiaries, it is only natural that they place great emphasis on evaluating their subsidiaries' performance by applying also non-financial criteria such as market share, various productivity ratios, quality control, personnel, and so forth.

We have also found that those foreign units required to supplement their "raw numbers" with key ratios depicting trends and budget variances and with narrative comments generally have a better grasp of their own financial condition than those that complete for corporate headquarters piles of forms which may be meaningless to them and do not help them run their business.

3. Proposals

3.1 Foreign Currencies

- Recasting the budget at the actual rate is proposed, and then comparing to actual results or to use projected exchange rates for budgeting purposes and actual end-of-period rates for comparison.
- Exchange gains and losses should be included in the operating results but excluded from foreign management and foreign subsidiary performance evaluation unless subsidiaries have a substantial amount of control over these gains and losses.
- Translation gains or losses should be excluded from operations and performance evaluation, similar to a Statement No. 52 treatment.
- Local management should be evaluated based on local currency results as opposed to home country currency.

- It is suggested that translation of foreign units' financial data take place at the current rate method.

3.2 Transfer Pricing

- To the greatest extent possible, foreign subsidiaries should be treated as independent third parties, and intercompany services and goods should be charged at arm's-length prices, and the bases for these prices should be reasonably documented.

3.3 Country Risk Analyses

- Should be used to develop more quantifiable country risk factors that would enable companies to incorporate these factors in their hurdle rates when making investment decisions and when evaluating the continued appropriateness of investments abroad. In using these analyses, macroeconomic data, as well as non-numeric intelligence combined with day-to-day information, should be evaluated.

3.4 Interest Cost

- Consideration should be given to charging subsidiaries for the use of corporate funds, for example, to impute interest based on local interest levels for net current assets, thus motivating local management to make optimum use of those resources it controls locally.

3.5 Inflation Accounting

- Foreign subsidiaries' results should be adjusted to local inflation and then translated into parent company currency at the current rate.
- Current cost measurements appear to be more readily accepted as an "accurate" measure of inflation than are constant dollars.
- Both headquarters and local management should be able to evaluate the results of operations separately from inflationary impacts and from currency changes.

3.6 Performance Criteria

- Always compare actual results with budget, both in relation to balance sheet and income statement items, supplemented by comparison to the previous periods' actual data.
- Expand the use of financial ratios and non-financial criteria in evaluating subsidiaries' performance.
- Place more emphasis on cash flow reporting and projected short-term cash needs.

Performance Evaluation of International Subsidiaries in the Case of Acquisition/Disposal and Annual Audits from the Point of View of a German Wirtschaftsprüfer

Josef Lanfermann

1. Introduction

In all major industrialized countries, one can identify the often significant impact of foreign investments on economic prospects within both the host and the originating country. In this context, independent accountants are increasingly concerned with the appraisal of financial information. This paper seeks to highlight the role the independent accountant can play with regard to cross-border acquisitions, disposals, and the annual audit from the viewpoint of a German professional.

2. Acquisition and Disposal of International Subsidiaries

2.1 General

Foreign investments may be influenced by various considerations or motives. Investment decisions may, for example, be taken with regard to the growth of the business and the necessity for worldwide operations, market opportunities for the products made or services rendered, safeguarding against protectionism, transfer of capital to countries with political stability, cost savings, supply of raw materials, availability of high technology and institutions for research and development, tax considerations, government grants for investment in assisted areas, and so forth, or a combination of these factors.

In all cases, the accountant should know the motive(s) of the potential buyer since that would assist him in meeting the requirements of his client and in determining the capacity in which he would act. Regardless of his motives, the acquirer will generally attempt to gather some basic information on the undertaking in question and may ask an independent accountant to provide assistance in this respect. In some instances, the client may consider it sufficient for the accountant to compile data regarding the performance of the entity in question, whereas in other instances, he would wish the accountant to prepare a valuation of the business. In the case of a disposal, the accountant would be involved only in the second stage (valuation of the business) since the basic information is already available to the vendor.

2.2 Gathering Information

2.2.1 Types of information. Basic information required for the evaluation of the performance of the entity may, inter alia, include the following:

1. Activity, main products, and market position
   - Development and analysis of turnover of the last five years (product groups, customers, domestic, abroad...)
   - Future-oriented analysis of the production program (weaknesses, strengths)
   - Job production or production for stock (in case of job production: current status of unfilled orders and development in recent years)
   - Competition
     Growth of the market (past/future)
     Own share in the market (domestic/abroad)
     Main competitors (share in the market)
     Stabilitiy of the market (entry of new/relegation of former competitors)
     Distinct characteristics compared with the competitors
     Utilization of production capacity of competitors
     Market barriers (financial, technological, legal)
     Alternatives (flexibility)
     Type of competition (secret price fixing, cartels...)
     Competition caused by substitutionary effects

- Sales
  - Dependence on business or seasonal trends
  - Extent of market research
  - Pricing policy (quoting keen or high prices, prices quoted by competitors...)
  - Description of sales force
  - Important customers or groups of clients
  - Uniform terms of delivery and payment
  - Dependence on bulk purchasers
  - Existence of permanent supply contracts
  - Warranties
  - Advertising compared to competitors
- Purchases
  - Description of purchase department
  - Main suppliers
  - Dependence on proprietary products
  - Existence of permanent delivery contracts

2. Costs and proceeds

- Measures taken within the last three years to increase efficiency and changes brought about
- Impact of extraordinary matters on the structure of cost during recent years becoming void in the future
  - Start-up expenses relating to problems meanwhile solved
  - R&D expenses
  - Financial assistance granted for a limited period (government grants, subsidies, exemption from duties...)
  - Activities involving losses that have been eliminated or could be eliminated respectively
- Inflationary tendencies expected
  - Wages and salaries
  - Cost of materials
  - Sundry
- How estimated increases in cost can be compensated for

3. Know-how, R&D, product innovation

- Impact of certain aspects of advanced technology on future earnings
  - Lead over competitors
  - Legal protection

- Aging and probable remaining lives of current products
  - Products whose competitiveness has come to an end
  - Marketable products
  - Pioneer products (exceptional yields)
  - Products being implemented (start-up expenses)
- Development of products for future demands
- Developments realized by competitors that may impinge on the enterprise's own market position
- R&D expenses over recent years
  - Exceptionally high
  - Failure do do so
- License contracts (processing and products)
  - Licenser/licensee
  - Possibility of intensifying license agreements

4. Personnel
   - Directors and senior management
     - Corporate organization
     - Age and average length of service with the enterprise
     - Average emoluments of directors and senior management
     - Reasons for recent management turnover
     - Extent to which the viability of the enterprise depends on their ability
   - Staff
     - Workers and employees (development during recent years)
     - Average length of service with the enterprise (fluctuation)
     - Age
     - Allocation with regard to divisions
     - Redundancies and bottlenecks
     - Labor market situation and market position of the enterprise
     - Unions, closed shop, influence of the unions
     - Strikes
     - Assessment criteria for staff review
     - Development of wages, salaries, and social security levies during recent years
     - Action scheduled to cope with the rise of employee benefits
     - Redundancy plans and severance payments

5. Assets
- Real estate
  Form of utilization
  Dimension and buildings thereon
  Description of place, surroundings, etc.
  Average market values per square meter (on the assumption that this land would be available to a willing buyer)
  Action scheduled (government, transfer of site...)
  Advantages and disadvantages of place or location
- Buildings
  Office, factory, or other buildings
  Date of construction
  Design of building with a view of production process
  Technical suitability for present requirements
  Possibilities of different forms of utilization
- Machinery and equipment
  Types (listed by groups)
  Effective useful lives and rate of depreciation for balance sheet purposes
  Average age by groups
  Technical developments
  Production capacity available and degree of employment
  Shifts (possible and actual)
  Times of stoppage and for repairs
  Expenses for repairs during recent years
  Possibilities of a different form of utilization
  Future capital expenditure for replacement and expansion
- Investments
  Percentage of equity
  Other shareholders
  Related party transactions
- Inventories
  Segregation of stock (finished goods, work in progress, raw materials)
  Physical conditions
  Obsolete stock
  Excess stock
  Inventory turnover
  Days' sales in inventory
  Valuation (net realizable value)

6. Contingencies
   - Tax position (tax audit)
   - Events after the balance sheet date
   - Guarantees and warranties
   - Forward contracts
   - Lawsuits, threatened or actual, or claims pending
   - Protection of the environment
   - Anti-trust law
   - Financial assistance

In practice, however, the matters listed will generally be described in even more detail by the accountant. Whereas the points listed will be applicable, in general terms, to domestic and foreign investments, the following matters will necessitate special consideration in the case of a foreign investment:

- Political stability of the country or region concerned;
- Current rate of inflation and its future development;
- Currency fluctuations, interest rate, and restrictions regarding transfer of capital;
- Tax considerations (existence of a double tax treaty or treaties, unit of taxation, unitary tax, availability of an imputation system to all types of investors, approach of the fiscal authorities concerning intercompany pricing, etc.);
- Range of activities permissible to foreign investors (discriminatory measures);
- Burden of statutory requirements (market economy, mixed economy, etc.);
- Travel distances, language problems, and mentality of local people; and
- Accounting principles (variances compared to home country).

2.2.2 Difficulties regarding the gathering of information. Generally, information can be generated externally or internally. As a rule, the vendor would not make available internal data to a potential acquirer. In addition to his professional duties, this fact mainly determines the involvement of the independent accountant.

Confidentiality. Internal data are often considered confidential by the enterprise in question. This particularly relates to information concerning projections and research and development. Projections are normally made within the constraints of an identified set of specific assumptions, for example, future productions or sales programs, restructuring to reduce production capacity or to improve efficiency, redundancy plans, financing considerations, and so on. As a rule, third parties and the work force should not become aware of the information concerned. Therefore, the vendor would normally furnish internal data only in those instances where a letter of intent has been duly signed by the potential acquirer.

The professional standards of the accountancy profession require, however, that the accountant expose the assumptions on which his report is based so that the recipients are in a position to assess the criteria used. The experienced professional will therefore attempt to find a compromise between his professional duties concerning information and documentation deemed necessary for this purpose and the legitimate interests of the enterprise under evaluation. Accountants are bound to secrecy by professional ethics and will normally determine the extent of information passed on to the users of the report in coordination with the officers of the enterprise in advance.

Reliability. Professional standards and accepted practice suggest that reports prepared by accountants must be based on audited information or other reliable data. A departure would be considered unprofessional even if it would be possible to make it clear to the reader that the report was not based on reliable documentation, for example, by using formulae along the lines of "as provided," and so forth. The accountant should always disclose the scope of his own appraisal to meet the expectations of the business community and society. The mere collection and presentation of data provided by third parties without subjecting it to procedures whether audit or otherwise would not be sufficient.

However, what could be considered as reliable documentation? Basic data on prior periods that have been derived from audited financial statements are viewed as reliable. This is particularly valid for adjusted past performance and the determination of the asset base. If the financial statements have not been audited, the accountant should follow procedures to satisfy himself as to the credibility of the main basic data. These procedures do not constitute an audit examination, however.

Documentation provided by the enterprise which by its very nature could not be subjected to audit procedures such as projections, market analyses, and such, should be critically reviewed by subjecting it to plausibility tests to determine the level of credibility.

Part of the information contained in a forecast could be reviewed by the application of existing procedures. This would include the following:

1. Forecasting techniques and methods of analysis, that is, the predictions are based on reasonable assumptions, the different assumptions are compatible with each other, and the computations made are accurately based on the assumptions;
2. Completeness of a forecast from a methodological point of view;
3. Matters already known affecting the future such as contracts signed, orders in hand, credit lines, capital expenditure, and so on;
4. Analysis of performance by source of profit (product and product groups, etc.), including comparisons with the budgeted amounts; and
5. The reasons suggested for deviations between budgeted and actual results.

However, it is not possible to review subjective information contained in a forecast, that is, quantities or values dependent on events yet to occur, such as sales, production, and supply forecast and the budgeted costs and revenues relating thereto; and long-range financing and liquidity plans. It is possible for the accountant only to perform plausibility tests and to check that the most important components of the overall plan are mutually consistent.

Letter of representation. Professional recommendations suggest that the accountant should obtain a letter of representation from the officers of the entity under evaluation with regard to the data supplied. It should contain a statement to the effect that the figures on which the evaluation is based reflect to their best knowledge and belief all economic, technical, and contractual matters which might affect the enterprise. The letter of representation does not, however, impinge on the accountant's duty to undertake his own appraisal but should make officers aware of the significance of the information provided.

2.2.3. Reporting. Professional standards require the accountant to submit a detailed written report in which he will present his findings, in particular with regard to the information underlying the evaluation, that is, availability and quality of the basic data (including the opinions of third parties); limitations of his responsibility for information obtained from others; assumptions and estimates; and simplifications. An illustrative example of the content of such a report is provided in Appendix A.

2.3 Valuation of an Undertaking

2.3.1 The conceptual approach. In Germany, independent accountants are viewed as the experts for conducting valuations. The profession has issued "Standards for the Valuation of Business Enterprises" (1983) which are widely accepted by the business community, legal bodies, and such. The European profession issued a similar statement in 1980 entitled "Procedure to Be Followed by Accountants in Valuing an Undertaking as a Going Concern."

According to these pronouncements, the capitalized earnings value method (the present value of future earnings) represents an adequate basis for business valuation. It is clear that this value of an undertaking is not determined by its net assets at present value but by the benefits which its owner can derive from it (his valuation and willingness to pay a certain price are determined by such subjective estimation of future benefits).

Other methods formerly used in practice such as the average value procedure, the temporary excess profit capitalization method, and others are no longer viewed as conceptually correct approaches. Therefore, the paper is limited to a discussion of the capitalized earnings value method.

2.3.2 The problem of subjectively different business valuations. Depending on the standpoint of the valuer, different business valuations reflecting variations in subjectively estimated future earnings may arise.

(i) "An objectively determined business value reflects the continuation of an existing business with existing policies by reference to an alternative capital market investment."

This value uses the assumption of the typified third party, that is, the average investor, and is of only limited relevance for the external accountant acting as an expert adviser to an acquirer or vendor. It is presented by an accountant acting as a neutral assessor, and it may serve as a starting point for price negotiations. The work of the external accountant acting in the capacity of a neutral expert should result in valuation findings that are generally defensible. (It may be interesting to know that in Germany, accountants are frequently assigned by both parties concerned to determine this value.)

(ii) "A subjectively determined value reflects the continuation of a business as a going concern under the different policies and investment alternatives that are peculiar to the case in point."

This decision value represents the maximum investment that an acquirer can make or the minimum that a vendor should demand. As an expert adviser, the accountant combines his findings with the perceptions and supplementary arguments of his client and thereby assists in determining the latter's subjective decision value. This will increase the client's scope for negotiation in price fixing.

Therefore, the value derived from (i) will simply serve as a means for discussion to determine the client's strategy and his decision value (ii). It should not be overlooked that both values are frequently submitted to the appropriate bodies of the company for approval of the scheduled acquisition/disposal. Hence, alternative going concern values are not a consequence of different procedures but of the application of different parameters. In conjunction with the motives of a potential acquirer as discussed in the General section on p. 189, however, it may be possible that these will influence his willingness to pay a price exceeding the aforementioned values.

The principles governing the mere compilation of data that is the kind of information to be used, confidentiality and reliability apply equally to the collection of data for valuation purposes.

2.3.3 Computation of capitalized earnings value. The following sequence of operations may be helpful in the computation of a capitalized earnings value.

Adjustment of past performance. In assessing the earning power (future earnings) of the undertaking to be valued, use should also be made of the adjusted past results that can be derived from financial statements for immediately preceding years. Normally, three to five previous years are used.

Past results are modified to allow for such changes influencing earnings that have become apparent meanwhile (adjusted by reference to actual conditions). This may, inter alia, include the following:

- Adjustment of accounting principles for valuation purposes (eliminating the effect of the concept of prudence, matching stocks and results, etc.);
- Adjustment of expenditure and income effects of long-term investment processes (depreciation based on replacement cost or charging reinvestment rates, R&D costs, restructuring expenditure, start-up expenses, etc.);

- Adjustment of accounting policies applied (setting-up and reversing provisions and reserves, etc.);
- Adjustment regarding items not included in the profit and loss accounts or to be excluded from them (proprietor's salary in the case of private companies, etc.);
- Adjustments necessitated by the techniques applied in business valuation (expenditure and revenue of non-operating assets); and
- Changes representing the results of these adjustments (in respect to taxation, interest payments, etc.).

The adaptation of past performance to the future will include the implications of adjustments to past performance for future performance; and considering changes to the profitability structure (production methods, increases in efficiency, cost, selling prices, elimination of unique, extraordinary influences).

These modifications result in adjusted past earnings which are normally computed prior to items such as depreciation, interest, extraordinary costs and service charges, taxes based on earnings, and so on.

Analysis of earning power (forecast). The present status serves as the starting point for all forecasts. The past and present results adjusted as described provide an orientation in relation to earning power at the valuation date. Starting from the adjusted past results, the periodic expenditure and revenue accounts for different future phases are estimated. It is not the object of this paper to discuss technical details with regard to the establishment of a forecast. Hence, the indications to be discussed here are more of a general nature.

Sales. The sales forecast reflects market analyses and other forecasting data and shows expected turnover by divisions. Exported goods sold in foreign currency will require special attention. The development of currency rates may have a decisive impact as to whether the enterprise will make a profit at all. The same is valid for imported supplies with regard to costs.

Costs. Valuation criteria are derived from the cost accounting system taking account of conceivable changes to the existing cost structure. Future cost changes reflecting inflation are normally ignored. Structural price changes affecting either cost or revenue should, however, be taken into account as far as possible. Costs that would need special consideration, such as depreciation, interest charges, retirement benefits, and taxes on earnings are discussed here.

Depreciation/capital expenditure. To determine the net distributable earnings, future depreciation is based on future capital expenditure. Projected capital expenditure should be classified according to its nature, for example, replacement investments, investments to increase efficiency, expansion investments, and so on, to facilitate an assessment of the related financing requirements and their impact on future sales and costs. In including expansion investment already in the course of being implemented, however, the principle of valuation by reference to existing earning power should be applied and an increased rate of future investments considered. Replacement cost depreciation in respect to previous capital expenditure and for future replacements should be determined by reference to the productive capacity which will maintain future earning power intact. For the computation of taxes on earnings, tax depreciation allowances should also be calculated.

Special considerations are required in those instances where enterprises have delayed necessary replacement investments due to their earnings position and have obsolete machinery at the valuation date. In these cases, the effects of the investments needed on future earnings must be considered.

Interest charges. The amount of funds tied up in net operating assets is subject to fluctuations, and the level of a firm's external financing varies continuously. It may frequently be the case that investment outlays and depreciation charges deviate from each other. For this reason, interest charges correctly computed by reference to a financing requirements table should be included in an expenditure and revenue account. In particular, the financing requirements table modifies interest charges in respect to borrowed capital in that future sales are always matched with the level of expenditure necessary to maintain production capacity and capital intact.

Long-term projections require detailed analyses of probable sources and applications of funds. Therefore, the existing equity capital is, as a rule, taken as an unvariable point of reference for valuation purposes which implies the assumption that all net earnings are distributable.

Accordingly, all financing requirements or surpluses will directly affect the raising or repayment of borrowed capital. It may also be necessary, however, to assume a different level of equity capital for the future compared to that existing on the valuation date. To this extent, the equity "shortfalls" or "surpluses" reduce or increase the value of an undertaking as a going concern. It should be noted that a decline in the equity ratio may increase both the burden of interest charges and financial risk to a disproportionate extent. There are considerable variations in the average equity ratio with regard to industry, country, and the like.

Retirement benefits/pension liabilities. Pension liabilities may also have a significant impact on financing due to the amounts involved. Problems will arise where pensions have been granted but not accounted for or only partially accounted for. The burden must be allocated to future periods. It may be described as a "shortfall" of equity and will in practice be deducted from the value of the undertaking as a going concern.

In that the burden put on future periods with regard to retirement benefits will vary, an additional problem is posed. Sophisticated actuarial computations are necessary to determine the annual allocations to pension reserves and the actual payments to be effected.

Tax implications. It would go beyond the scope of this paper to treat tax considerations in detail since taxation may pose a magnitude of problems in the case of cross-border acquisition/disposal. Instruments such as unitary tax or imputation requirements for foreigners may highlight some problems. Statements of general relevance are not possible. To the extent that taxes on earnings should be considered, however, they could normally be determined as a given percentage of the result of the valuation computed so far.

Performance forecast. Future performance is estimated as a range by reference to the foregoing considerations and assuming a full distribution of attainable earnings and the maintenance of full operating capacity. Known risks and recognizable uncertainties as to future developments, other than general entrepreneurial risk, and their quantitative effect on future performance will be considered in forecasting future results. The concept of prudence as applied to commercial accounting is not applicable, however, since it would favor one of the two parties interested in the valuation.

The often strong dependence of earning power on the talents of management and on family ties, and so on, must be considered. Those value elements must be eliminated if such personnel are not to remain with the firm after a change of ownership. In practice, however, this can be based only on guesswork.

Furthermore, it is important to know the combination or synergistic effects resulting from the unification of firms or proprietary interests therein since such a combination may cause a change in their earning power. This is the case when the merger of an acquired firm with an existing undertaking results in a higher combined capitalized earnings value than the sum of the two individual values. Examples of synergistic effects related to technical matters are improved utilization of capacity, investments waived, cost savings related to purchases and sales, increased revenues, improved financing opportunities, and so forth. The overall criterion is that the single entity would not be able to take advantage of the matter concerned. It should not be overlooked, however, that subsidiaries are normally charged with parent company overheads for accounting, tax, legal and electronic data processing services, R&D, etc., which may outweigh the costs incurred by independent entities.

Capitalization and alternative investments. Future earnings should be compared with surpluses derived from an alternative investment to determine the capitalized earnings value. Generally, no information is available regarding alternative investments. Therefore, investments offered by the money market represent the standard of comparison. The interest rate for fixed-interest bearing long-term securities will serve as a basis; factors that may have an impact on future earnings of the enterprise to be valued should be reconciled with those influencing the long-term average interest rate.

The approach is based on the assumption that the interest rate on the money market include a bonus for inflationary tendencies. This entails assessing the extent to which the enterprise will be able to pass increasing costs to customers — not only in absolute terms but on a percentage basis. To the extent to which this is deemed possible, the bonus for inflation is deducted from the interest rate for fixed-interest bearing long-term securities. It is obvious that some scope for estimation is involved.

Moreover, professional practice suggests consideration of the fact that future earnings of the enterprises to be valued are different from future interest rates on the money market in that the degree of risk involved differs. It is for this reason that a surcharge is levied on the money market interest rate to consider the general entrepreneurial risk and thus achieve comparability. Based on the principle of taking risks and opportunities equally into account, this premium recognizes different attitudes toward taking risks. Here, too, some scope for estimation is involved.

Needless to say, the accountancy profession views this scope for estimation in determining the capitalization rate as *the* problem of the capitalized earnings method. It is therefore advisable for the accountant to expose the components of the capitalization rate and their underlying assumptions in his valuation report.

2.3.4 Liquidation Value. The discounted net cash surplus realized through the liquidation of an undertaking with a weak capacity may exceed its value as a going concern. Regardless of whether the intention of an acquirer is to continue to operate or to liquidate a firm, the vendor will normally ensure that, after comparing its capitalized earnings value and liquidation value, the higher of the two (mutually exclusive values) be adopted as the basis of its total value.

Given the multiplicity of possible ways of disposing of assets, no general prescriptions and valuation principles for the determination of an undertaking's liquidation value can be promulgated. The net discounted cash surplus arising from the disposal of assets, discharge of liabilities, and resolution of all contractual claims (for example, redundancy payments plan and other costs associated with closing the business, including taxes) must be computed. Thus, considering the time available, the best possible realizable value of the business's assets should be planned and a hypothetical disposal strategy should be developed accordingly.

2.3.5 Other conceptually adequate procedures. In the case of international acquisitions, time constraints and a lack of information sometimes make it difficult to conduct a valuation according to the principles described here. In those instances, the independent accountant may conduct "valuations" commissioned by the party interested in the valuation and by reference to special criteria. Such values are frequently derived from earnings by reference to similar transactions or to the price/earnings ratio of other listed companies (x times earnings method). Such simplified price determinations should be treated with caution since they would only be valid as long as the earnings level would not fundamentally change.

The role of the independent accountant is similar to the assignment described earlier as gathering information. In particular, the accountant is required to ascertain the reliability of the data provided.

2.3.6 Reporting. The standards of reporting as described in the section on Reporting (p. 196) apply equally to the independent accountant's report on valuation. Additionally, the accountant must state a definitive value or value range and provide substantiation due to the very nature of his assignment. An illustrative example of the content of such a report is provided in Appendix B.

3. Annual Audit

3.1 General

Following the completion of an acquisition, parent company management assumes increased responsibilities and must cope with a variety of problems, in particular regarding maintaining or strengthening profitability. Success or failure of the investment made is often determined by the ability to analyze the activities of the acquired entity: weaknesses must be identified and corrected, whereas strengths should be exploited.

Management may use a number of tools for their analysis: interim and year-end financial statements, statements of source and application of funds, ratios, cash flow budgets, common-size and trended financial statements, management audits, and such. The accountancy profession is in a unique position to assist management in fulfilling the stewardship role and should do so. The independent accountant may conduct statutory audits and may accept special scope assignments within the limits of professional standards and his expertise.

By their very nature, the conditions governing the latter type are freely contractable in their entirety. Therefore, it would be impossible to derive common features for these engagements given the variety of objectives possible.

The following discussion is restricted to the impact an annual audit may have on the evaluation of company performance.

3.2 Audit Requirements Determined by Local Law and/or Parent Company Management

Depending on the country involved, most modern-day entities are required by law to have their financial statements audited. The objective of an audit of financial statements, prepared within a framework of recognized accounting policies, is to enable an auditor to express an opinion on such financial statements. The responsibility for the preparation of the financial statements is that of the management of the entity; the audit of the financial statements does not relieve management of its responsibilities.

In the absence of any such legal requirements, parent company management will nevertheless impose an audit on the respective group companies. This follows from the concept of accountability. It should also be remembered that parent company management may wish to complement local statutory requirements by group requirements. In this case the auditor's task will be twofold: (1) to perform an examination for local purposes and in accordance with local professional standards; and (2) to determine that the financial statements prepared for the purpose of consolidation ("consolidation package") are drawn in accordance with the group accounting requirements (including, where applicable, the legal requirements of the parent company's home country).

Moreover, parent company management may wish to broaden the scope of the audit prescribed by local requirements by including specific matters such as particular features of internal control and internal reporting, analysis of director's emoluments, and so on into the scope of the examination. Therefore, the approach used in international audit engagements should be responsive to the characteristics of a multinational entity.

3.3 Organization of International Audit Engagements

International audit engagements will require the group auditor to use the work of other auditors in foreign countries who may be members of his international firm or otherwise. In all cases, administration of international audit engagements requires careful planning and effective communication between the group auditor (also referred to herein as the instructing or originating office) and the foreign colleague (also referred to herein as the participating or receiving office). A number of problems peculiar to international audit engagements exist; some have already been outlined in the section on Types of Information, page 190, from the point of view of the acquirer. From the auditor's viewpoint, these issues include such matters as differences in corporate legislation between countries of operation of the parent company and individual components, differences in accounting requirements or practices, often as a result of legal or fiscal regulations; differences in auditing standards or practices so far as the local profession is concerned in various countries; differences in reporting format; difficulties arising on translation of component financial statements into the reporting currency of the parent company; and so on. It is therefore particularly important for the various responsibilities of the originating and receiving offices to be clearly defined by stating the scope of the audit to be performed and the nature, form, and date of reporting.

The ultimate responsibility for the audit of an international group rests with the instructing office which must ensure that (1) the overall audit scope of the examination is adequate to support its opinion on the consolidated financial statements; and (2) the accounting principles followed throughout the group are consistent with those of the parent company, or that where a component adopts differing accounting principles, these differences are identified and appropriate instructions given as to their treatment.

It follows that the receiving office must be furnished with complete instructions as to accounting principles to be followed and auditing procedures to be applied. It is often necessary to supply detailed charts of accounts, accounting manuals, or similar information. Instructions as to the scope of the audit and the procedures to be followed must be stated in as much detail as necessary to prevent misunderstanding and to identify clearly those procedures considered mandatory by the originating office but which are not necessarily required by local legal or professional requirements. If there are any queries, the participating office should not hesitate to request interpretations or additional information to meet the client's expectations regarding performance. The instructing office must establish lines of communication with all participating offices to achieve effective administration of the engagement. If there are accounting, auditing, or other problems which could affect the particular assignment, prompt communication between the originating and receiving offices is essential. Matters such as (1) significant unexpected accounting or auditing problems which may require the scope of the engagement to be substantially revised; (2) accounting or reporting problems which require reference to parent company management; (3) proposed adjustments which may significantly affect financial information previously submitted by the component; (4) material weaknesses in internal control; and (5) reporting deadlines which may not be met or potential qualifications arising from the aforementioned issues would be communicated to the instructing office on a timely basis. The course of action scheduled would depend on the particular circumstances of the individual issue.

The originating office should arrange for a copy of each management letter issued by the participating office to be forwarded at the conclusion of each assignment. These documents are of particular importance in the context of international audit work and provide the instructing office with meaningful information as to developments in the business of the component, as well as an insight into the accounting, auditing, and tax problems encountered during the audit.

As outlined earlier, components will often be required to prepare a number of different financial statements or reporting packages, for different purposes, each of which may be reported on by independent accountants. As a general rule, unless there is a specific reference to the contrary in the auditor's report, it is implicit in issuing of financial statements that (1) they be prepared in accordance with accounting principles, standards, or practices of the country of the participating office; (2) they comply with the specific reporting requirements of that country; (3) the scope of the audit examination has been determined by reference to local requirements; and (4) the audit examination has been conducted in accordance with local auditing standards.

Where the auditor reports on financial statements prepared in accordance with another country's accounting principles, standards, or practices and/or in accordance with the accounting requirements of the parent company — which are frequently determined in close coordination with its auditor — and audited in accordance with auditing standards applicable in the parent company's country, it is essential for that fact to be perfectly clear to the reader of the report, so that the reader is aware of the framework within which the auditor reached his professional opinion.

The auditor may also be asked to report on financial statements prepared within the aforementioned context and translated into the currency used by the parent company. These statements may form part of standard company forms used to facilitate reporting and consolidation of components with the parent company ("consolidation packages"). Because of the restricted purpose for which they are designed, however, such forms may not give a true and fair view of the component's financial position, and it is quite likely that they do not comply with local statutory requirements. The reporting accountant would give appropriate recognition to the restrictions under which his report is to be issued. It is normally restricted to the confirmation that the package has been prepared in conformity with parent company accounting instructions since separate opinion examinations are rarely performed given that packages, as a rule, do not meet statutory disclosure requirements. Reports on audit packages are normally in the form of clearance type communications transmitted by whatever suitable means from receiving offices to the originating office.

The message that should have emerged from the detailed discussion described here is that the group auditor will normally have at his disposal a variety of financial information concerning components. In many countries, company law and the standards set by the professional bodies require the adjustment of financial statements to be included in the consolidated accounts in accordance with accounting principles and policies generally accepted in the country of the parent company. These adjustments may have been made at the local level and covered by the audit report issued by the participating office. They may also be performed at parent company level and checked by the group auditor, however. The group auditor would then be responsible for determining whether the adjusted financial statements meet these criteria.

Most international organizations of accountants have partners and/or managers who may be designated "expatriates." This designation is used where the persons concerned work or will be working in the country of another member or representative firm for a specified time. In the event that there is an expatriate partner from the originating country at the receiving firm, he will normally be involved in the referred work. The nature and degree of this involvement may vary according to the circumstances. It may vary from the situation where the expatriate partner is in charge of the engagement and the involvement of the national partner is restricted to matters where local expertise is needed, to the situation where the national partner is the engagement partner and the expatriate partner is acting in a liaison and review function only. Factors that ordinarily would determine the nature and degree of involvement of the expatriate partner and of the national partner include the wishes of the parent company and/or the originating office, the views of the subsidiary, the knowledge of the expatriate of the local legal and professional requirements, and the reporting and disclosure requirements. (For this purpose, Klynveld Main Goerdeler, the international organization of accountants coordinating the international work of this author's firm, has formed units to conduct international work which are supported by expatriates.)

3.4 A Practical Approach to the Audit of Consolidated Financial Statements of a German Parent Company

Let us consider a German stock corporation preparing group accounts in accordance with International Accounting Standard No. 3, "Consolidated Financial Statements." Foreign group companies submitting financial statements for inclusion in the consolidated accounts are required to prepare those statements in accordance with the German Stock Corporation Law, that is, in many cases they will have to prepare so-called "HB II" accounts (commercial accounts prepared for consolidation purposes). The HB II is based on the financial statements prepared for statutory purposes which must be audited and reported on by (local) independent accountants (so-called "HB I"). Variances are recognized through adjustments; explanations with regard to the amounts involved form an essential part of the set of financial statements to be submitted by foreign group companies.

It follows from the overall responsibility of the group auditor that he is required to check all accounts to be included in the consolidated financial statements. The procedures applied for the review of HB II accounts may, inter alia, include the following.

Annual review procedures. During the course of the audit of the consolidated accounts at parent company premises, the auditor reviews the completeness of the adjustments made and the plausibility of the explanations given for accounts to be included in the consolidated financial statements.

It may be helpful to send a questionnaire to local auditors including such matters as completeness, accounting policies applied, fair presentation of financial position, and so on. Such a list may also include issues enabling the group auditor to arrive at an opinion regarding the quality of the audit work performed by local auditors. The interpretation of the questionnaires will focus on completeness, presentation, and the performance of the audit work. Special consideration will be given to qualified audit opinions and the impact these may have on the HB II. A disadvantage of the approach is that the questionnaire will be worded in general terms to achieve worldwide applicability.

Cyclical reviews. Based on the size and complexity of the entity concerned, the "quality" of the accounting department and his appraisal of the "quality" of the local auditor, the group auditor will subject group companies to review in rotation. The review will be designed to verify the adjustments recognized with regard to the preparation of the HB II.

In view of the gathering of information and as a matter of professional courtesy, it is essential for the review team to have full and frank communication with local auditors to obtain knowledge regarding the object and scope of the local audit. The form of consultation will depend on the cirumstances and might, for instance, follow the procedures set in International Auditing Guideline No. 5, "Using the Work of an Other Auditor." The work described there should enable the group auditor to satisfy himself that he can accept the figures as in the HB I set of financial statements for his review.

Based on the information gathered, the group auditor will determine the scope of his review of the HB II set of financial statements and the approach responsive to the particular circumstances. The written report by the group auditor will describe the scope of his work and his findings, including a summary of the communications he had with the local auditor.

3.5 The Audit of International Subsidiaries in Germany

The German profession has issued standards on auditing and reporting which are also applicable to the audit examination of international subsidiaries in Germany. The auditor is generally required to issue a long-form report on the results of his work. An illustrative example of the content of such a report is provided in Appendix C.

Reporting on the development of the economic conditions and on the changes in the legal situation including the current year, if applicable, is standard practice. The scope of this reporting is guided by the value of such information to the recipients of the report. Moreover, the changes in the financial position and results of operations are analyzed in detail in the report. This is done by comparison of summarized figures of the financial year with those of the preceding year and by making appropriate comments. In this context, discussion of liquidity, the presentation of statements of source and application of funds, cash-flow analyses, statements of changes in financial position, as well as comments on the maintenance of operating capacity, and so on, will also serve this purpose. In those instances where the subsidiary is required to publish its financial statements including a directors' report (providing a business review and an indication of likely future developments), the auditor must review the information given in the report for consistency with the accounts. He is furthermore required to ensure that the information is not misleading.

3.6 Completing Special Assignments

During the course of providing their services to the client, both the local and the group auditor sometimes become aware of illegal or questionable payments, questionable practices, violations of codes of conduct of the parent company, violations of exchange control regulations and entering into secret price fixing or market sharing agreements, and so on. Such situations will necessitate an in-depth study of the applicable professional recommendations and the potential legal implications and may often result in special scope assignments.

3.7 Going Concern Considerations

Doubts may arise as to whether a subsidiary company is a going concern. Where there is uncertainty as to the company's ability to continue as a going concern, the general standards of reporting require the auditor to issue a qualified opinion in his report on the financial statements. Where the local auditor may have to qualify his report, this would entail the group auditor's immediate attention as the lines of communication established with the instruction letter would require participating offices to notify the group auditor on any such matters promptly. The going concern basis may be appropriate only because the parent or a fellow subsidiary is able and willing to provide support. Professional standards will require the local auditor to obtain a letter from the supporting company confirming its intention to keep the subsidiary afloat.

It may happen that going concern problems come to light only at HB II level, that is, during the course of the group auditor's review. In these instances, effective coordination between parent company management, the group auditor, and the participating office is needed to ensure an appropriate course of action based on materiality considerations. Regarding an international subsidiary in Germany, the auditor is required to report in writing on certain facts ascertained in the performance of his work in addition to his reporting on the accounts, namely those which may either endanger the enterprise's existence or may substantially impair the enterprise's progress.

4. Conclusions

It is obvious that there is a need for accountants to assist their clients both at domestic and international levels in acquisition and disposal talks within the realm of their professional skills. In many countries, the profession is attempting to broaden its so-called merger and acquisition services. This ranges from strategic planning to assistance with the completion of contract. As a rule, German accountants do not identify acquisition or disposal candidates. They would be subject to disciplinary measures for accepting any commission resulting from the implementation of advice which they had given to a client.

An annual audit should provide both local and parent company management of an international group with reliable information regarding the performance of the subsidiaries. An international audit engagement hence requires effective coordination and communication between group auditor and local auditors. This is a major reason for the establishment and success of international firms of accountants.

Appendix A.

Information Gathering Report (Specific Example)

Content

Appendix B.

Valuation Report (General Structure)

A. Scope of work
B. Legal background and economic bases
C. Valuation bases and policies
D. Valuations
   I. Introductory remarks
   II. Value of operating assets
      1. Capitalized earnings value
         (a) Analysis of past performance
         (b) Forecasts
         (c) Determination of capitalization rate
         (d) Result of computation of capitalized earnings value
      2. Liquidation value (as appropriate)
   III. Value of non-operating assets (as appropriate)
   IV. Determination of business enterprise
E. Conclusion

   Appendices
   1. Adjusted performance data and forecasts
   2. Comparison of book and actual values as at the valuation date
   3. Synopsis of book and actual values of non-operating assets
   4. General conditions of assignment

Appendix C.

Auditors' Report (Long-Form Report)

Contents

The Present State of Performance Evaluation in Multinational Companies

Hanns-Martin W. Schoenfeld

1. Introductory Remarks on the Method Used

After a brief look at the history of performance evaluation in a multinational environment, the presentation of several company cases, and the observations of indepent accounting firms, an attempt shall be made to show the present state of the art in this field. The following remarks are based on these presentations and the findings of a research project undertaken by this author during 1983 and 1984. As previously noted in connection with the case selection, the project was based on the analysis of fourteen European and six U.S. companies. Each of the participants agreed to an interview, usually conducted in the presence of the chief financial officer and several staff specialists. Additional materials are scheduled for later publication.

This research approach was chosen to ensure accurate representation of actual systems. The participants in the various countries (the United States, West Germany, the Netherlands, and Switzerland) were chosen on the basis of their known expertise in the field of performance evaluation and their willingness to participate in the project. That almost all companies contacted agreed to participate should be mentioned. The approach chosen definitely has the advantage of disclosing a great number of details as to company procedures and the rationale which led to the selection of specific methods. The fact that different industries were selected also appears to be an advantage, since the results show — despite procedural differences — a surprisingly high degree of similarity in the basic concepts used — and also relatively few differences between countries. This suggests a convergence of needs or ideas determined by operations in a multinational environment. Notable differences existed due to the type of approach prevailing in certain accounting systems, which was not altogether unexpected.

To minimize biases which seem to exist in surveys due to a limited number of questions and the inability to use a term which fits the individual "in-house" terminology of companies, a relatively unstructured interview procedure was chosen. This permitted the participants to describe their system fully before the interviewer asked questions — which might be leading. Although no interviewing procedure can fully eliminate a degree of subjectivity, it is felt that this approach minimized possible distortions.

A selective interview approach normally does not lead to results which can readily be generalized; however, due to the prevailing similarities found, it is relatively safe to assume that the findings from these interviews, together with the cases presented here, can be accepted as a comprehensive — although not exhaustive — description of the state of the art. To increase the usability of the results, brief comments will be inserted to indicate differences wherever these were found.

2. Factors Complicating Performance Evaluation in a Multinational Environment

Conceptually, multinational companies can be classified into two groups:

1. Operating multinationals which enter a market to remain permanently, thus displaying features similar to domestic operations. This classification is applicable, regardless of whether the specific purpose for establishing a subsidiary was its securing a raw material basis, extending the market, and so forth. The IBM case discussed earlier in this publication is a typical example for such a company.
2. Multinational financial conglomerates, whose purpose largely consists of participating in short-term financial gains; such companies concentrate more on immediate results and can be expected to focus their evaluative efforts on a different set of criteria.

Although it is tempting to classify business efforts into categories with distinctly different goals, it must be stated that most companies may shift from one classification to another as far as individual subsidiaries are concerned. This is largely due to changing political, economic, and other environmental conditions. It is, therefore, not unusual to find in every system evaluation measures which represent both types of approaches.

Much has been written about the difficulties multinationals encounter when attempting to measure the performance of their subsidiaries accurately. This is due to the fact that all conditions, which in a domestic environment are relatively similar, are subject to frequent non-homogeneous changes. How many of these factors may be present in every situation is apparent — without any further explanation — from the following figures. Although not all of these influences are subject to change at any given time, it can be expected that many of them are dissimilar for most of the subsidiaries. Translating these influences into factors directly affecting a subsidiary in operational terms, the following reasons for non-comparability of measurement or data can be compiled. Some of these are unavoidable; others are imposed by headquarters as part of the long-term mission of a particular subsidiary or as part of the short-term operating policies. Either way, these influences on the operating results are constant for a particular operating period and will result in distortions which cannot be avoided. As a consequence, the performance measurement system

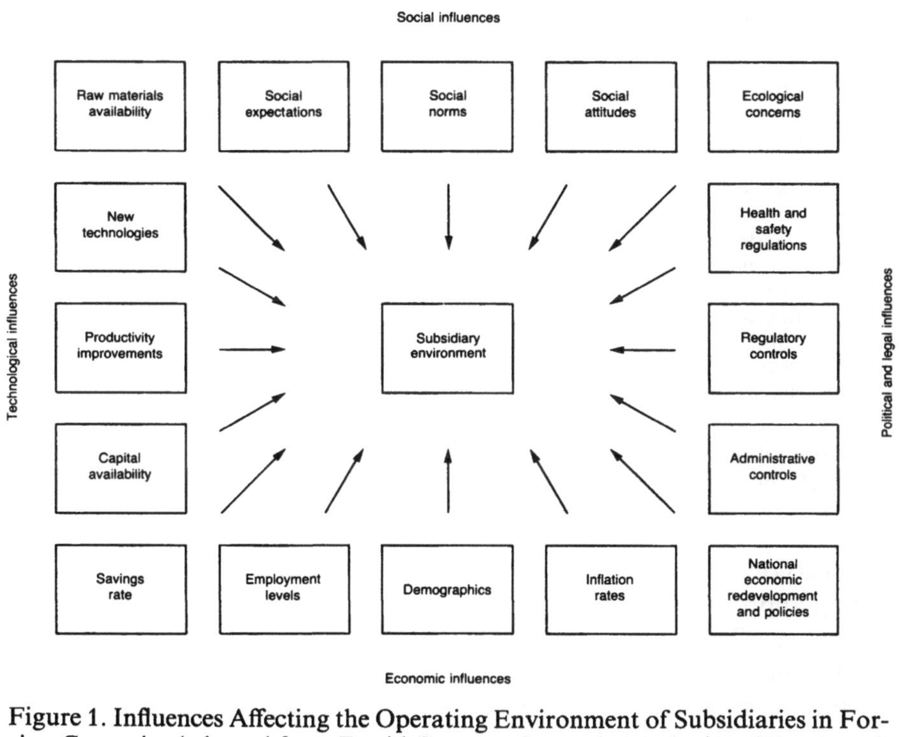

Figure 1. Influences Affecting the Operating Environment of Subsidiaries in Foreign Countries (adapted from David Cravens, Strategic Marketing, Homewood, Ill., 1982, p. 104)

1. Mission of subsidiary
   (raw material acquisition vs. low cost production vs. market presence; growth area vs. cash cow)
2. Stage of development
   (newly established vs. fully developed)
3. Organizational structure
4. Functional development
   (limited function vs. all function subsidiary; centralization of selected functions at headquarters)
5. Societal impact on organization
   (managerial hierarchy, working traditions, fringe benefits, etc.)
6. Distribution channels, service function requirements
7. Regulatory environment
8. Capital structure (equity vs. borrowed capital)
9. Financing methods
   (foreign sourcing, collateral support from headquarters, tightness of financial planning and clearinghouse function, currency convertibility)
10. Price structure of foreign market
11. Cost structure
    - Wages and fringe benefits
    - Training cost
    - Productivity level
    - Technology level
    - Non-income taxes
    - Product modifications
    - Operating conditions (climate, restrictions, local customs)
    - Capacity utilization levels
    - Ecomomies of scales
12. Conditions imposed by headquarters
    - Transfer prices
    - Headquarters allocations
    - Know-how fees, service charges
    - Purchase/sales requirements
    - Capital expenditure restrictions
    - Funds repatriation requirements
13. Growth rate
14. Inflation rate

Figure 2. Some Factors Responsible for Non-comparability of Operating Data in Foreign Subsidiaries (non-exhaustive listing)

must account for them properly. This can be accomplished only by developing appropriate, highly individualized measurement systems for each subsidiary. This — in operational terms — requires a much more detailed budgeting process as needed for domestic operations. Since development of foreign subsidiaries usually is a process extending over several years, the tie-in with the strategic planning process is inevitable.

There is also a consensus that all influencing factors eventually will be reflected in managerial or financial accounting data. It is also apparent that neither problems nor long-term approaches to problem solutions will be immediately reflected in such data. Typical examples of the existence of such lags are measures to improve quality (not necessarily recognized immediately by customers, however, as directly reflected in cost) or to upgrade managerial personnel. As a consequence, multinationals show a growing tendency to integrate non-accounting and qualitative indicators into their budgeting and evaluation process. This development has been confirmed by recent surveys (Czechowicz, Choi, Bavishi 1982: 23–28); they give as an example one company's selection of indicators as shown in Figure 3.

The utilization of this type of information will be demonstrated in greater detail; it should be noted, however, that such data do not have the same accuracy as accounting data. Nevertheless, their rapidly growing application suggests that they are regarded as indispensable by management. This point was made by many multinationals in stressing the fact that without such information, operating improvements within the organization can not be controlled.

3. The Parts of the Performance Evaluation Process in Multinationals

3.1 The Overall Process

The process which ultimately leads to performance evaluation follows traditional control procedures consisting of several steps:

1. Long-range and strategic planning;
2. Preparation of short-term budgets (operative planning);
3. Routine reporting at predetermined intervals requiring financial, managerial, and qualitative data originally included in the strategic plans/budgets; in most cases, reports are submitted monthly (for management accounting and qualitative data and information) and quarterly for financial data. U.S. companies showed a higher frequency of reporting for financial data due to the practice of publishing quarterly financial statements. Most reports, in addition to specified data, also require verbal statements of deviations from the basic assumptions which were used for the strategic planning and budgeting process.

A major MNC in the consumer products durable business uses the following checklist to evaluate its managers. It includes many nonfinancial measures.

	Evaluation		
	I Methods, systems, procedures, or techniques	II Specific targets and reporting systems	III Results achieved
General			
Revitalize cost reduction programs			
Identify short-term profit opportunities			
Simplify your business			
Maintain or improve gross margins			
Reduce break-even point			
Improve cash flow			
Improve inventory turns			
Control investment in receivables			
Plan future directions for the company			
Improve product planning and development systems			
Prune unprofitable product lines			
Replace unproductive people with better performers			
Continually train and upgrade key people			
Provide incentives for creativity			

Evaluation Codes (To be used in each column)

Current Status
A. Excellent – No changes required.
B. Good – Minor modifications required.
C. Fair – Some significant effort required to improve.
D. Poor – Major improvements and effort required.
E. No system, no direction, no targets, poor results.

Change since last review
J. Improved
K. No change
L. Worse

Figure 3. General Manager's Checklist for Improved Performance

	Evaluation		
	I Methods, systems, procedures, or techniques	II Specific targets and reporting systems	III Results achieved
Marketing Identify new product opportunities, short- and long-range Aggressive promotions Competitive analysis to identify weaknesses Improve relationships with key customers Selective price increases Sell obsolete or slow-moving inventories Plans for improved market share Improve sales forecasting Insure on-time deliveries Manufacturing Improve productivity Improve quality and reliability Increase capacity utilization Improve plant loading Take on outside work to better utilize equipment Improve methods and processes			

Evaluation codes (To be used in each column)

Current status
A. Excellent – No changes required.
B. Good – Minor modifications required.
C. Fair – Some significant effort required to improve.
D. Poor – Major improvements and effort required.
E. No system, no direction, no targets, poor results.

Change since last review
J. Improved
K. No change
L. Worse

Figure 3. (continued)

	Evaluation I Methods, systems, procedures, or techniques	II Specific targets and reporting systems	III Results achieved
Reduce warranty costs Eliminate unbalanced stocks Identifiy alternative suppliers Improve reject rates			
R & D			
Shorten product development cycle Identify less expensive alternative materials Apply latest technology to our business			
Finance			
Improve cash management Develop and monitor early warning systems Identify impact of inflation on plans and decisions Improve credit and collection operations			
Overal evaluation			

Evaluation Codes (To be used in each column)

Current Status

A. Excellent — No changes required.
B. Good — Minor modifications required.
C. Fair — Some significant effort required to improve.
D. Poor — Major improvements and effort required.
E. No system, no direction, no targets, poor results.

Change since last review

J. Improved
K. No change
L. Worse

Figure 3. (continued)

4. Evaluation of subsidiary results by headquarters staff and jointly with subsidiary managers (in special meetings).

To describe the procedures, each of these parts will be analyzed separately.

3.2 Long-Range and Strategic Planning

The long-range planning process in most multinational companies is continuous and consists of several distinct parts — at least conceptually. In reality, many of these steps are performed at the same time. Each step serves a distinctive diagnostic and analytical purpose. The steps of the process are these:

1. Formulation of strategic objectives;
2. Environmental analysis;
3. Market and product analysis;
4. Competitor analysis;
5. Analysis of subsidiary's strength and weaknesses; and
6. Formulation of key strategies, individual plans, and budgets.

3.2.1 Formulation of strategic objectives. The formulation of strategic objectives must be regarded as the key issue in the whole process. This is confirmed by all top managers. That this process depends on the prevailing value structure in a given organization is generally agreed. Since this process is directly related to subjective assessments of the future and the attitude toward risk taking, very little could be found regarding the workings of such processes. The only manifestations are regular strategic meetings with a wide variety of participants. There are notable differences between companies with regard to who provides inputs, ranging from the existence of a formal strategic planning group to the less formalized use of staff members. Since this process was not analyzed in this study, it can only be noted that all companies claim to have a long-term strategy development procedure. They also claim that the mission of individual subsidiaries is derived directly from these ideas. No attempt was made to ascertain and classify whether the plans used were aggressive or merely reactive. For shorter time periods, however, all companies utilized narrowly defined statements of operational goals (objectives) to be achieved within the next operating period(s). In most cases, particular emphasis was placed on specifying conditions which might have a major influence on goal attainment. In all cases, management personnel of the subsidiaries (business units) participated in the goal determination process; however, it is impossible to determine how much weight was attached to their inputs. Only general statements concerning the underlying philosophy of decentralization could be obtained.

The process of obtaining inputs showed differing degrees of formalization, ranging from the requirement of short verbal descriptions of the various areas (as discussed later) to detailed manuals, which specified all items to be analyzed and provided forms for reporting of such planning data and their sources. In several cases, it was obvious that companies were experimenting with these systems (going through the stages from informal, to highly standardized, and then back to selected standardized items, because an all-encompassing standardized set of procedures was regarded as too costly). In diversified multinationals, requirements imposed by headquarters and by various product divisions differed substantially.

It is also noteworthy that most companies reported they had gone through a cycle which initially extended the planning period over a long time horizon (up to ten years); this range was gradually reduced to the presently prevailing three-year period. Planning data beyond the three-year horizon — although sometimes included — were frequently rated as less important because of their low reliability.

3.2.2 Environmental analysis. Analyzing the business environment serves several purposes: (1) determination of the status quo; (2) diagnosis of existing trends and their implications for operations; (3) forecasting future trends; and (4) determining particular opportunities and threats.

All companies included the following environmental areas in their analysis, although the degree of details varied substantially, depending on the products manufactured or marketed. Since in some companies a distinction is made between macro- and microanalysis, some of the items mentioned here were assessed under different subheadings; diversified multinationals tend to make a clear distinction between macro- and microanalyses, whereas single (or limited-range) product companies did not use such a differentiation. All data are collected from available published materials and enhanced by integration of views held by executives and consultants. This applies particulary to forecasting and opportunity assessment.

Economic environment. Data collected usually contain information about the gross national product (GNP), growth rates, currency stability, inflation trends, income distribution, economic cycles, import/export incentives and restrictions, raw materials and energy availability, industry structure, development of private versus public sector, level of employment, changes in labor supply, union attitudes, strike propensity, expected wage trends, government support and investment incentives, taxation, subsidies, industrial policies, etc.

Political environment. The most frequently collected information consists of some historic data, description of government policy changes, prevailing attitudes in the population, interest groups, critical power groups, political stability or unrest and resulting business risk, attitude toward foreign companies, favored industrial sectors, requirements for domestic participation, priorities in fiscal policies, monetary policies and their continuity, restrictions on transfer payments, tax system and tax preferences, infrastructure and planned development, competition policies, preferences for national enterprises, political parties and their attitudes, relations to other countries, etc.

Societal environment. Data usually reported are demographics, cultural traits and features, ethics, attitude toward foreigners, language and ethnic problems, changes in social responsibility perceptions, social safety network, attitude toward employment in multinationals, and training and educational levels.

Regulatory environment. Data encompass the legal system, expected changes and their timing, regulatory agencies, their policies, new regulations and standards (safety, pollution, etc.), including compliance requirements, standard-setting process, patent and trademark protection, industrial policy, export support, currency convertibility, capital market intervention, central bank policies, consumer protection, insurance requirements, and so on. Some of these details were included under a different heading because it is not always clear under which classification a diagnosis of joint events can be accomplished most efficiently.

Technological environment. This analysis attempts to assess the complexity and maturity of the technological environment, its volatility and the availability of new technologies, their protection, proliferation, technological support from research institutions (domestic and foreign), etc. This is one of the most likely parts of the analysis to be moved from this classification into the area of product analysis.

Some companies attempt to summarize the evaluation of these data using

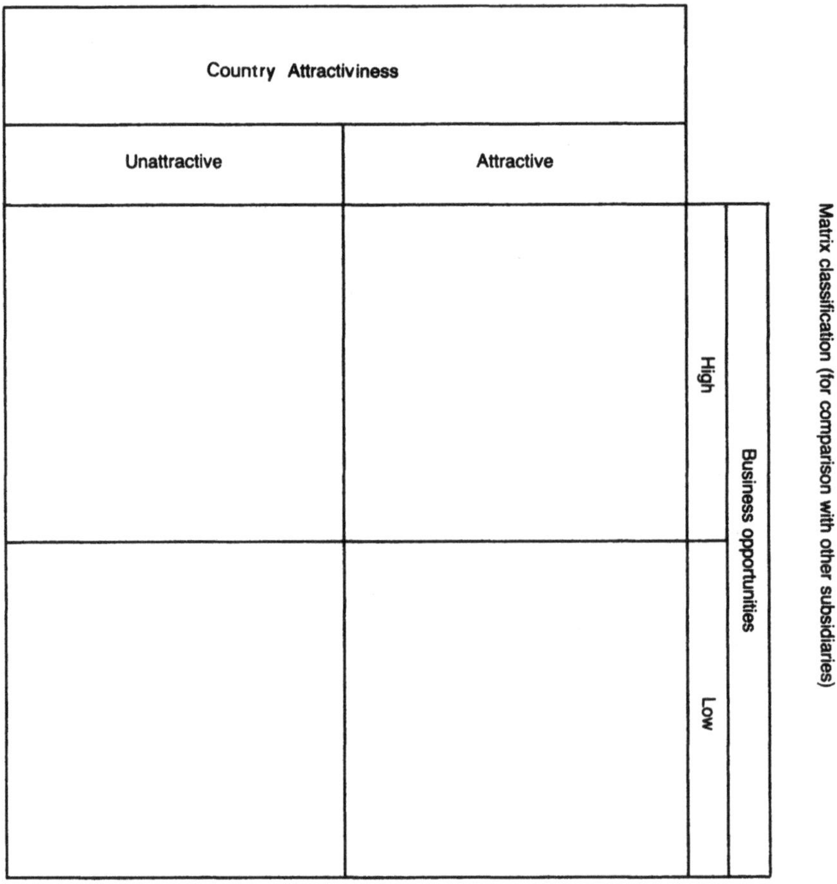

Business opportunity / Strategic elements	Permissible weight range	Assigned weight	High opportunity	Low opportunity
Demand Competitive position Returns	0–60 0–60 0–60	to be assigned by subsidiary		
Totals	100			
General assessment (verbal explanation):				

Figure 4. Country Analysis

Country attractiveness Strategic elements	Permissible weight range	Assigned weight	Attractive	Unattractive
Economic environment Political environment Competitive structure Sociological characteristics	20–60 20–60 20–60 10–20	to be assigned by subsidiary	assigned weights may be split between attractive and unattractive if the need arises	
Totals	100			
General assessment (verbal explanation):				

Figure 4. (continued)

a formalized approach which also integrates some of the findings from the steps to be described (competitive position) to allow a synopsis of their findings. Such a plan is shown in a generalized form in Figure 4.

3.2.3 Market and product analysis. The market analysis phase best demonstrates the approaches used in microanalysis. It requires a strict product orientation, because otherwise existing trends can not be distinguished. Sometimes it is consolidated in a last step to show the impact on an entire multiproduct subsidiary. Data are collected for all products and markets (or market segments), which eventually are combined into a portfolio-type review. For each market/product (or in some cases product lines), two areas are analyzed: (1) markets for products (or product lines) and (2) industry attractiveness.

Market analysis for products (product lines). Data to be collected — usually for several past years and projections for period t (first year) to t + n (n = last year) of planning horizon — consist of market size, growth rates, relative or absolute market shares, expected market development, breadth and depth of product (product line) offered, quality requirements, product positioning, service capabilities and demands, product innovation requirements, product substitution, cyclical trends, captive customers, competitive structure, expected future competitors, market entrance restrictions, price developments, capacity utilization, distribution channels, availability of materials input, energy, etc.

Industry attractiveness. Industry attractiveness data are based on information already collected as part of the environmental and market analysis. The objective of this assessment is to determine the desirability of continued operations in this market/country. This frequently requires the utilization of the competitor analysis. Not all companies interviewed used this type of analytic category; nevertheless, the basic idea (even if only as a verbal nonsystematic description) surfaced in every analytical scheme. To summarize the findings, most companies use charts similar to the example shown in Figure 5, which permit a quantification of findings to some degree.

Product line (or subsidiary) ________________ Country ________________

	In percentage					
	Company data	Weight range	Selected weight	Highly attract.	Moderate attract.	Lower attract.
1. Historic (last 5 years) market growth, % in constant $		5–15		>5	3–5	<3
2. Projected market growth, % in constant $		10–20		>5	3–5	<3
3. Industry return on average capital employed (after tax)		10–20		>8	5–8	<5
4. Industry cash-flow return on average investment (inflation adjusted)		10–20		>9	5–9	<6
Environmental factors						
5. Market factors		5–15				
6. Industry factors		5–15				
7. Competition		5–15				
8. Customer factors		5–10				
9. Technology		5–10				
10. Government factors		5–10				
11. Economic factors		5–10				
12. Changing social attitudes		0–10				
Total			100			
General verbal assessment:						

Figure 5. Industry Attractiveness Analysis

3.2.4 Competitor analysis. Competitor analysis considers all aspects of competition and attempts to determine the strengths and weaknesses of all major competitors. This calls for a diagnosis of all business functions and even an assessment of the strategy pursued by these firms. Therefore, data concerning the historical development, objectives, financial performance and structure, importance of particular products in competitors' portfolios, research and development (R & D) policies, manufacturing plants, labor problems, cost structure, marketing approach, sales force, market development activitities, expected product line changes, as well as management abilities, reward systems, and so on, are usually included.

	Company data	Permissible weight range	Selected weight	In percentage Strong	Medium	Weak
				(usually values are prescribed)		
Divisions absolute market share		10–20		>35	25–35	<25
Divisions relative market share		15–25		>1.2	.8–1.2	<.8
Product line or division return on average capital employed (after taxes)		10–20		>8	5–8	<5
Divisional cash flow return on average investment (inflation adjusted)		10–20		>9	6–9	<6
Cost position vs. industry leader		10–20		>110	90–110	80–90
Internal factors						
R & D engineering factors		5–10				
Manufacturing factors		5–10				
Marketing factors		5–10				
Management factors		5–10				
Total			100			
Verbal summary:						

Figure 6. Analysis of Subsidiary Strength and Weaknesses

3.2.5 Subsidiary's strength and weaknesses. To analyze the individual subsidiary, all factors previously mentioned for competitor analysis should be considered. Frequently, companies develop a plan for their own analysis which is later applied to competitors. This system actually represents a comprehensive management audit of all functions and resources available. In this context, specific emphasis is placed on the ability to respond to future challenges. In addition, the dependence on other subsidiaries of the multinational to fulfill a particular strategic mission (products from other divisions, headquarters financing) are included. The internal audit group of the multinational frequently assists in the analysis to develop comparative assessments or is instrumental in developing systematic corporation-wide analytic plans. This often takes the form of issue catalogues and development of specific analytical methods which permit (partial or subjective) quantification of findings. For summary purposes, charts or profiles are employed as shown in Figure 6.

3.2.6 Formulation of key strategies, individual plans, and budgets. To arrive at basic strategies and a definition of the long- and short-term mission of a subsidiary (or its various product segments), the information collected in the previous steps is usually shown in graphic summaries which utilize the typical matrix approach prevalent in strategic planning. Systems with either a four- or a nine-quadrant approach were the only ones found. Companies also seem to prefer the typical terminology (stars, problem children, cash cows, dogs) included in Figure 7. The nine-quadrant approach (with green, yellow, and red zones) is shown in Figure 8. In most cases, not only the present position but also expected future results of the adopted strategy were included in these charts (usually for year $t + 3$ or $t + 5$).

The relationship between the position of certain subsidiaries and the product life cycle theory is usually contained (explicit or implicit) in these charts. The basic idea of this relationship is summarized in Figure 9. Several companies stated that they had difficulties in determining the exact positioning of certain products along the life curve due to frequent product modifications.

These charts were frequently used in different versions, plotting various types of data against each other. To indicate some of the approaches found, several paired data combinations are listed in Figure 7. It is also important to mention that the detailed analytic steps are not normally undertaken in annual intervals. The prevailing pattern was the annual

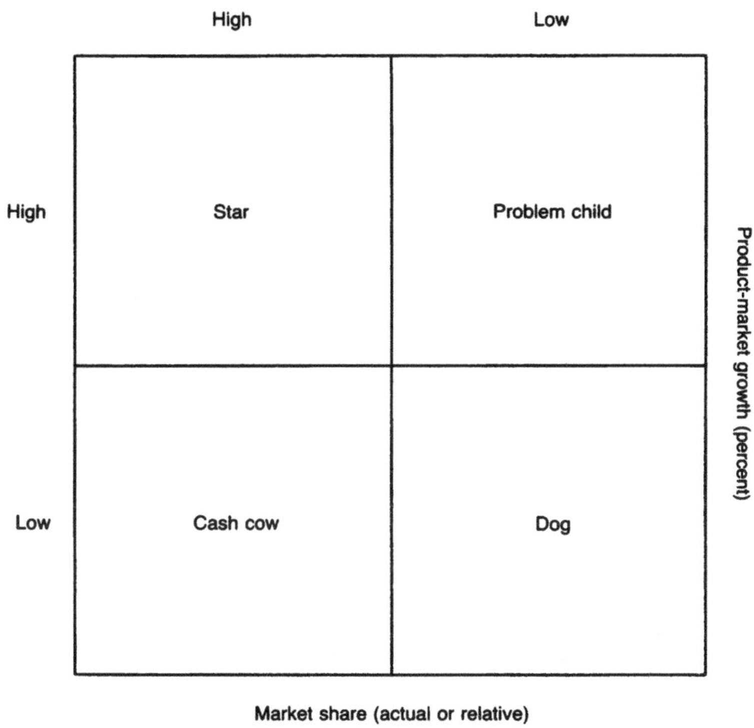

Other paired data combinations frequently used:

Vertical	Horizontal
Market growth rate	Relative market share (share relative to largest competitor)
Market attractiveness	Business position
Country attractiveness	Business position'
Industry attractiveness	Business position
Country attractiveness	Business opportunities
Cash use	Cash generation

Figure 7. Four-Cell Matrix Analysis

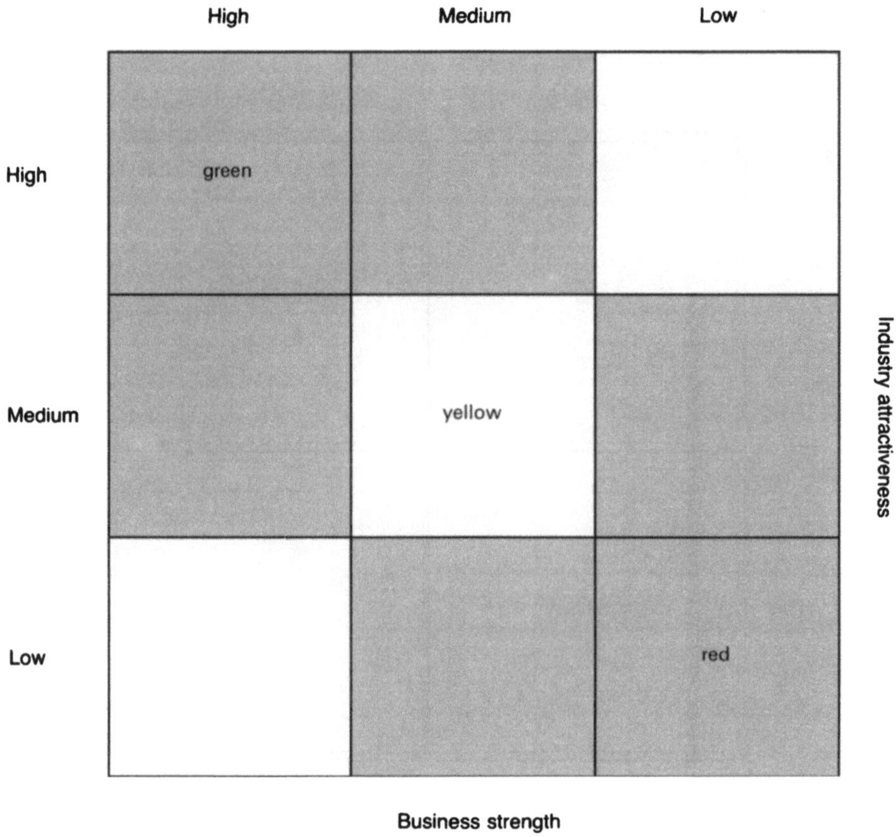

Figure 8. Nine-Cell Matrix Analysis

updating of all variables included in previous years. Sometimes variables not assessed in earlier periods were added, however. The whole approach can, therefore, be regarded as a continuing process with an increasing quantity of information.

Another approach found in several companies was the so-called gap analysis, which is applied either to revenues of entire subsidiaries or to individual products (product lines). This represents a simple attempt to show the difference between developments without interference, the desired outcome, and the expected outcome after integrating the proposed or approved strategic measures for each subsidiary. A typical gap analysis chart is shown in Figure 10. Some companies go beyond the basic ap-

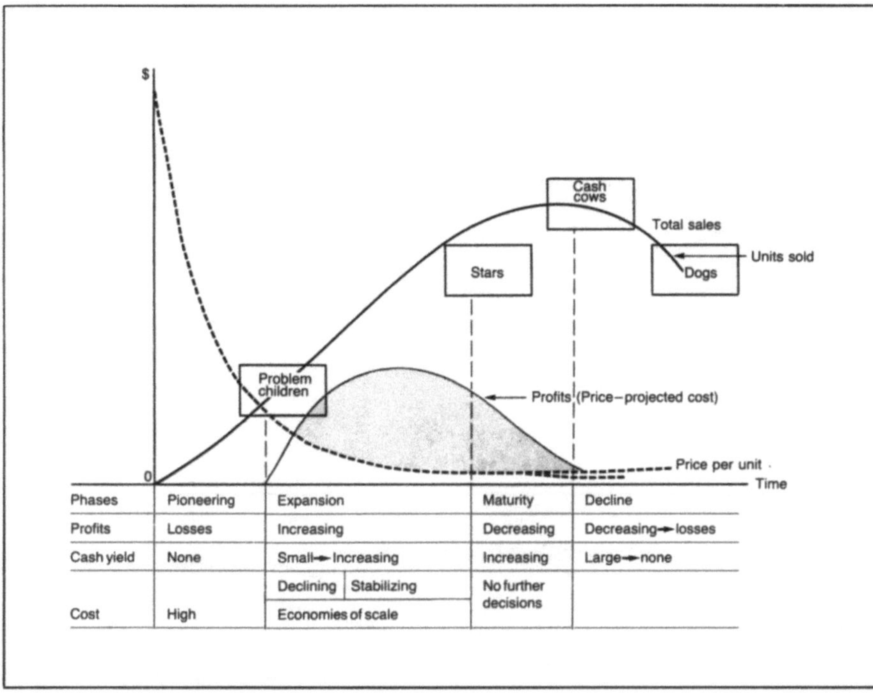

Figure 9. Relationship between Product Position on Life Curve and Financial Results

proach and require specification of the expected results at various confidence levels (usually 90, 70 and 50 percent) to give the management of the subsidiary an opportunity to express its expectation more clearly.

From the analysis of individual subsidiaries emerges a picture of the portfolio of units or product lines held by a multinational company (or parts thereof). The objective assigned to each subsidiary must be consistent with its position in the matrix (see Figure 7), It is, however, usually a top management decision to which extent disinvestment, gradual withdrawal of cash, aggressive pursuit of new marketing goals, etc., will become the specific objective of the next period(s). Only after this general determination has been made is each subsidiary able to proceed with its budget preparation.

Budgets contain a brief summary of the assumptions made concerning changes in the economic, political, and societal environment as well as the projected competitor strategy. Examples are contained in the Philips (Fi-

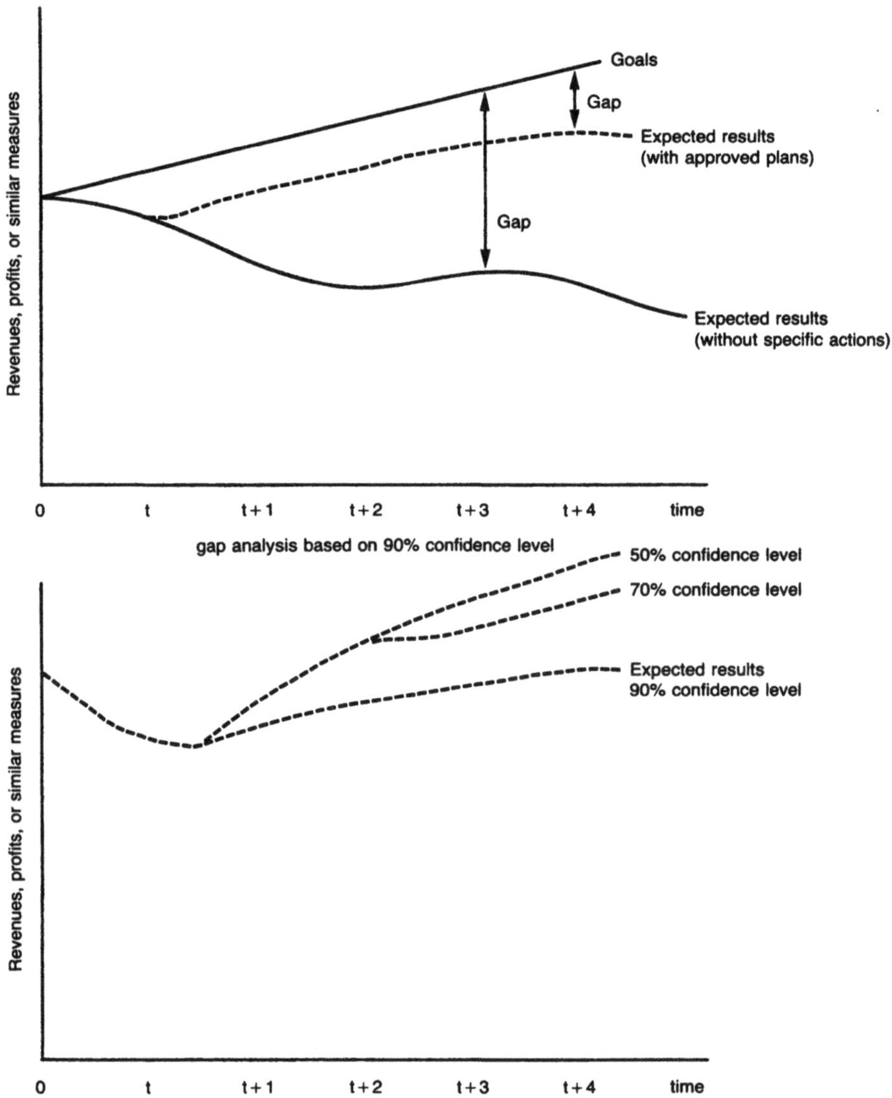

Figure 10. Gap-Analysis

	Strategic summary				
Product line	Competitive position	Strategic objective	Resource allocation	Life cycle position	% of current year's sales

Example for strategy designation:

Functional area	To support proposed strategy, the following changes are to be implemented during the planning period	Headquarters support needed
R&D		
Manufacturing		
Marketing		
Human resources		
International		
M.I.S.		
Others		

Resource requirements

Critical success factors	Resources available	Additional resources needed	Source of new resources	Cost of new resources	Individual responsible	Completion date

Figure 11. Strategic summary report.

gures 1–3) and Nixdorf (Section 3) cases. As the next step, actions to be pursued by the subsidiary are outlined. Most budgets not only state the strategies but also the individual measures to be undertaken with specific dates for their initiation and their end as a means to allocate expenditures. This is closely connected with capital expenditure projects (which are normally analyzed individually and are approved separately by top management, regional management, or the manager of the subsidiary in accordance with previously assigned powers of authorization). The usual capital budgeting procedures are followed; the level of adherence to such analysis, however, differed between companies.

Several companies require for planning purposes the identification of primary and supporting strategies, together with the resources needed and the expected results. As a summary, some comprehensive — though abbreviated — reports were submitted by subsidiaries. The basic approach used — although there are substantial differences — is shown in Figure 11. These data are carried over into the detailed budgets; sometimes summaries for functional areas are included in the budget package. The details required in each report are closely tied to the budget data, thus permitting an analysis of policy changes and their budgetary impact whenever some of the underlying assumptions have changed.

3.3 Reporting by Subsidiaries

3.3.1 Reporting procedures. The reporting procedures found in our sample were all based on the existing accounting data. For U. S. – based companies, reports and evaluative measures are more closely tied to financial accounting information than in the case of European-based multinationals. As Morsicato has found (Morsicato 1980: 135), reporting for U. S. companies occurs either in U. S. dollars alone or in both U. S. dollars and foreign currency, whereas the prevailing pattern in Europe was reporting in local currency; conversion to headquarters currency was frequently performed by headquarters staff. The reason given for this procedure was the lack of control over currency fluctuations by the subsidiary. Whether the subsidiary management was held — at least partially — responsible for currency gains or losses depended on the organizational and financing structure of the individual company. Regardless of the solution to this problem, all European companies clearly distinguished between operating (= local currency) and other results.

Frequency and comprehensiveness of reporting varied widely within each multinational. A prevailing pattern required monthly reporting of key data, usually a two-step process, including a so-called flash report on the second or third working day of the next month with detailed data following with a few days' delay. The detailed report was waived in cases in which headquarters had direct on-line access to the data of subsidiaries. In all cases, more detailed quarterly reports are required. All reports included so-called "prognosis data," which were used to state actual expectations without modifying all budget data. In most cases, different sets of data were required by central headquarters (more condensed and more oriented toward financial accounting information) and by the product divisions. The latter require detailed operational information to follow the cost development in functional areas closely. This pattern existed in all multiproduct multinationals which usually have a matrix organization.

European companies which use different data for cost accounting and financial reporting require data which become an integral part of their financial statements usually on a quarterly basis. This distinction does not exist in U.S. – based companies.

In summary, all multinational companies required reports containing the following:

1. Financial statement data (based on acquisition values and national valuation rules; at least once annually these data are adjusted to headquarters' format and valuation requirement for consolidation).
2. Income statement data adjusted as above.
3. Cash-flow data in local currency (mostly combined with an assessment of future cash flows) and expectations concerning currency exchange and interest rates. These data also include monthly reports on accounts receivable and payable, as well as detailed inventory reports.
4. Managerial accounting data showing details for products and functional areas. All European and some U.S. companies require inflation adjustments in these data. The required details and frequency of reporting were substantially different depending on the management style of the company. The report content is prescribed by headquarters in all cases and has evolved in complexity over time.
5. Financial and managerial ratios are either included in the appropriate reports or submitted as separate reports. Ratios varied widely between companies. U.S. companies showed a stronger inclination to use mainly financial ratios.

6. Verbal explanations of all deviations and detailed assessments, whenever assumptions used in the planning process had changed (together with suggestions on how to cope with the new conditions).

3.3.2 Computation of return or residual income. The key figures to measure results are return on investment (ROI), return on assets (RONA), or return on sales (ROS). It must first be noted that "return" for these purposes is determined in many different ways by various multinationals. This corresponds to the "residual income" idea, that is, the common factor in all cases is the before taxes figure. Residual income is, however, subject to a wide variety of adjustments. Taxes, headquarters' allocations, and extraordinary items were added back to net profit in all cases before arriving at residual return. European companies — in addition to these items — add back all actual financing expenses because they apply "imputed interest" as an operating cost factor. This does not prevent them from eliminating this item at a later stage of the evaluation process (to determine net profitability). Management performance, however, is regarded as separate from financial performance, and the use of imputed interest permits the introduction of a measure reflecting capital utilization in an economically realistic way (as suggested in the European cost accounting literature).

In most cases, charges by headquarters are — at least initially — excluded from the computation of residual income, since these items are beyond the control of subsidiary management and — if desired — headquarters can always calculate the necessary adjustment.

All companies interviewed used arm's-length transfer prices. This approach did not require an adjustment of prices charged within the multinational. If it were necessary to introduce price allowances to penetrate new markets or to adjust to prevailing national price levels, these adjustments were handled by clearly identifiable allowances which were included in materials (or product) cost before assessing the operating return of the subsidiary.

No uniformity could be found in determining a *satisfactory* rate of return for each subsidiary. Most companies have subjective benchmarks for each subsidiary which depend on country risk, stage of development, particular mission and so forth. For these benchmark returns, no uniform computational procedures could be found. Only some comparisons frequently mentioned could be identified. Overall profitability of the multinational, typical profitability rates for the specific type of industry in the host country, and other comparable subsidiaries in the same state of development and country risk are mentioned as factors contributing to the assessment of the situation before determining — in advance — a target rate for one or more operating periods.

As implied in these comments, in many cases several different return measurements are applied. The following definitions were found; some companies used several of them in consecutive evaluation steps. These analyses are always performed in local currency and sometimes (U.S. companies) after translation:

Return I	=	Sales revenues minus total operating cost including pertinent administrative and general expenses (without adjustments for inflation).
Return II	=	Results from above minus total operating cost adjusted for inflation.
Return III	=	Results from above minus total operating cost without actual financing cost; these are replaced by imputed interest.
Return IV	=	Results from above minus adjustments for corporate expenses and allowances for transfer price and marketing adjustments.
Return V	=	Results from above minus extraordinary expenses (= net return before taxes).
Return VI	=	Results from above minus taxes (= net return after taxes).

3.3.3 Computation of capital usage and inflation impact. One of the most difficult issues lacking a uniform solution at this time is the determination of capital employed by the subsidiary. This amount is crucial for the computation of either ROI or RONA. All companies computed for this purpose an *average amount* of capital or assets; however, differences exist in determining averages ranging from a simple average (beginning balance plus ending balance/2) to improved approaches using the beginning balance and twelve monthly ending balances/13 to account for seasonal variations.

The computations are either based on the capital side or the asset side of the balance sheet. The latter approach prevailed with German companies, since the asset-based determination of capital utilization is a practice used for several decades (Schoenfeld 1974: 18–24). Some U.S. companies use both methods (see FMC case).

Since the inflation impact causes severe additional difficulties in measuring capital usage, some U.S. and all European companies require inflation adjustments for the determination of capital utilization. The approaches range from detailed adjustments prescribed by corporate manuals as described in the case of Philips N.V. to more ad hoc procedures used by other companies. All European companies applied current cost methods (with the exception of some South American subsidiaries, where this method proved to be too expensive and unreliable). Depending on the rate of inflation, adjustments were made quarterly or annually. The inflation-adjusted asset values in all cases were utilized as a basis to compute the amount of imputed interest, which becomes part of the product cost for pricing purposes. The same inflation-adjusted basis is also used to compute current value depreciation, which in turn is charged to products. For measuring performance, the imputed interest and depreciation amounts remained as part of the operating cost; this is a typical practice of companies based in Germany (which are otherwise tied by taxation requirements to depreciation rates imposed by the revenue service). U.S.–based companies used an inflation-adjustment approach as prescribed in SFAS 33; however, they also preferred the current cost approach over an adjustment in constant dollars. This method leads to different results, particularly in all cases in which the dollar is considered the functional currency.

To avoid currency fluctuation influences, most European multinationals measure performance of subsidiaries only in national currency; they include a separate measurement after translation only at the headquarters staff level.

In one case, a rather unusual approach was applied: the company, in addition to the steps mentioned earlier, defined capital also in terms of transfers from headquarters only, thus treating their foreign subsidiaries similarly to a simple investment in stock.

Capital, therefore, is defined by multinationals in several ways which are used individually or jointly for performance analysis both in local currency and after translation. In some cases, one or more of these capital values was used for assigning appropriate capital amounts to product lines or product groups (a method which raises the issue of proper assignments for common assets or capital amounts):

Capital I	=	Net transfer from headquarters only.
Capital II	=	Net capital without inflation adjustments (book value).
Capital III	=	Net capital with inflation adjustments.
Capital IV	=	Capital equals the net value of all assets without inflation adjustments. This may also include downward adjustments for obsolescence and productivity increases.
Capital V	=	Book value of all assets plus a uniform inflation surcharge of a percentage assigned by headquarters.
Capital VI	=	Acquisition value of assets plus some uniform surcharge.
Capital VII	=	Capital equals the net value of all assets after adjustments for inflation.

3.3.4 Determination of interest rates. All companies which use imputed interest rates and treat actual interest paid as an extraordinary item are faced with the problem of selecting an appropriate interest rate. To solve this problem, several basic approaches seem to prevail.

In all cases in which no inflation adjustment is made, companies attempt to compensate for the lack of an adequately computed capital basis by requiring interest in the amount of the *inflation rate plus a factor* which reflects either (1) their internal cost of capital, (2) the typical national interest rate applying to the specific industry, (3) the typical national overall interest rate plus a surcharge for the industry risk factor, or (4) the interest rate prevailing in the country of headquarters with, in this author's opinion, a subjective risk surcharge for the country.

In all cases in which inflation-adjusted capital or asset data are utilized, the need for imputing the inflation rate into the interest rate does not exist. Therefore, companies solve the problem by computing the appropriate amount by using only the non-inflation part of the four different methods mentioned previously.

Since some managers were not convinced that the use of a single interest rate is sufficient for all types of decisions, headquarters' staff frequently performs one or more additional analytic computations: most frequently assessments are made by using a typical country interest rate for comparisons within the national environment, and a multinational specific interest rate is applied for comparisons with other subsidiaries in a similar line of business and state of development.

3.4 Evaluation Procedures

3.4.1 Evaluation patterns. For the evaluation of their subsidiaries, most multinationals use as a minimum an analytic procedure comparing:

1. Actual results with past periods (up to three years)
2. Actual results with original budget and adjusted budget data
3. Actual results with results of
   (a) comparable competitors in the same country;
   (b) averages and published data in the same country;
   (c) results of subsidiaries in other countries;
   (d) overall multinational results.

3.4.2 Evaluation data. In all cases evaluations are performed using the following:

1. Traditional financial accounting data;
2. Extensions of accounting data such as ratios for turnover, days covered by inventories, percent of order backlog in terms of sales, and all other financial ratios, such as ROI, RONA and ROS;
3. Managerial (cost) accounting data, whenever this information is on a different value basis. Differences in the value basis occur with inflation adjustments or with different allocation patterns (as in the case of Philips with allocations of R&D on a unit of product basis);
4. Additional data in use within the company to measure performance in other than strictly accounting terms. These data will be discussed in the section on evaluation measures beyond accounting.

Top management of all companies stressed that reliance on accounting data alone was not sufficient because it was not always possible to generate early warning signs or insights into the actual trouble spots from this information. There seemed to be agreement that this is due to the existing accounting conventions and also to the fact that subsidiary data are highly aggregated and therefore may permit the recognition of problems, however, not necessarily the identification of their causes. Consequently, additional data are used frequently as interpretive measures. There seemed to be agreement also that no single set of data exists which will contain by itself all the information needed. Therefore, management interprets sets of data from different sources jointly.

It was also stressed that the comparison between actual and budget in most cases yielded the best insight because budgets represent realistic, mutually agreed outcomes which are based on a set of environmental conditions; these were initially assessed jointly, however, and cannot be monitored very closely from headquarters. Changes in actual performance are frequently attributable to certain causes whenever a comparison between original assumptions and the status quo of the real world is undertaken. Although some of these assumptions are necessarily subjective, they are regarded as more reliable than explanations after the fact only, because they force local management into a detailed analysis and projection of a developing situation. In view of these arguments, it is not surprising to see multinationals rely so heavily on a (more or less) formalized system of strategic planning. The entire procedure can therefore be compared to an attempt to perform a factor analysis (testing for variables which explain performance changes) without resorting to statistical means in all cases, because some of the factors involved cannot be quantified readily at this time.

Few of the companies participating in this survey contributed or received data from Profit Impact of Marketing Strategy (PIMS) project (Abel, Hammond 1979: 271–89), which is based on the information of a large number of firms and attempts to attribute the impact of certain factors on profits. Nevertheless, evaluations performed by individual companies — at least conceptually — suggest the realization that any evaluation based on accounting alone is not sufficient in a multinational situation. Since this is an insight shared by all accountants, it is not surprising that performance evaluation at this time has all the features of an incomplete search process; companies rely on data, which in the past have proven to contain information — which is not necessarily the same data set in each industry. Since other information might be needed in the future, a tendency to include more and more data in the process is at least understandable, although it results in information overloads which have been experienced by all participants and have resulted from time to time in a reduction of reporting requirements.

Examples of the type of data routinely reported for evaluation purposes are contained in the cases presented in these proceedings; they show the diversity of inputs used — and also a certain uniformity in the area of traditional accounting data.

3.4.3 Evaluation measures beyond accounting. Evaluation measures beyond accounting fall generally into three groups: (1) other quantitative data collected during operations, (2) subjective assessments of project progress, and (3) support through management auditing techniques. The latter are not directly meant to provide performance measurement, but rather represent actions initiated by headquarters or subsidiaries to improve lagging performance and transfer effective procedures from one location to another.

Non-accounting data are based on measured or observed operating results. Such data cannot be detected by the accounting system, however, because they do not lead immediately to recordable transactions (for example, capacity utilization, downtime). There is a wide range of such data which defies classification. Usually companies attempt to find measurements for potential output quantities and compare these in the form of ratios with actual output. This is simple in a single product situation, but causes difficulties when more than one product can be produced and the output mix can be chosen arbitrarily. The resulting capacity utilization measure frequently yields information of developing problems much earlier than does accumulated cost. Most European companies also include utilization data for their work force, ranging from turnover information to comparisons of actual hours utilized for key tasks with budgeted hours. To determine the effectiveness of work performed, indicators for outcomes are also sought in the quality control area (see Phillips case, p. 116); all quality-related problems (measured by returns or service calls, regardless of who eventually pays for these) are monitored and charted over time to measure fluctuations in performance. More recently, companies have been experimenting with productivity data; the latter are measured in terms of man hours (or labor cost) occurring at critical stages in the production or service process. The Nixdorf case illustrates such attempts — although Nixdorf uses relationships such as percentage of employees for certain functions, which is effective in fairly homogeneous situations. Another example of the use of performance indicators can be found in the case of the GoldStar Corporation (see Tables 5 and 6). Instead of using a long list of performance indicators, the company applies a limited set selected from accounting and other data, which measures results. Depending on the special needs of certain operations, this set can be changed when the need arises. It even seems highly likely that the choice of indicators may be extended in the future, since GoldStar is a relatively young company.

Philips, for example (see p. 135) has attempted to introduce a set of performance indicators which will — though not in all instances — measure certain operations which are regarded as critical for the overall results. This is perceived as an effective approach to monitor performance and, at the same time, reduce the potential overload of data; some of these indicators may be used as a shortcut for interim performance reporting. Such indicators may even be effective when monitored only at the subsidiary level and reported to headquarters whenever fluctuations beyond a predetermined range occur. It should also be recognized that a variety of performance indicators (specifically various productivity measures) can serve as early warning systems, because they are likely to reflect changes much earlier than accounting data. (For more detailed information, see Sudit, Ch. 3–4).[1] A combined function is probably served by items such as the booking/billing ratio used by Nixdorf (Nixdorf case: Table 1, p. 147), which not only measures past performance but also permits improved budget data for the next period; it unquestionably has early warning sign characteristics.

The second approach consists in identifying specific projects in the planning stages. At this point, actions to be taken are identified and, in addition to identifying managers responsible for the project, completion dates are established. Reports of deviations are required. In some cases also, desired results are specified in qualitative (descriptive) terms; the latter approach is regarded as a first step toward measurement in all cases in which quantitative measures do not yet exist. Some companies suggest that this approach — if accompanied initially by a ranking scale for expected results — will improve the evaluation process appreciably, because arguments in the follow-up phase are minimized. At the same time, it improves the planning process by providing a sharper focus on certain hard to describe goals. This type of evaluation is applicable to measures as listed in Figure 6. Not yet fully developed but discussed by some companies are attempts to analyze goals in greater detail to improve their priority ranking and thus tie them more closely to resource allocation. Methods available for this purpose can be found in the literature (Sinden and Worrell 1979), and need testing for our purposes.

The last approach mentioned is utilization of accumulated experience with the assistance of internal audit teams. Undeniably, the success of many multinationals can be attributed to their management know-how and experience. Such experience is available within the organization, not necessarily in each subsidiary, however. The results of utilization of this experience are qualitative improvements in individual activities. In all cases of lagging performance — or even suspected inefficiencies — subsidiaries in some companies are able to use management audits provided by headquarters. It is obvious that such actions will not work when applied only in the case of insufficient performance — and if accompanied by direct or indirect penalties. If applied as a consulting function in the best interest of both headquarters and the subsidiary, improvements can be expected and such teams will be called in. The Control Evaluation Review Technique as practiced by Borg-Warner Corporation (p. 88) is a good example of this approach. It is also obvious that in this particular area, much additional work is needed to upgrade the knowledge transfer process systematically.

4. Conclusions and Future Directions

The cases in previous sections of these proceedings and this discussion have shown that the performance evaluation process in multinational companies at the present time has progressed beyond the procedures used in — mostly smaller — national companies. The greater emphasis on the strategic planning and budgeting process is especially such an extension. It may be argued that all the steps taken do not represent a radically new approach — and this is definitely true if one assesses the techniques used. It does, in my opinion, represent a departure from traditional methods because it addresses a problem not present to the same extent in national companies. This problem is the communications gap within management. Due to the variety of different environmental problems and the different educational background and day-to-day information inputs in various countries, many operating problems are not fully understood when viewed only as aggregate outcomes from the top. To overcome this type of communications gap, additional information inputs are required as illustrated in the previous cases. This process may not yet be fully accomplished — nevertheless, it can be seen that significant steps have already been taken in this direction. It can hardly be expected that this process has already reached a stage of perfection in view of the fact that most management groups have had only a limited experience in this area.

Returning to the set of unresolved issues summarized at the beginning (p. 10), it is apparent that not all of these issues are near a resolution. Most companies do make a distinction between subsidiary and executive evaluation (only the former has been investigated); executive evaluation proved to be a highly sensitive issue because of the compensation problems in volved for which no standard approaches could be found. Companies in most cases indicated only that such issues were handled separately. Transfer prices were presented in all cases as arm's-length prices with properly disclosed adjustment and seemed to be regarded as less of a problem than initially thought. The highly sensitive nature of this problem must be assumed to have produced this outcome. The monitoring of progress toward goals — although measurement is subjective — is substantially upgraded by using an explicit strategic planning system which enumerates goals and environmental influences as clearly described as possible; the search for more appropriate measurement methods is continuing in this area. The inclusion of nonfinancial criteria into the process is clearly expanding, as some of the cases indicate. Some of the traditional performance indicators together with nonfinancial criteria are used even for explicit motivational purposes (see p. 199). As far as accounting data are concerned, a picture emerges showing that European companies increasingly utilize local currency residual income rather than translated amounts and that assessements are made at various levels of residual income, depending on the purpose of the analysis (performance evaluation versus investment/divestment decisions). Allocation of corporate cost and price adjustment are also handled separately. In regard to inflation assessments, it can be said that most companies attempt to integrate these; however, procedures in Europe are more company individual, whereas in the United States, guidelines established by SFAS No. 33 seem to dominate for compliance reasons and because the separation of the financial and managerial accounting systems is not such a routine accounting procedure as in German companies (for discussion, Schoenfeld 1984: 41–51).

In concluding the analysis of the state of the art in performance evaluation for multinational subsidiaries, some additional observations beyond the technical discussion seem to be in order. Accounting approaches to performance evaluation have by-and-large concentrated on specific methods and their adequacy for this purpose. Most of the methods have been criticized — even if used only in a less complex national environment (Dearden 1969: 124–33) on technical and more importantly on motivational grounds. All these arguments are still valid and improvements can be expected only from more sophisticated methods. It is questionable whether even this will solve the problem. Studies in organization theory suggest that performance in any organization is dependent on a large number of variables whose impact can be proven empirically (for a

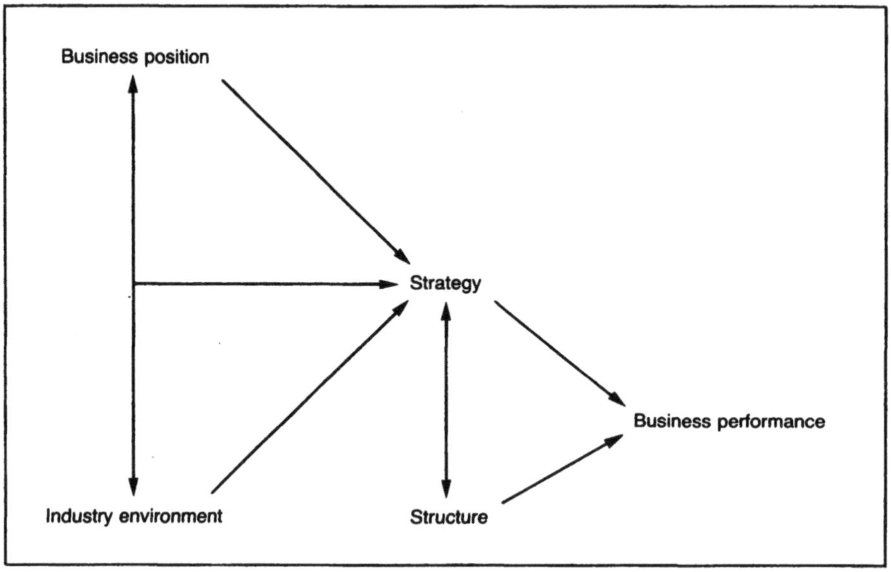

Figure 12. Integrative Model of Performance (White and Hamermesh, 1981)

comprehensive analysis, see White and Hammermesh 1981); the PIMS method is partially based on these observations. This suggests that the presently existing performance evaluation method will remain insufficient so long as no correction in the inputs of these methods can be accomplished. After reviewing the existing literature and research, White/Hammermesh (pp. 16–18) suggest that actual performance of a company or parts thereof depends on the interaction of outside (business position and industry environment) and inside variables (organization structure and strategy adopted by the company). Their congruence and timing will determine the success of the operation. Although intuitively obvious, such a model (or even a more exhaustive one) may not even fully describe the actual interrelationships. It is, however, also obvious that the inputs of the accounting-based performance evaluation models do not attempt to integrate some of these variables into the measurement process. Granted the difficulties of using additional sets of input data which are not based on the same measurement system, an evaluation system which does not integrate all the variables present in a given situation cannot be expected to yield satisfactory results. The attempts to integrate additional information by companies practicing performance evaluation in a multinational setting appear to be much more understandable in the context of these arguments. The future task, therefore, will consist of finding satisfactory procedures for this type of comprehensive analysis. The factor-analysis approach employed by PIMS may offer one of the possible solutions. The search for methods which will encompass all contributing variables, therefore, must continue because at this point, evaluation will always remain in part subjective and depend to some extent on the intuition of top management. It can even be argued that this situation will prevail permanently, because not only past results but also the impact of future directions (goals) are part of the performance picture — and the future remains unpredictable without making subjective assumptions. The task at hand therefore consists — at least for the accountant — in attempting to improve measurability of additional variables, particularly in the area of budgeting. This will, it is hoped, improve the assessment of outside impacts and the adjustment of internal variables such as organization structure and strategy.

Notes

[1] The study by Friedlaender et al. provides a good example for this case (Sudit: 38–40). In their study, the researchers estimated the total productivity growth for General Motors, Ford, and Chrysler between 1969–1979. Their results indicate that Ford and, to some extent, GM have enjoyed productivity growth, whereas Chrysler has experienced substantial cost increases and productivity decreases during this period. They state that "... these results are important. Since they suggest that even if Chrysler did not suffer a competitive disadvantage with respect to its recent scale of production, it would still be at a competitive disadvantage vis-à-vis Ford and GM." Sudit's comment on this issue, "It would be interesting to speculate whether Chrysler's executives could have averted financial crisis by initiating preemptive corrective actions" points in the direction of utilizing additional variables.

References

Abell, Derek F., and John G. Hammond: *Strategic Market Planning Problems and Analytical Approaches* (Englewood Cliffs, N.J.: Prentice-Hall 1979)

Czechowicz, James I., Frederick D.S. Choi, and Vinod B. Bavishi: *Assessing Foreign Subsidiary Performance: Systems and Practices of Leading Multinational Companies* (New York, N.Y.: Business International Corporation 1982)

Dearden, John: "The Case against ROI Control". *Harvard Business Review* (May-June 1969: 124–35)

Morsicato, Helen G.: *Currency Translation and Performance Evaluation in Multinationals* (Ann Arbor, Mich.: UMI Research Press 1980)

Schoenfeld, Hanns-Martin W.: *Cost Terminology and Cost Theory: A Study of Its Development and Present State in Central Europe* (Urbana, Ill.: Center for International Education and Research in Accounting, 1974).

– : "Financial and Managerial Accounting — Causes for the Separation of the Two Systems". *Issues in Accountability No.* 10 – *Financial and Cost Accounting – Are They Compatible?* Paris: D.A.R. Forrester (Ed.) (Symposium at University of Dauphine 1984)

Sinden, J.A., and A.C. Worrell: *Unpriced Values* (New York, N.Y.: Wiley 1979)

Sudit, Ephraim F.: *Productivity Based Management* (Boston: Klumer-Nojhoff Publishing 1984)

White, Roderick E. and Richard Hammermesh: "Toward a Model of Business Unit Performance: An Integrative Approach". *Academy of Management Review* (1981, Vol. 6, No. 2: 213 ≧ 23)

Comprehensive Bibliography

Abell, Derek F. and John G. Hammond: *Strategic Market Planning Problems and Analytical Approaches* (Englewood Cliffs, N.J.: Prentice-Hall 1979)

American Accounting Association, Committee on Non-Financial Measures of Effectiveness: "Report of the Committee on Non-Financial Measures of Effectiveness". *The Accounting Review* (Supplement to Vol. 46, 1971)

– : "Report of the Committee on International Accounting". *The Accounting Review* (Supplement to Vol. 48: 120–67, 1973)

– : "Report of the Committee on International Accounting". *The Accounting Review* (Supplement to Vol. 49: 250–69, 1974)

Anderson, Carl R. and Carl P. Zeithaml: "Stage of the Product Life Cycle, Business Strategy and Business Performance". *Academy of Management Journal* (1984, Vol. 27, No. 1: 5–24)

Barefield, R. M.: "Comments on a Measure of Forecasting Performance". *Journal of Accounting Research* (Autumn 1969: 323–27)

Baur, Paul C. Jr.: "Profit Performance Index". *NAA Bulletin Management Accounting* (March 1965: 17–20)

Branch, Ben: "The Impact of Operating Decisions on ROI Dynamics". *Financial Management* (Winter 1978: 54–60)

Brandt, William K. and James M. Hulbert: "Pitfalls in Planning for Multinational Operations". *Long Range Planning* (1980, 13, No. 6: 23–31).

Brooke, Michael Z. and Lee H. Remmers: *The Strategy of Multinational Enterprise.* (New York: Pitman 1978)

Burlew, Raymond E.: "Accounting Problems — Foreign Operations". *NAA Bulletin* (Sec. 3, September 1956)

Burns, Gene A.: "Strategy for Financing Multinational Business". *Management Accounting for Multinational Corporations* (New York: National Association of Accountants 1974)

Bursk, Edward C., John Dearden, David F. Hawkins and Victor M. Longstreet: *Financial Control of Multinational Operations* (New York: Financial Executives Research Foundation 1971)

Buzzell, Robert D., Bradley T. Gale and Ralph G. M. Sulton: "Market Share, Profitability and Business Strategy." *Working Paper* (Cambridge, Mass.: Marketing Science Institute, August 1974)

Choi, Frederick D. S. (Ed.): *Multinational Accounting: A Research Framework for the 1980s* (Ann Arbor, Mich.: UMI Research Press 1981)

– : "Multinational Challenges for Managerial Accountants". *Journal of Contemporary Business* (Autumn 1975: 52–67)

– and Gerhard G. Mueller: *An Introduction to Multinational Accounting* (Englewood Cliffs, N.J.: Prentice-Hall, Inc. 1978)

– and I. J. Czechowicz: "Assessing Foreign Subsidiary Performance: A Multinational Comparison". *Management International Review* (1983, Vol. 23, No. 4: 83)

Clark, Kim and Zvi Griliches: "Productivity Growth and R&D at the Business Level: Results from the PIMS Data Base". Working Paper No. 916. *National Bureau of Economic Research* (Cambridge, Mass. 1982)

Cocks, Douglas: "The Measurement of Total Factor Productivity for a Large U.S. Manufacturing Corporation". *Business Economics* (September 1974: 7–20)

Cowen, Scott S., Lawrence C. Phillips and Linda Stillabower: "Multinational Transfer Pricing". *Management Accounting* (January 1979: 17–22)

Craig, Charles E. and R. Clark Harris: "Total Productivity Measurement at the Firm Level". *Sloan Management Review* (Spring 1973: 13–28)

Creamer, Daniel, A. D. Apostolides and S. L. Wang: *Overseas Research and Development by the U.S. Multinationals: 1966–75 Estimates of Expenditures and a Statistical Profile.* (A Research Report from The Conference Board's Division of Economic Research 1976)

Czechowicz, I. James, Frederick D. S. Choi and Vinod Bavishi: *Assessing Foreign Subsidiary Performance Systems and Practices of Leading Multinational Companies* (New York: Business International Corporation 1982)

Darby, James J.: "Some Suggestions for Budgetary Control of Foreign Operations". *NAA Bulletin* (May 1962: 67–70)

Dearden, John: "The Case Against ROI Control". *Harvard Business Review* (May-June 1969: 124–35)

Douglas, Susan P. and C. Samuel Craig: "Examining Performance of U.S. Multinationals in Foreign Markets". *Journal of International Business Studies* (Winter 1983: 51–62)

Eilon, Samuel (1978): "Some Useful Ratios in Evaluating Performance". *OMEGA* (1978, Vol. 7, No. 2: 166–68)

–, Bela Gold and Judith Soesan: *Applied Productivity Analysis for Industry* (Great Britain: Pergamon International Library 1976)

Enthoven, Adolf J.H.: "International Management Accounting — A Challenge for Accountants". *Management Accounting* (September 1980: 25–32)

Fantl, Irving L.: "Control and the Internal Audit in the Multinational Firm". *International Journal of Accounting Education and Research* (Fall 1975: 57–65)

Gale, Bradley T.: "Market Share and Rate of Return". *Review of Economics and Statistics* (November 1972: 412–23)

Goggin, William C.: "A Decade of Progress: Multinational Organization Structure". *University of Michigan Business Review* (1979, No. 2: 8–13)

Gold, Bela: *Foundations of Productivity Analysis: Guides to Economic Theory and Managerial Control* (United States: University of Pittsburg Press 1955)

– : *Explorations in Managerial Economics* (Great Britain: Basic Books Inc. 1971 a)

– : "Technology, Productivity and Economic Analysis". *OMEGA* (1971 b, Vol. 1, No. 1: 5–24)

Gorelik, George: *Accounting Measurements in Planning and Control Decisions: Comparative Study of Soviet and American Industrial Enterprises*. Ph. D. Thesis (Ann Arbor, Mich.: University Microfilms 1973)

Gotcher, J. William: "Strategic Planning in European Multinationals". *Long Range Planning* (10 October 1977: 7–14)

Gray, Jack and Deigan Morris: "Comprehensive Controls for Multinational Corporations". *Managerial Accounting: An Analysis of Current International Applications*. V. K. Zimmerman (Ed.) (Urbana, Illinois: Center for International Education and Research in Accounting, University of Illinois 1984)

Hawkins, David F.: "Controlling Foreign Operations". *Financial Executive* (February 1965: 25–32, 56)

Hayes, Robert H.: "Why Japanese Factories Work". *Harvard Business Review* (July-August 1981: 57–73)

Holzer, H. Peter (Ed.): *International Accounting* (New York: Harper & Row Publishers 1984)

Hutchins, David: "Organization of Company Wide Quality Control". *The Japanese Approach to Product Quality: Its Applicability to the West*. Naoto Sasaki/David Hutchins (Eds.) (Oxford: Pergamon Press 1984)

Ijiri Y., T.C. Kinard, and F.B. Putney: "An Integrated Evaluation System for Budget Forecasting and Operating Performance with a Classified Budgeting Bibliography". *Journal of Accounting Research* (Spring 1968: 1–12)

Kaplan, Robert S.: "Management Accounting and Manufacturing: The Lost Connection." *Working Paper* (Pittsburg, Pa.: Carnegie-Mellon University, October 1982)

– (1984): "The Evolution of Management Accounting". *The Accounting Review* (July 1984: 390–419)

Karatsu, Hajime: "Quality Control — The Japanese Approach". *The Japanese Approach to Product Quality — Its Applicability to the West.* Naoto Sasaki/David Hutchins (Eds.) (Oxford: Pergamon Press 1984)

Kearney, William J.: "Value of Behaviorally Based Performance Appraisals". *Business Horizons* (June 1976: 75–83)

Kelly, Marie Wicks: *Foreign Investment Practices of U.S. Multinational Corporations* (Ann Arbor, Mich.: UMI Research Press 1981)

Kendrick, John W.: *Improving Company Productivity: Handbook with Case Studies* (Baltimore, Md.: Johns Hopkins University Press 1984)

Kim, Seung and Stephen W. Miller: "Constituents of the International Transfer Pricing Decisions". *Columbia Journal of World Business* (Spring 1979: 69–77)

Kuin, Pieter: "The Magic of Multinational Management". *Harvard Business Review* (1972, 50: 89–97)

Lessard, Donald and Peter Lorange: "Currency Changes and Management Control: Resolving the Centralization/Decentralization Dilemma". *Accounting Review* (July 1977: 628–37)

Lester, Ronald H., Norbert L. Enrick and Harry E. Mottley: *Quality Control for Profit* (New York: Industrial Press Inc. 1977)

LeCraw, Donald J.: "Performance of Transnational Corporations in Less Developed Countries". *Journal of International Business Studies* (Spring/Summer 1983: 15–33)

Mammone, James L.: "A Practical Approach to Productivity Measurement". *Management Accounting* (July 1980: 40–44)

Mauriel, John J.: "Evaluation and Control of Overseas Operations". *Management Accounting* (May 1969: 35–39, 52)

– and Robert N. Anthony: "Misevaluation of Investment Center Performance." *Harvard Business Review* (March-April, 1966: 98–105)

Mays, Robert L.: "Divisional Performance Measurement and Transfer Prices". *Management Accounting* (April 1982: 20–24)

McInnes, J.M.: "Financial Control Systems for Multinational Operations: An Empirical Investigation". *Journal of International Business Studies* (Fall 1971: 11–28)

McIntyre, Edward V.: "Interaction Effects of Inflation Accounting Models and Accounting Techniques". *The Accounting Review* (July 1982: 607–17)

Mikhail, Azmi I. and Hany A. Shawsky: "Investment Performance of U.S. – Based Multinational Corporations". *Journal of International Business* (Spring/Summer 1979: 53–65)

Miller, Elwood L. (Ed.): *Responsibility Accounting and Performance Evaluations* (New York: Van Nostrand Reinhold Company 1982)

Moncur, Robert H. and Robert Sweiringa: "Relationship Between Managers' Budget Oriented Behaviour and Selected Attitude, Position, Size and Performance Measures". *Empirical Research in Accounting* (1974: 19A–21A)

Morgan, Robert A.: "The Multinational Enterprise and Its Accounting Needs". *International Journal of Accounting Education and Research* (1967, 3, No. 1: 21–28)

Morsicato, Helen G.: *Currency Translation and Performance Evaluation in Multinationals* (Ann Arbor, Mich.: UMI Research Press 1980)

– and Michael Diamond: "An Approach to Environmentalizing Multinational Enterprise Performance Evaluation Systems". *International Journal of Accountancy* (Fall 1980: 247–66)

Nash, Michael: *Managing Organizational Performance* (United States: Jossey-Bass 1983)

Persen, William and Van Lessig: *Evaluating the Financial Performance of Overseas Operations* (New York: Financial Executives Research Foundation 1979)

Plasschaert, Sylvain R.F.: *Transfer Pricing and Multinational Corporations* (England: Gower Publishing Co. 1980)

Robbins, Sidney M. and Robert B. Stobaugh: "The Bent Measuring Stick for Foreign Subsidiaries". *Harvard Business Review* (September/October 1973: 80–88)

Seashore, Stanley E. and Ephraim Yuchtman: "Factorial Analysis of Organizational Performance". *Administrative Sciences Quarterly* (1967, Vol. 12, No. 3: 377–95)

Schendel, Dan and Richard Patton: "A Simultaneous Equation Model of Corporate Strategy." *Management Science* (1978, Vol. 24, No. 15: 1611–21)

Schneeweis, Thomas: "Determinants of Profitability: An International Perspective". *Management International Review* (1983, Vol. 23, No. 2–83: 13–21)

–, Robert D. Buzzell and Donald F. Heany: "Impact of Strategic Planning on Profit Performance". *Harvard Business Review* (March-April 1974: 137–44)

Schoenfeld, Hanns-Martin W.: "Financial and Managerial Accounting — Causes for the Separation of the Two Systems". *Issues in Accountability No. 10 — Financial and Cost Accounting — Are They Compatible?* Paris: D. A. R. Forrester (Ed.) (Symposium at University of Dauphine 1984)

– : "International Accounting: Development Issues and Future Directions". *Journal of International Business Studies* (Fall 1981: 83, 100)

Smith, St. Elmo V.: "Accounting Problems Peculiar to Multinational Business". *Canadian Chartered Accountant* (December 1967: 420–24)

Solomons, David: *Divisional Performance: Measurement and Control.* Homewood, Ill.: Richard D. Irwin 1965)

Steffy, Wilbert and Daniel R. Darby: *Performance Evaluation Systems* (Ann Arbor, Mich.: Industrial Development Division: Institute of Science and Technology — The University of Michigan 1969)

Sudit, Ephraim F.: *Productivity Based Management* (Boston: Kluwer-Nijhoff Publishing 1984)

Sumanth, David J.: "Productivity Indicators Used by Major U.S. Manufacturing Companies: The Results of a Survey". *Industrial Engineering* (May 1981 a: 70–73)

– : "Survey Results: How Major Non-Industrial Corporations Measure Their Productivity". *Industrial Engineering* (September 1981 b: 32)

– and Norman Einspruch: "Productivity Awareness in the U.S.A. — Survey of Some Major Corporations." *Industrial Engineering* (October 1980: 84–90)

Terleckyj, Nestor E.: "Effects of R&D on the Productivity Growth of Industries: An Explanatory Study". *National Planning Association Report* (1974, No. 140)

Tse, Paul S.: "Evaluating Performance in Multinationals." *Management Accounting* (June 1969: 21–25)

van Loggenberg, Bazil J. and Stephen J. Cucchiario: "Productivity Measurement and the Bottom Line". *National Productivity Review* (Winter 1981/82: 87–99)

Weiner, Nan and Thomas A. Mahoney (1981): "A Model of Corporate Performance as a Function of Environmental, Organizational and Leadership Influences". *Academy of Management Journal* (September 1981: 453–70)

White, Roderick E. and Richard Hammermesh: "Toward a Model of Business Unit Performance: An Integrative Approach". *Academy of Management Review* (1981, Vol. 6, No. 2: 213–23)

Yoshina, M.Y.: "Toward a Concept of Managerial Control for a World Enterprise". *Michigan Business Review* (March 1966)

Zander, A.F. (Ed.): *Performance Appraisals* (Ann Arbor, Mich.: Foundation for Research on Human Behaviour 1963)

Zenoff, David: "Profitable, Fast Growing but Still the Stepchild." *Columbia Journal of World Business* (July/August 1967: 51–56)
Zimmerman, Vernon K. (Ed.): *Managerial Accounting: An Analysis of Current International Applications* (Urbana, Ill.: Center for International Education and Research in Accounting-University of Illinois 1984)

Brief Biographical Sketches of Authors

Leisa B. Aiken earned her B. A. degree from Oklahoma State University and her M. B. A. degree from the University of Chicago, after spending a year as an ITT Fellow in Chile. She is currently employed as a Staff Accountant in the Chicago office of Deloitte Haskins and Sells where she has served in engagements for several diversified clients.

Eric F. Evans is a member of Operations Analysis at FMC Corporation, having been with FMC since 1983. He has three years' experience as senior auditor of the accounting firm Laventhol and Horwath (the accountants of the Illinois State Lottery). Mr. Evans received his B. A. from Dickinson College and his M. B. A. from the Amos Tuck School of Business Administration — Dartmouth College.

John C. Fletcher is the Corporate Director of Control Evaluation and MIS Consulting at Borg-Warner Corporation in Chicago, an international manufacturing and financial service organization. In 1984 he was given additional responsibility for the corporate telecommunications function. Before joining Borg-Warner, he was Executive Director for the Institute of Internal Auditing and Director of Auditing for the Union Pacific Railroad Company.

A certified international auditor, Mr. Fletcher also is a CPA, holds the CISA certificate, and was recently certified in Production and Industry Management (CPIM) by the American Production and Industry Control Society.

He completed his doctoral studies at the University of Colorado in 1981 after receiving his B. S. and M. B. A. degrees from Arizona State University in 1967 and 1970. Mr. Fletcher now lectures on management control and operations management for the Lake Forest Graduate School near Chicago.

H. Peter Holzer is the Deloitte Haskins & Sells Professor of Accountancy at the University of Illinois at Urbana-Champaign. He received his doctorate from the Graduate School of Business Administration, Vienna, Austria, and is also a CPA. He is campus coordinator of the World Bank – financed Indonesian Accountancy Education Training Project.

He recently served as Visiting Professor at the Technical University of Berlin, Germany, and lectured at several other European universities. Previously, he served as Project Adviser and Visiting Professor of the National Institute for Development Administration in Bangkok, Thailand, and as Chief of Party and Visiting Professor of the Tunisian Business Education Project, University of Tunis. He has repeatedly served as a consultant to the World Bank and other international organizations. He has written extensively, particularly in the areas of international and managerial accounting.

K. Won Kang, Executive Vice President, GoldStar Co., Inc., is responsible for marketing, finance, planning and evaluation, and administrative human resources. He received his doctorate degree in Economics from Dong-A University in Korea and is currently on the campus of the University of Illinois as a Visiting Scholar at the Center for International Education and Research in Accounting. The major area of Dr. Kang's personal interest is in strategic planning and performance evaluation. During his study leave from GoldStar, Dr. Kang is studying business practices in the United States compared to those of Korea and Japan, and the future prospect of China as a major trade partner. He believes a good understanding of these areas is essential for his long-range planning responsibilities, not only for GoldStar, but also for the Lucky-GoldStar Group.

Josef Lanfermann is Managing Partner of Deutsche Treuhand-Gesellschaft and also Klynveld Main Goerdeler in Duesseldorf. He studied business economics at the University of Cologne and became a Wirtschaftspruefer in 1973.

He is a member of various national and international committees in the field of accounting and auditing and is a member of the examination board for the Land Nordrhein-Westfalia. He was a member of the Auditing Statements Board of the Union Europeenne des Experts Comptables Economiques et Financiers (U.E.C.) from 1973 to 1982 and was its Chairman in 1981/82. He has lectured in Germany and abroad.

Elwood L. Miller is Professor of Accounting and International Business, as well as a former Chairman of the Department of Accounting, at Saint Louis University. Prior to joining the faculty of Saint Louis University in 1975, Professor Miller served as Chairman of the Business Department and Dean of the Evening College at Lindenwood College for three years.

Prior to entering academia, Professor Miller's business experience encompassed some thirty years, including more than a decade in international management.

He earned his undergraduate degree in Accounting from Southern Illinois University and graduate degrees from Saint Louis University, also in Accounting. He is a member of the American Institute and Missouri Society of CPAs, as well as the National and American Accounting Associations.

During the past five years, Dr. Miller has written three books dealing with international accounting, furnished chapters for others, and contributed articles to several journals, domestic and overseas.

Lenz Neuhauser is a Partner in Peat, Marwick, Mitchell & Company. As an audit partner, he specializes in international business with particular emphasis on U.S./German accounting and financial reporting requirements.

He holds a doctorate degree in Economics (1968) and a Master of Business Administration (Diplomkaufmann degree 1966) from the Hochschule fuer Welthandel in Vienna, Austria. Mr. Neuhauser is a Certified Public Accountant, a member of the American Institute of Certified Public Accountants and the Illinois and Minnesota Societies of Certified Public Accountants. He also serves as Vice-President and Treasurer of the German-American Chamber of Commerce in Chicago and is an active member in the World Trade Council of the Chicago Association of Commerce and Industry, the International Business Council Midamerica and the Chicago Council on Foreign Relations. He has lectured extensively in North America and Europe and has published articles on international business practices and accounting issues.

Soong H. Park, Assistant Professor of Accountancy at the University of Illinois, was born in Korea and received his higher education in the United States, earning his Ph.D. in Business Administration from the University of Iowa. His teaching and research interest is in managerial accounting, especially in managerial decision making using accounting information. His current research interest topics are the performance evaluation of parties in international joint ventures and the impact of microcomputers in administrative resource planning. Recently, he taught for two years at Korea University in Seoul and was involved in the design of performance evaluation systems at GoldStar.

Richard J. Rubino joined IBM World Trade E/ME/A Corporation in July 1983 as an E/ME/A accounting practices and manufacturing accounting representative. He entered the E/ME/A Balance Sheet function in February 1984, with responsibilities including inventory and allowance accounting, and overall balance sheet analysis.

Mr. Rubino received his B.S. degree in Accounting from Manhattan College, New York City, from which he graduated Magna Cum Laude in 1979. He was employed by Price Waterhouse, New York, from 1979–83, where his responsibilities included audit senior in charge of multinational manufacturing and multinational banking engagements.

Hanns-Martin W. Schoenfeld is the H. T. Scovill Professor of Accountancy and Business Administration and has served as Director of the Office of Western European Studies at the University of Illinois at Urbana-Champaign. Professor Schoenfeld received a doctoral degree (D. B. A.) from the University of Hamburg and a Ph.D. (Habilitation) from the University of Braunschweig. He taught and worked in public and industrial accounting and as a consultant in Germany and several Western European countries before coming to the United States in 1962. He has served as a visiting lecturer at many European universities and executive development centers. Professor Schoenfeld has published several books, among others, *Kostenrechnung, Rechnungswesen, Die Fuehrungsausbildung im betrieblichen Funktionsgefuege*, and is the author of numerous articles in American and German periodicals. He is the author of the Center for International Education and Research in Accounting monograph, *Cost Terminology and Cost Theory: A Study of Its Development and Present State in Central Europe*, and has held both the Weldon Powell and Roedger Professorships in Accountancy.

Armin C. Tufer, who earned his bachelor's and M. B. A. degrees from the University of Michigan, started his public accounting career in the Detroit office of Deloitte Haskins and Sells and subsequently transferred to the firm's executive office in New York to assist in the coordination and development of the firm's auditing procedures. He became a partner in 1969 and was in charge of the firm's research department for three years and has also served in the firm's Accounting and Auditing Services Group. He presently serves as Deloitte Haskins and Sell's Chicago office Accounting and Auditing Coordinator. During his thirty years in public accounting with DH & S, he also has served a large number of diversified clients.

Mr. Tufer is currently a member of the Ethics Code Implementation Ad Hoc Committee of the National Accounting Association and recently completed a six-year term as a member of the Committee on Management Accounting Practices, a senior technical committee of the NAA. He is a past chairman of the AICPA Information Task Force and has served on the AICPA Committee for Voluntary Health and Welfare Organizations and Real Estate Accounting. He has also been active in a number of other professional societies.

Index

Bei Fragen zur Produktsicherheit wenden Sie sich bitte an:
If you have any questions regarding product safety,
please contact:

Walter de Gruyter GmbH
Genthiner Straße 13
10785 Berlin
productsafety@degruyterbrill.com